INSTITUTIONALIZATION OF AUTHORITY
AND THE NAMING OF JESUS

Institutionalization of Authority and the Naming of Jesus

∽

YOLANDA DREYER

∽PICKWICK *Publications* • Eugene, Oregon

INSTITUTIONALIZATION OF AUTHORITY AND THE NAMING OF JESUS

Copyright © 2012 Yolanda Dreyer. All rights reserved. Except for brief quotations in critical publications or reviews, no part of this book may be reproduced in any manner without prior written permission from the publisher. Write: Permissions, Wipf and Stock Publishers, 199 W. 8th Ave., Suite 3, Eugene, OR 97401.

Pickwick Publications
An Imprint of Wipf and Stock Publishers
199 W. 8th Ave., Suite 3
Eugene, OR 97401

www.wipfandstock.com

ISBN 13: 978-1-61097-809-5

Cataloging-in-Publication data:

Dreyer, Yolanda.

Institutionalization of authority and the naming of Jesus / Yolanda Dreyer.

xiv + 162 p.; 23 cm. Includes bibliographical references and index.

ISBN 13: 978-1-61097-809-5

1. Bible. N.T. Gospels—Criticism, interpretation, etc. I. Title.

BT198 D75 2012

Manufactured in the U.S.A.

Contents

Preface vii

Abbreviations xi

1. Naming Jesus—A Matter of Political Maneuvering 1
2. A Synchronic Test Case: Q and the Synoptic Gospels 15
3. The Institutionalization of Charismatic Authority 73
4. From Names to Political Titles: Jesus the Son of Man as Test Case 107

Bibliography 139

Preface

IN THIS BOOK THE Jesus tradition is interpreted ideological-critically and socio-politically. Military power and literacy were products of an advanced agrarian society. Powerful people (elite) employed scribes and soldiers (retainers) to exercise authority. The late Jewish New Testament scholar, Anthony Saldarini ([1988] 2001:266), in his pioneering "sociological analysis" of *Pharisees, Scribes and Sadducees in Palestinian Society*, deemed scribes one of the "learned groups par excellence" in Second Temple Palestine. Saldarini connected scribes "both with village life and the leaders in Jerusalem." Scribes usually stemmed from the group of sages and seers. They often used honorary titles to praise their employers.

Jerome Neyrey (2004:3) highlights Plutarch's "most comprehensive, native discussion of names in antiquity" (see Plutarch, *Marcus Coriolanus* II.2–3, in Ziegler 1969:183–226). The first name was a male person's proper name. The second indicated the family or clan to which he belonged, whereas the third name was an "honorary title" bestowed on him because of some achievement, good fortune, physical attribute or "special excellence." Examples of such "third names" or "honorary titles" are *sōtēr* (savior), *euergetēs* (benefactor).

Neyrey (2004:15) also highlights Daube's (1973:158–63) insights into the Babylonian Talmud (*Niddah* 69b–70a) concerning rabbinical interaction. Rabbis would challenge their peers with twelve questions divided into four categories: conduct (*halakah*—how to apply the Torah to life), erudition (*haggadah*—trying to trap the opponent into contradicting the Torah), mocking questions (ridiculing the opponent's convictions of the Torah), and questions regarding theoretical conceptions of the Torah. In such a "challenge-riposte" situation opponents label each other. If this label (either derogatory or honorable—albeit intended ironically) sticks, it becomes the "third name" to which Plutarch refers. Malina and Neyrey

Preface

apply these insights to the Jesus tradition in their work, *Calling Jesus Names: The Social Value of Labels in Matthew*. They explain the challenge-riposte between opposing groups as follows:

> These attacks come from the outside and the inside: (1) *From without*—the Jesus-movement group is challenged by another Jewish reform group, the Pharisees, whose members disparage allegiance to Jesus and his teaching. (2) *From within*—some members are perceived as not living up to Torah perfection, and behavior rooted in undisciplined enthusiasm threatens to displace Torah observance as the group's ideal. Against these it must be affirmed, that it is not those who say "Lord, Lord," nor those who "prophesy in my name and do mighty works" who will enter the kingdom, but only those "who do the will of my father who is in heaven" (7:21–23//Luke 6:46 and 13:25–27). The system, then, is under siege from within and without. (1988:11)

Honorary titles were attributed to Jesus mostly after his death. This was often the case with sages. The process of attributing honorary titles to Jesus gained momentum after the destruction of the Jerusalem temple by the Romans during the Great Jewish Revolt in the late sixties of the first century CE. This period became known as "formative Judaism" and "formative Christianity." Pharisees began a process of spiritual, economic and political reformation. Destroyed and damaged cities and villages were restored. Scribes became involved in the restoration of villages. They were called "village scribes," an Egyptian title brought to Palestine and Syria by the Ptolemies. Village scribes who conserved the Mosaic legacy ("the great tradition") and those bound to the wisdom of Jesus ("the little tradition"), came into conflict. In order to survive, the little tradition adopted aspects of the language of the great tradition. In this process *names* that were used for and by Jesus were infused with the values of the great tradition and gradually became honorary titles. Because of this history, the titles could be used either to amplify Jesus' wisdom and empower people, or as instruments of power.

The book confirms that the followers of Jesus acknowledged and expressed his authority by means of naming. The names of Jesus therefore have a tradition history that should be interpreted on different levels of contextualization. This pertains specifically to the four canonical gospels. The biographical genre and the narrative structure of these gospels confirm that the authors applied the words and deeds of Jesus to their own post-Easter context in new ways. Names used for Jesus within the narrative structure reveal the evangelists' points of view.

In this book the tradition history of the names used for Jesus, as well as the function of these names in the plot of the narrative, are explained by means of the postmodern perspective of demystification, the social scientific theory of conflict, and the social theory of the institutionalization of charismatic authority. Such an interpretation can be defined as ideological-critical or political exegesis. In this process the words and deeds of a charismatic figure were believed to be relevant and meaningful to others even after his death. The charismatic leader had a new vision: to redefine the existing reality in terms of subversive wisdom. The followers verbalized his wisdom and transformed the ideals of the new order into collective goals and norms which were seen as powerful and authoritative. The transformation, articulation and codification are part and parcel of the process of the institutionalization of rites and ceremonies. Such a social universe was supported by a symbolic universe which legitimated the articulation and codification. The result is a "sacred canopy" that regulates people's lives.

Institutionalization strengthened the identity of a group over against opposing groups. Authors of institutionalization remained anonymous but their writings became normative. Often these authors referred back to authoritative figures (*Erinnerungsfiguren*—see Kirk 2005:191–206; cf. Assmann 1992), such as "apostles" or "missionaries," by means of pseudonyms. In the process of legitimation, value-systems were constructed on the proverbial sayings and teachings for which the founder of the cult was known. The legitimators were the scribal experts and in their scribal activity the "little tradition" of the peasantry merged with the "great tradition" of the élite. Antagonism among groups, opposition and incompatibility were expressed in terms of interests, goals, values and expectations. Power was acquired and maintained to the benefit or at the expense of others. Authority was used to dominate. Positively seen, conflict functioned to strengthen cohesion and to develop new rules, norms and values.

This book aims to expose the ideological and political mystification of Jesus concealed in the transmission of the tradition about him. It illustrates the exegetical relevance of:

- the social history of formative Christianity;
- the diachronic investigation of the evolution of the Jesus traditions;
- the synchronic investigation which unfolds the Jesus tradition by focusing on the genre of biography;
- the theory of the institutionalization of charismatic authority and conflict theory for understanding the process of naming Jesus.

Abbreviations

AASF	Annales Academiae Scientiarum Fennicae
AGJU	Arbeiten zur Geschichte des Antiken Judentums und des Urchristentums
AGSU	Arbeiten zur Geschichte des Spätjudentums und Urchristentums
ANRW	*Aufstieg und Niedergang der römischen Welt*
ATANT	Abhandlungen zur Theologie des Alten und Neuen Testaments
BETL	Bibliotheca Ephemeridum Theologicarum Lovaniensium
BHT	Beiträge zur historischen Theologie
BJS	Brown Judaic Studies
BR	*Biblical Research*
BTB	*Biblical Theology Bulletin*
BWANT	Beiträge zur Wissenschaft vom Alten und Neuen Testament
BZNW	Beihefte zur Zeitschrift für die neutestamentliche Wissenschaft
CBQ	*Catholic Biblical Quarterly*
CBQMS	Catholic Biblical Quarterly Monograph Series
CRINT	Compendia Rerum Iudaicarum ad Novum Testamentum
EdF	Erträge der Forschung
EvT	*Evangelische Theologie*
FRLANT	Forschungen zur Religion und Literatur des Alten und Neuen Testaments
GBS	Guides to Biblical Scholarship
GNT	Grundrisse zum Neuen Testament
HRWG	*Handbuch Religionswissenschaftlicher Grundbegriff*
HTS	Harvard Theological Studies
HvTSt	*Hervormde Teologiese Studies*

Abbreviations

HvTStSup	Hervormde Teologiese Studies Supplement Series
ICC	International Critical Commentary
IRT	Issues in Religion and Theology
JAAR	*Journal of the American Academy of Religion*
JBL	*Journal of Biblical Literature*
JSNT	*Journal for the Study of the New Testament*
JSJSup	Supplements to the Journal for the Study of Judaism
JSNTSup	Journal for the Study of the New Testament Supplement Series
JSOT	*Journal for the Study of the Old Testament*
JTS	*Journal of Theological Studies*
KEK	Kritisch-exegetischer Kommentar über das Neue Testament
LCL	Loeb Classical Library
NICNT	New International Commentary on the New Testament.
Neot	*Neotestamentica*
NovT	*Novum Testamentum*
NovTSup	Supplements to Novum Testamentum
NTL	New Testament Library
NTOA	Novum Testamentum et Orbis Antiquus
NTS	*New Testament Studies*
NTTS	New Testament Tools and Studies
OBT	Overtures to Biblical Theology
ÖTK	Ökumenischer Taschenbuchkommentar zum Neuen Testament
PTMS	Princeton Theological Monograph Series
QD	Quaestiones disputatae
SBS	Stuttgarter Bibelstudien
SemeiaSt	Semeia Studies
SNTSMS	Society for New Testament Studies Monograph Series
SSN	Studia Semitica Neerlandica
SUNT	Studien zur Umwelt des Neuen Testaments
TDNT	*Theological Dictionary of the New Testament*. 10 vols. Edited by Gerhard Kittel and Gerhard Friedrich. Translated by Geoffrey. W. Bromiley. Grand Rapids: Eerdmans, 1964–76.
Teubner	Bibliotheca Scriptorum Graecorum et Romanorum Teubneriana
TS	*Theological Studies*

Abbreviations

WMANT	Wissenschaftliche Monographien zum Alten und Neuen Testament
WUNT	Wissenschaftliche Untersuchungen zum Neuen Testament
ZNW	*Zeitschrift für die neutestamentliche Wissenschaft und die Kunde der älteren Kirche*
ZTK	*Zeitschrift für Theologie und Kirche*

CHAPTER 1

Naming Jesus—A Matter of Cultural and Political Labeling

IN THE MIDDLE OF the previous century Thomas W Manson ([1937] 1949) wrote the book, *The Sayings of Jesus* in which he emphasized Q as a very old source of the teachings of Jesus from which the evangelists Matthew and Luke derived a major part of their material. According to Manson the two most certain facts in the gospel tradition are that Jesus taught and that he was crucified. In Mark Jesus is called "teacher" twelve times and four times "Rabbi," the usual name for a teacher of Israel. Manson raised the question whether Jesus, so to speak, was "academically qualified for the title of Rabbi?" The impression left is that Jesus was deemed not a "village craftsman turned amateur theologian but rather a competent scholar who had developed heretical tendencies" (Manson 1949:11).

Though Manson takes the history of the Jesus tradition in Q and the synoptic gospels into account, these *diachronic* insights do not function heuristically. Diachronic exegesis means that texts are seen as the products of a writing process that takes place *over a period* (*dia* + *chronos*) – in other words literature that is produced in an evolutionary fashion by means of either an anonymous group who transmitted their story orally or literarily or individuals who added, modified and interpreted received traditions, and in doing so changed their meaning. An exegete who takes this process seriously is engaged in a "diachronic" discovery of plausible meanings.

However, Manson's interpretation of the gospel traditions was rather an early example of *synchronic* exegesis. This means that he inferred the meaning of the traditions from what they communicated *within a particu-*

lar period (*sun + chronos*) rather than what they could have meant during earlier stages of transmission. It is such a type of interpretation that places the relevance of the theme of "Jesus as teacher" in the spotlight because it functioned within the specific social context of synagogical controversy. Manson's conclusion was that Jesus had "authority" on account of his being a "competent scholar" and therefore he was a Rabbi.

Yet, a somewhat different picture of Jesus the teacher can also be painted. Christopher Tuckett (1996:283), for example, takes the context of conflict in which Jesus found himself, into account. According to Tuckett, "much of the Christological awareness in Q focuses on the hostility and rejection experienced by Jesus . . . and the same experiences will come to his followers."

These views of Manson and Tuckett differ substantially. According to the first, Jesus is *subject* of personal agency. According to the second, Jesus is *object* of affected interpretation. Nearly a decade before Tuckett pointed out the development in the Q tradition from the conflict experienced by Jesus to the conflict experienced by Jesus' followers, Vernon K Robbins (1984) explored a similar development in the Markan tradition. This was the development from the pre-Easter Jesus as teacher, to a reflection of the post-Easter Jesus movements on the relevance of Jesus' teaching for them. Robbins discussed various aspects of this development, for example the "validation" of Jesus' authority in order that the followers of Jesus could be prepared for their own vindication. He also indicated how "Christological titles" were used as a means to validate Jesus' authority and vindicate the post-Easter Jesus movements.

Validation and its opposite defamation are means of social labeling, either as an act of honoring or as an act of stigmatization. In Jesus studies Bruce Malina and Jerome Neyrey (1988:x–xi) refer to "naming as labeling" as a "Christology from the side", that is how Jesus would have been experienced by his contemporaries rather than how his later followers theologized about his words and deeds. One of the reasons for Jesus' followers calling him "Teacher", "Prophet", "Messiah", "Son of Man", "Kyrios", "Saviour" and "Son of God" could be that Jesus spoke and acted in a such a compelling way that they expressed their experience of him by honoring him with these "predicates of value" (in German: "Würdeprädikationen").

This book explains why and how the earliest followers of Jesus attributed titles such as "Rabbi" to Jesus. It aims to do so in terms of a particular

Naming Jesus—A Matter of Cultural and Political Labeling

social theory. A diachronic investigation will be done and a synchronic description given of the Jesus tradition, to explain the social dynamics of such attribution. I will make use of the work of the Swedish Biblical scholar, Bengt Holmberg. In his pioneering work in the field of Pauline studies, Holmberg showed what the role of power is in the process of the ligitimation and institutionalization of authority (Holmberg 1978:125). An example of this process is when the authority of a leader is accepted as legitimate. Holmberg's case study in this regard is Paul, an apostle of Jesus, whereas Jesus himself is the case study of this book. In a brief overview of the research of the past half a century I explore why research on Q and the synoptic gospels have changed so substantially in a time-span of fifty years.

From the perspective of postmodern values, I aim to demystify the process of the validation of authority. Jesus' authority was grounded in his wisdom. In this regard, Anthony Thiselton (1994:453-472) suggests a useful perspective for studying the titles of Jesus. Thiselton (1994:465) "borrows" the concept of institutional authorization "from social history or from sociology". He describes what was "implicit" about Jesus, as the state of affairs concerning the identity, role, and authority of Jesus (Thiselton 1994:461).

The model Thiselton employs to work out the concept of institutional authorization is literary theoretical rather than social-scientific. He explains the development of "implicit Christology" to "explicit Christology" in terms of "speech-act theory."[1] Thiselton argues that the "performing of acts on the basis of *causal force* constitutes in essence an *act of power through self-assertion*. On the other hand, illocutionary acts which rest on institutional roles serve the purpose as *acts which point by implication away from the self to some source of authority which lies beyond the self alone* (Thiselton 1994:462-463; his emphasis). With regard to the study of Christological titles, Thiselton does not attempt to work out the "evolution" or the "unfolding" of the "illocutionary" (Christological) statements about Jesus. He also does not discuss the social dynamics of institutional authorization.

I argue that the Q tradition (and Mark and Matthew) originated within the context of scribal activity. For the demystification of scribal

---

1. For speech-act theory, see J R Searle 1969; 1979:58–75, J L Austin 1962; N Wolterstorff 1980:198–239, and F Recanati (1987:260–66).

activity, I employ conflict theory to interpret scribal activity in the Middle-East.

The general dynamics of social conflict illuminates the specific conflict situations of both Jesus and his followers. A socio-historical approach sheds light on the pre-industrial agrarian context of Jesus and his followers. Narrative criticism provides the interpretative instrument to explore the biographical nature of the gospel tradition and to explain the polemics in the plot of the relevant stories. The main objective of the book is to trace the development of the Jesus tradition from an earlier to a later context in terms of the process of the institutionalization of charismatic authority. It illustrates how through this process titles were attributed to Jesus from a post-Easter perspective in order to validate his authority.

Power is part of the process of institutionalization. My focus is on the dynamics of authority and power in the transmission of religious traditions in order to better understand the relationship between authority, institutionalization and Christological titles used for Jesus. Such a theoretical approach calls for an evolving and flexible design by means of which the Jesus tradition is interpreted ideological-critically and socio-politically. Military power and literacy were products of an advanced agrarian society. Powerful people (élite) employed scribes and soldiers (retainers) to exercise authority. Scribes, who usually came from the group of sages and seers, often used honorary titles to praise their employers.

My thesis is that scribes attributed honorary titles to the sage Jesus of Nazareth after his death. This process gained momentum after the destruction of the Jerusalem temple by the Romans during the "Great Jewish Revolt" in the late sixties of the first century CE. This period became known as "formative Judaism" and "formative Christianity". Pharisees began a process of spiritual, economic and political reformation. Destroyed and damaged cities and villages were restored. Scribes became involved in the restoration of villages. They were called "village scribes", an Egyptian title brought to Palestine and Syria by the Ptolemaians. Their Hellenistic administrative structures were continued under Roman rule. After the battle of Actium in 31 BCE the "Roman government restored free economic enterprise, but maintained the existing oppressive range of taxation, and much of the Ptolemaic bureaucratic administration" (Appelbaum 1976:704). According to Fiensy (1991:160–61), the so-called "nomes" were the basic social unit:

Naming Jesus—A Matter of Cultural and Political Labeling

The land in Egypt was organized administratively for tax purposes along the lines of the ancient divisions, called "nomes". Each nome was divided into toparchies, with the smallest administrative unit being the village. Palestine had a similar organization[2] Each large administrative unit had both a military and economic overseer, and the smaller units had probably only one administrator.[3] Over the entire administrative complex stood the second most powerful man in Ptolemaic Egypt, the Dioiketes, whose job was to oversee all the finances of the king, both his private estates and his tax revenues.[4]

These "overseers" were previously categorized as elders (*presbuteroi*), leaders (*proestotes*), first men (*protoi*), notables (*gnoromoi*), powerful ones (*dunatoi*), the most honourable (*time, genos*), and honored men (see Fiensy 1991:160–61). These names refer to people in powerful positions. Village administration in first-century Galilee, modeled after the Egyptian system, had already advanced from *simple agrarian* to *advanced agrarian*. The earlier system based on kinship structures developed into a bureaucratic organization on village level, which meant that a number of extended families were clustered together (cf. Lenski et al. 1995:182). William Arnal (2001:151–52), in his extensive study on scribal activity in antiquity, shows how the phenomenon of names used as honorable titles in the Egyptian bureaucratic tradition, was brought to Palestine by the Ptolemees and became a writing technique among the scribes. The following quote explains the process:

> "This kind of phenomenon must necessarily have been somewhat variegated: more or less absent or unofficial in tiny settlements, exaggerated or formalized in larger ones, and shared by a greater or smaller number of prominent families. In the case of larger villages and towns, with several prominent families, with diverse economic circumstances and plot sizes, with tenancy, and with at least nominal attachment to an outside power (Egypt, Syria, Judea, depending on circumstances), a local administrative apparatus was required. The necessarily limited political affairs of such communities were conducted by a collection of elders, some of whom, perhaps, from time to time bore the title of village leader (*komarches*) or something similar, their legal affairs settled by magis-

---

2. Cf. Hengel 1974:20.
3. Cf. Tcherikover and Fuks 1957; Hengel 1974:21; Rostovzeff 1922:80.
4. Cf. Rostovzeff 1922:26; Hengel 1974:19; Tarn 1952:196.

trates, while their total polity and community life was expressed in gatherings of village assemblies.

Under such circumstances, even the most de facto autonomous of towns required various official and witnessed bills of sale, petitions, contracts, marriage agreements, wills, and so forth, as well as an apparatus for the administration of justice. Thus, in addition to local strong men and affluent families, a small class of literate administrators was essential to the smooth functioning of the region even prior to Roman-Herodian city building. Such a role was normally filled by the so-called village clerk (*komogrammateus*). We have extensive evidence from Egypt for the presence and function of these figures, and some indications that they were a feature of Palestinian village life as well. As their title indicates, their primary task was writing: composing various official documents for those unable to write; forwarding petitions to appropriate officials; ensuring the execution of legal responsibilities; and serving as witnesses, middlemen, or accountants for persons with extensive business dealings.

These administrators would not be found in every settlement and could not have been very numerous even in larger settlements. Thus a single scribe might very well have serviced a cluster of villages, and inhabitants of smaller settlements, when seeking justice, preparing documents, or pursuing other official business, had to travel to the nearest settlement that had a scribe. These duties did not occupy the scribes full-time. They were as engaged by agricultural production as their fellow villagers and were drawn from the local peasantry itself, with whom they probably, to some degree, identified. At the same time, however, their roles involved a measure of prestige and power, at least within the village and its immediate area. These administrators thus occupied a middle position between the average smallholder and the larger landowners who dominated village life and whose interests the scribes tended to represent. They therefore formed something of a rudimentary retainer class, who mediated between the ordinary people and the upper classes, and who, in so doing, sought to maximize their own power and privileges."

This Egyptian influence forms the basis of my thesis (cf. Horsley 2007:74–76). Structures of Egyptian village administration provide insights for understanding village administration in Galilee during the first half of the first century CE (cf Schams 1998:88–90, 125–27, 326). On account of Hellenistic influence since 300 BCE, the economic structure of the Palestinian society was similar to that of the rest of the Graeco-Roman world. Increasingly land was owned by rich families who mostly lived in the cities. The clan and extended family systems crumbled (Holmberg 1990:26). Hans Kippenberg (1978) describes in detail how the dispossession of land took place and how it became increasingly necessary for peasants to make their living as day labourers. Theissen (1983:142–59) explains the differences and tensions between the Judean élite and the peasants in the rural regions. ". . . Jerusalem dominated the rest of the land economically, politically, and culturally." The social class, status and power of the élite in Jerusalem and also in other cities like Sephoris, were not determined by political power and wealth. These desirable qualities were determined by factors such as purity of heritage, profession, and "academic"/"theologico-judicial proficiency".

When Nero came into power (54 CE) the whole administrative system changed extensively. In 54 CE Nero transferred Tiberias and Magdala-Tarichaeae to the jurisdiction of Agrippa II (see Jos Ant 20.1.59 – cf Kloppenborg 2000:235). One of the consequences of these changes was that many scribes in Palestine were replaced and this changed the character of scribal activity. Perdue (2008:19-20) describes the social role of "sages and scribes in Egypt" as follows:

> "Scribal careers normally took two paths: royal or temple administration. The administration of the kingdom was highly bureaucratic and required scribes at every level of civil life. Scribes were in charge of building projects including tombs, temples, and cities . . . and in operating the kingdom's administration, including the activities of the military, correspondence, diplomacy, and the writing and archiving of records . . . The social status of Egyptian scribes was a coveted one. In essence, the scribes were responsible for the development and transmission of Egyptian culture, ranging from building projects to literary texts."

Scribes were generally also people of influence, though they could be found in all walks of life: they could be from priestly or Levitical families, both the higher and lower ones, they could be traders, artisans or even day workers (see Jeremias 1969:264). As patrons or benefactors they had a "political position" which in the village would mean a position of leadership (Arnal 2001: 150151). According to Holmberg (1990:27), even scribal activity became institutionalized: "In the time of Jesus and the early church, the scribes formed an influential part of the highest Jewish authority, the Sanhedrin, and after the catastrophe of AD 70 this body was reconstituted as a purely scribal council" (Holmberg 1990:27).

From the time of Jesus to the destruction of the temple in 70 CE the struggle for supremacy between the scribes of the ruling class and those of lesser nobility escalated (see Jeremias 1969:233). This could be seen especially within the cultic setting of Jerusalem. Since academic proficiency (knowledge) bestowed social power, a scribe underwent many years of training before being officially accepted as an ordained (*semikah*) scholar or *hakam*. A non-ordained scholar was known as a *talmid hakam* (see Jeremias 1969:235). A person who was still training to be a scribe, was called a pupil, *talmid*. There was much personal contact between pupil and teacher. In an oral culture the teacher spoke and the pupil listened attentively. When a pupil had mastered the teachings of the master and was able to reach independent decisions and judgements on religious matters, he was acknowledged as *talmid hakam*, an ordained scholar. Jesus, son of Sirach, was a well-known *hakam*.[5] In his work, Ecclesiasticus 38:24-39 (in Moore 1962:40-41), Sirach paints the following portrait of a scribe:

> Learning is the privilege of leisure. Husbandmen and artisans are the support of the social structure, but, wholly occupied as they must be in their several callings and often highly expert in them, they have no time for the wide-ranging studies that make the scholar. They are therefore not qualified to be called to the council or to take the lead in the assembly; they cannot sit on the judge's bench, for they do not understand the principles of the law, and cannot bring out the rights of the case and a just judgement. Different is the case of the man who gives his whole mind to it, and concentrates his thought on the law of the Most High. He will seek out the wisdom of all the ancients, and occupy himself with the study of prophecies, and pay attention to expositions of famous men, and will penetrate into the elusive turns of parables. He will search out the hidden meaning of proverbs, and will be versed in the enigmas of parables.

Sirach also describes the influence and power of scribes since the beginning of the second century BCE (Sir 37:33—39:11). As the sages of the past, the scribes enjoyed precedence in the assemblies of the people. They were the judges and the legal experts. They had knowledge of traditional wisdom which they could apply to the situations of their times.

5. See Moore ([1927] 1962:37-41; cf. Davies 1992:132).

Naming Jesus—A Matter of Cultural and Political Labeling

Their knowledge of the "laws of the Most High" gave them access to great men and rulers (see Schürer [1885-1924] 1979:323). The function of the scribes was to enable those in power to maintain their control: control over the economy (keeping commercial records), control and possession of the past and of literature (keeping the archives and writing history), control over the future (predictive writing), and maintaining the social values of the élite classes. Though the scribes worked for people in power positions, they themselves also formed a privileged class. They did not necessarily agree with the authorities, but disagreements would always be expressed "in the words of an earlier prophet, so that no direct criticism of the current authorities is explicit. The scribes, retainers of the governing institutions, were in large measure insulated from the majority of the population [peasantry]; physically (they lived in cities), economically (they were supported by the taxpayer) and culturally" (Davies 1992:107-8).

In New Testament times the scribes were the undisputed spiritual leaders. In Greek they were called *grammateis* (Scripture experts). The Latin title for these scholars was *homines literati*, which is the equivalent of the Hebrew *soferim*. Besides this general description they were more specifically called *nomikoi*, in other words interpreters of the law (see Matt 22:35; Luke 7:30; 10:25; 11:45-46, 52; 15:3). Scribes were also known as *nomodidaskaloi* (teachers of the law—see Luke 5:17; Acts 5:34). Josephus (*War* 6.5.3) calls them, among others, *hierogrammateis* (holy scribes) and "narrators of the law of the fathers" (*Ant.* 17.6.2). According to Schürer (1979:325), the "extraordinary respect which these sages enjoyed among the people finds expression even in the titles given them." The reduction of honour was also expressed by a change in title. Kloppenborg (2000:200 note 42) puts at as follows: "This is probably the level of minor village official that Josephus has in mind when he records the threat of Herod's sons Aristobulus and Alexander to reduce their other brothers to the status of 'village scribes' (*kōmōn grammateis*, War 1.479; *kōmogrammateis*, Ant. 16.203)."

Rabbis enjoyed a high social status (cf Jeremias [1962] [1967] 1969:244). Pupils were even encouraged to honour their teachers more than their own fathers and mothers (see Schürer 1979:327): "In the study of the Torah, if a son acquired much wisdom while sitting before his teacher, his teacher precedes his father, for both he and his father are obliged to honour the teacher" (*m. Ker.* 6:9; translation in Schürer 1979:327). This respect for the rabbis is also portrayed in Matthew 23:6-7; Mark 12:38-39; Luke 11:43; 20:46: "they love the place of honor at banquets and the most important seats in the synagogues, they love to be greeted in the marketplaces and to have men call them 'Rabbi'" (Matt 23:6-7 NIV). Their clothes were even similar to those of the priests and the nobility (*stolas*—Mark 12:38//Luke 20:46; *ampechonas* and *dalmatikas*—Epiphanius, *Haer.* 15).

Though there were similarities between scribes, priests and the nobility, not all scribes were of noble or priestly origin (see Davies 1992:107). Stern (1976:621) points out that extensive knowledge of scribes during the period 2 BCE to 1 CE is available to us. Scribes came from all over Palestine and the Diaspora: the regions of Judea, Jerusalem, Samaria, and the Arbel mountains in Galilee (Stern 1976:621). Their social backgrounds varied: some were from the peasantry and others even came from the families of proselytes. Though the insider nobility would be naturally reluctant to acknowledge the scribes of lower and outsider origins (they had no ascribed honor; see Malina 1993b:8), sometimes outsider patrons, for instance Roman authorities, would ascribe honour to these scribes. This, of course, contributed to the tension between the insider and the outsider scribes. In time Roman authorities began to acknowledge sages as official leaders of the people (see Urbach 1968:38ff). "[A]s early as 200 B.C.E. 'the scribes of the Temple' formed a privileged group in the Temple hierarchy" (Bickerman 1988:163). "In the Herodian temple it was the *grammateus* (the *sofer*) and not the priest who sat in Moses' seat." *Soferim* refers to "penmen, drafters of documents, and teachers of elementary reading and writing" (Bickerman 1988:163). Scribal activity differed from those priestly schools (e.g. the Qumran community) where wisdom/knowledge was often seen as esoteric insider information.

> The scribe had to be able to write for everyone and to read anything written. His art was needed for the conduct of public affairs and private affairs, for temples, for accounts, and for correspondence. For this reason, schools in our sense of the term existed for the scribal profession from the beginning. Furthermore, because writing and books were the proper subjects of instruction in these schools, it is understandable, for instance, that the Egyptian literature that has been preserved for us has come mainly from school texts (Bickermann 1988:164).

Naming Jesus—A Matter of Cultural and Political Labeling

It has become clear that knowledge of the structure of village administration in rural Galilee is necessary in order to understand the context of Jesus' message. One can assume that the transmitters of the Jesus traditions had an intimate knowledge of his frame of reference. They would know that, when Jesus spoke of God, it would be in terms of the structure of village administration rather than in terms of the power structures of the emperor. In the process of encountering God through Jesus, the followers of Jesus transferred the symbols he used for God to Jesus himself. These symbols often come from the realm of village administration.

During this period the first written traditions about Jesus originated in Galilee. An example of this is the Sayings Gospel Q (see Kloppenborg 2000:87). Village scribes who conserved the Mosaic legacy ("the great tradition") and those bound to the wisdom of Jesus ("the little tradition"), came into conflict. In order to survive, the little tradition adopted aspects of the language of the great tradition. In this process names that were used for and by Jesus were infused with the values of the great tradition and gradually became honorary titles. Because of this history, the titles could be used either to enhance Jesus' wisdom and empower people, or as instruments of power. Attempts to study the phenomenon of exploitation are frustrated by the reality of the silenced voices of the oppressed. That means that there is no material to study. Only what had been written, can be studied. The officials were responsible for written records. They were the representatives of the rulers and in that capacity the facilitators of the manipulation and exploitation of the masses. It follows that a change of ruler would have a downward spiraling effect on the ruling class and the officials. Officials who did not adapt to the new policies and interests were replaced by others or they themselves withdrew as official retainers (e.g., the Essenes withdrew from Jerusalem when the Hasmonean élite began collaborating with the Greeks—see Davies 1987:16). The written records or the new regime would differ in content from what was previously documented.

I intend to argue that "texts" (e.g., those that originated in the pre-70 CE Jesus community in Jerusalem, independent of the temple), that were transmitted orally and found their way into texts like the Gospel of Matthew, can be attributed to such scribal activity. Documents such as for instance the Sayings Gospel Q are products of scribal activity outside of Jerusalem. Some scribal activity therefore functioned independently of a temple environment and the priestly classes. That this became possible can be attributed to the Egyptian Ptolemaic heritage (see Bickerman 1988:69-80). Bickerman (1988:79) puts it this way: "The evaluation of the psychological impact of Ptolemaic domination is even more difficult. The essential and immeasurable factor was the secular character of Greek civilization, a civilization that had neither a priestly caste nor priestly scribes, and that was represented by an intelligentsia independent of both palace and temple... It was precisely the secular quality of Greek civilization that made the impulses coming from it so powerful" (Bickerman 1988:79).

The wisdom of the sages was heard on the streets, the market places and the households (see Neusner [1984] 1988:38). Scribes from the lower social classes could rise in social standing because of their popularity or for other reasons. The families of well-known scribes (whether of noble or humble origins) would share in their public honour and/or upward mobility. During the Second Temple period the family of Jesus is a good example of this. During Jesus' lifetime his family (his mother and brothers) were not supporters and advocates of his message (see Mark 3:31–35). However, after Jesus' death things changed. On account of the tradition of his resurrection, his honour increased dramatically. In the Graeco-Roman world resurrection meant that someone was taken up into the divine realm.

Even though the members of Jesus' family were originally "outsiders" from Galilee, their standing and public acknowledgement, rapidly increased after the death of Jesus. James, the brother of Jesus, in particular, enjoyed respect and upward social mobility in the cultic setting of Jesus followers in Jerusalem. He became a leading figure of scribal activity in the Jesus community in Jerusalem. This can be seen in the authorship of a later canonical document being attributed to him pseudepigraphically. James' popularity in Jerusalem culminated in his being put to death by the Sadducean High Priest (see Jos Ant 20.200-201). Eusebius (*Hist. Eccl.* III.11.1—see Stern 1976:576) refers to a tradition that one of James' cousins became his successor as a "Christian" leader in Jerusalem. The earliest witness attesting to James' highly respected position is 1 Corinthians 15:7. Galatians 2:9 also mentions James as one of the "pillars" of the Jesus group in Jerusalem whose opinions were highly valued. According to 1 Corinthians 9:5 other brothers of Jesus also played an active part in this community. The influence of James and the family of Jesus cannot, however, be attributed to Jesus having shown them any preference whatsoever. "James did not play a leading part in the affairs of the Christian community just because of his personal talents. It is to be attributed to his association with Jesus' family as such. His enlistment in the ranks of the new community entailed, in accordance with the practice of the time, a certain hegemony of Jesus' family in the Christian community" (Stern 1976:574).

My focus is on the process of *naming*. New Testament authors, on account of their particular observations, used symbols of power and authority to legitimize new structures of power. These structures of power were analogous to existing power structures in society. In the past the titles have been studied mainly from a diachronic (historical-critical) or synchronic (literary-theoretical) perspective. However, as Kloppenborg (2000:114) puts it: "Despite their differing approaches, diachronic and synchronic approaches are not opposed but complementary. They serve to corroborate, supplement and correct each other, since, after all, both seek to understand the construction and intent of the gospels, merely from different perspectives. Most actual analyses of gospel literature will involve both forms of analysis."

My argument is that the allocation of "power" to Jesus was in effect an attempt to affirm the self-respect, authority and power of the "leaders" and "scribes" of the earliest Jesus groups. The insight that underlying power relations exist in all forms of communication, however innocuous they may seem, is the product of the postmodern paradigm, in which we increasingly find ourselves. This book confirms that the followers of Jesus acknowledged and expressed his authority by means of naming. These "names" developed into "titles" when the post-Easter followers of Jesus allocated power to him. It therefore contributes to our understanding:

- of the relevance of the social history of formative Christianity;
- that diachronic and synchronic approaches to the text can be used in a complementary way;
- of the relevance of the diachronic investigation of the evolution of the Jesus tradition (by focusing on the Son of God title);

Institutionalization of Authority and the Naming of Jesus

- of the relevance of the synchronic investigation in unfolding the Jesus tradition in the genre of biography (by focusing on the Sayings Gospel Q and the synoptic gospels);
- of the relevance of institutionalization of authority in formative Christianity.

CHAPTER 2

A Synchronic Test Case: Q and the Synoptic Gospels

IN THE SYNCHRONIC INVESTIGATION of the names of Jesus, the Sayings Gospel Q will be used as case study along with the synoptic gospels. The aim of this chapter is to describe and explain the relationships between the names of Jesus as worked out in the Sayings Gospel Q and the synoptic gospels. Names of Jesus are investigated primarily from a synchronic perspective. The Sayings Gospel Q does not have a narrative structure like the biographical gospels, but consists of clusters of *logia*. This gospel is considered to be the oldest of all the canonical and extra-canonical gospels. Q is "written evidence" of the Jesus tradition and contains traces of an oral phase. Much later the oral tradition was written down in the form of narratives. The redactional work done on Q shows the beginnings of a narrative framework, but the Gospel of Mark is the first available example of a biographical gospel (a complete narrative). In the Gospel of Mark the sapiential and kerygmatic traditions were merged. The sapiential tradition in Mark was derived from Q, pre-Marcan sources and common oral traditions. The kerygmatic tradition in Mark was derived from the Jesus faction in Jerusalem and Pauline Christianity in Antioch/Damascus. It is not known how Mark came into contact with these two relatively independent traditions. According to Richard Burridge ([1992] 1999) Mark followed the narrative form also found in Graeco-Roman parallel texts (cf. Vorster 1980:46–61).

In this chapter the following four matters will be discussed:

- the nature of narrative poetics;
- the transmission from oral tradition to written evidence;

- the "biographical" nature of the gospel genre;
- a synchronic analysis of the Sayings Gospel Q, Mark, Matthew and Luke.

The aim of these four sections is to demonstrate that the transmission from oral tradition to written evidence did not take place without deliberate ideological interventions by the transmitters and copyists. A second aim is to indicate that narrative analyses often do not uncover these interventions. I focus on the names used for Jesus in the written evidence. As far as Q is concerned, a synchronic description of the composition of Q will be given and the tradition history of Q will be investigated.

The term "poetics" comes from the Greek ποιεῖν (to make). It refers to the literary theory by means of which the organization of a discourse is investigated (see Gräbe 1986:156). The gospels are regarded as narratives since the elements of a narrative are present: a narrator, a story and a reader. Analyzing a narrative comprises investigating the elements of author, narrator, implied reader, real reader, characters, time and space in their various relationships (see Moore 1989:41–55). The plot (how events are structured) of a story can be simplex or complex. Characterization is essential to the plot, which is determined by the relationships between the characters. Intrigue is created by elements of surprise and tension. The *point of view* of the narrator is the way in which the story is presented. The point of view refers to the perspective of the narrator, in other words how the world is seen and presented to the reader. It also refers to the ideological perspective which determines how the narrator evaluates the world (see Sternberg 1985:129). Because the gospels are religious texts, the narrator's ideological perspective is, simultaneously, the theological perspective. In the analysis of narrative strategies, the narrator's ideology/theology is revealed (see Van Aarde 2005:161–78). In other words the underlying "idea" can be identified.

The gospels are narratives of a simplex nature: the perspective of the author, the narrator and the main character (protagonist) are the same (see Petersen 1978a:97–121). All events are presented from one perspective, that is the perspective of Jesus. However, the nature of this dominant ideological/theological perspective differs in the various gospels. Once written, a story has a life of its own: its own world, design and inner harmony. The gospels are such stories (see Vorster 1986:42–62). They are not pure fiction, however, but are the literary products of a narrator who is, at the same time, also a redactor. The work of the redactor is to gather material from traditions and rework them in a creative way. The final product articulates the theology and ideology of the narrator. A narrative interpretation of the text is not so much interested in the historical author or reader, but rather in the narratological techniques the author uses (cf. Moore 1989:38). These techniques reveal the ideological motives behind the redactional work. Phraseology (or diction) refers to the choices made when editing the source material: what is included, left our, expanded or reduced? Sometimes the author is not completely successful in harmonizing the source material with the story and then the source becomes more visible to the analyst.

A story mirrors its world and so do the gospels. The socio-political, economical, religious and cultural context in which the story was born, is revealed. The gospels, as redaction of earlier traditions, reveal two social realities: the world of the earlier period of the transmission of the traditions, and the world of the later period when the story was written. The traditional material was selected and used in such a way that it could contribute to the process of meaning making and interpreting the social world of the author. The following are examples of elements from the Jesus tradition used by the evangelists in this way:

- Jesus' conflict with scribes and village leaders concerning the interpretation of the Torah sheds light on the rift in the post-Easter community of Jesus followers between the synagogue and the Jesus factions which led to the reorganization of Pharisaism at Jabneh and other centres in Galilee and Syria.
- Jesus' claim that God is his Father is used to ascribe authority to Jesus and those who proclaim the *kerygma* about him, and evolves to the canonization of the New Testament documents in the early Christianity.

The gospels were written from the perspective of hindsight (post-Easter) and are left open ended. The story does not end with the end of Jesus' earthly life, but is only completed when the Jesus movements take it further. The story is aimed at convincing the reader to do exactly that. Narrative strategies are employed to draw the reader into the story in order to experience and become actively involved with the story. The author's intention is to change the social world. With this in mind, the narrative strategy is chosen.

Not only the text itself, but also the strategy the author uses to communicate, are products of the social environment. In order to investigate the poetics (strategy) of a text, both the macrosocial context (extratextual, e.g. the first-century Mediterranean environment) and the microsocial context (intratextual, e.g. how the first-century Mediterranean environment is mirrored in the narrative world of the text) should be taken into account. The text is not equal to the reality of its surrounding world, but presents a *perspective* on that reality. The gospels narratives each have their own unique theological/ideological approach.

The gospels are related as third person narratives. The choice of this narrative strategy means that the narrator's position is outside of the story (not as in a first person narrative where the narrator is a character in the story). Therefore the author *refers to* the characters by giving them names: proper names (e.g., Peter), personal pronouns (e.g., she or he), and titles (e.g., Son of God) (cf. Petersen 1978a:112; Moore 1989:27). A third person narrator chooses the strategy of either an *omniscient point of view*, or a *limited point of view*, creating respectively distance or proximity between characters and author/reader (see Uspensky 1973:83). An investigation of this strategy can elucidate whether a character acts according to the ideological/theological perspective of the narrator (and becomes a bearer of it—Uspenski 1973:97-98), or in opposition to it.

The *psychological* narrative situation is about the narrator's choice whether to describe the character internally (describing the characters' innermost, thoughts, feelings and observations) or externally (the acts of the character are described in an impersonal manner).

The narrator also makes a choice concerning *time*: either story time (the chronological, linear reconstruction of events) or plotted time (cf. Brink 1987:92; Petersen 1978a:47-48). The latter pertains to how the narrator manipulates time in order to emphasize certain events. The study of how time is employed as a narrative strategy will reveal the narrator's ideological/theological focus. There is a similar distinction concerning *space* in a narrative: whether it simply indicates location, or whether the spaces in the story have some functional significance (see Van Eck 1995:137). The latter being the case, an analysis of space in the story will also reveal the narrator's ideological/theological perspective. The choice of narrative strategy will emphasize a tendency toward either consensus or opposition/conflict in the story.

An analysis of phraseology reveals how characters are portrayed and gives clues as to the ideological perspective(s) of the narrator (cf. Vorster 1987a:57-76). There are two types of characters (see Kenney 1966:29-30). The simplex character presents only one ideological perspective throughout the story. The complex character, on the other hand, often acts in an unexpected way, is at times hesitant, uncertain and full of doubts. This creates tension. Some characters merely play a "decorative" role and are not important to the development of the plot. They can fulfill the function of, for instance, creating the norms for judging the main character. The ideological perspective of the narrator is revealed in the way in which the characters relate to one another. The ideological perspective of the narrator can be seen in the emotions, observations, insights and thoughts that the author ascribes to the characters.

Naming can be used by the narrator to express the characters' perspectives on their relationships (see Uspenski 1973:22, 25-27). In the gospels, for instance, the names used for Jesus (e.g., Son of God, Kyrios, Son of Man) function as *Würdeprädikationen*. These *titular* names given to a character by others, are expression of their relationship with and perspective on the character.

From Oral Tradition to Written Evidence

The discussion of narrative poetics in this chapter is focused on the final redaction of the Sayings Gospel Q and the synoptic gospels. However, the tradition history of Q cannot be understood from a narrative perspective, since Q is not a biographical gospel type but a sayings gospel type. The interpretation of the tradition history necessitates insight into the development from the oral tradition of Jesus' sayings and deeds to the written evidence. In this regard Funk and Hoover (1993:16) note: "Because the evidence [see Geyser 1999b:3-21] offered by the gospels is hearsay evidence, scholars must be extremely cautious in taking the data at face value." The criteria are based on "observations regarding the editorial habits of Matthew and Luke as they make use of Mark and the Sayings Gospel

Q" as well as on "a scholarly assessment of the general direction in which the tradition developed" (Funk and Hoover 1993:17, 19).

Funk and Hoover (1993:19–25) list the following as some of what they call "the rules of written evidence":

- clustering and contexting;
- revision and commentary;
- false attribution;
- difficult sayings;
- christianizing Jesus.

Following Funk and Hoover, the "rules of written evidence" or criteria for distinguishing earlier from later strata in the Jesus tradition, will be briefly discussed.

Clustering and Contexting

After some time had passed and the sayings of Jesus had been repeated many times, these saying would probably not have been remembered in the exact context in which Jesus spoke them. In order to remember the sayings, they were clustered together according to themes or forms. This already happened fairly early on in the oral stage. This means that the sayings were not transmitted in their original context. In the process of grouping the "contextless" sayings, new contexts were created and with that new meanings and new interpretations of saying were inevitably created. "The tendency to cluster and compound often obscures the original sense of particular sayings or parables" (Funk and Hoover 1993:19). This was not only a passive process of something *happening to* the sayings. It could also be actively controlled. The grouping of sayings and parables could be used to control the interpretation. An example is how the phrase "son of man" (meaning humanity) was clustered (e.g., first within the theme of discipleship) and "reclustered" (referring to the title Son of Man). This process will be discussed further in the final chapter.

The clusters already present in the oral stage, were expanded in the written stage. In the process of writing the gospels, new *narrative* contexts were created for the sayings and deeds of Jesus. Their placement within the story serve the purpose of the narrative line and the author's intention (theology/ideology). The location of sayings and deeds are therefore different in the different gospels. That the contexts were created artificially, becomes obvious in that certain elements of the story are not congruent with what scholars know about the actual situation. There are, for example, instances in the gospels when the disciples were criticized for seeking positions of power. In reality this did not happen until after Jesus' death. The conflict revealed by this "new context" indicates a post-Easter setting and a process of institutionalization of the Jesus movements. Another example: In the gospels the Pharisees are depicted as Jesus' opponents, but in actual fact the Pharisees as a group only came onto the scene in Galilee after the destruction of the temple in 70 CE. Jesus' opponents would rather have been groups such as the pre–70 CE village leaders and scribes. Another indication of an artificially created context is when proof texts are cited from the Hebrew Scriptures in order to claim authority for the argument. This points to scribal activity. Funk and Hoover (1993:21) call this "the community's search in the scriptures for legitimacy." Legitimacy was an ideological concern which would have been of more importance to the later Jesus followers than to Jesus himself. In the process of institutionalization the ideological concerns of the followers of Jesus led to their attributing authority to Jesus.

Revision and Commentary

Whereas the first criterion discussed is concerned with *context*, revision and commentary are concerned with *content*. According to Funk and Hoover (1993:21–22), the evangelists modified sayings or controlled their interpretation in the following ways:

- The evangelists expanded sayings, or provided them with an interpretative overlay or comments.
- The evangelists revised or edited sayings to conform to their own individual language, style or viewpoint (Funk and Hoover 1993:21).

An example of this is Jesus calling God "Father" against the background of his *Vaterglaube*. Under the influence of Hellenism in a post-Easter setting the followers of Jesus called him "Son of God" (Mark 5:7).

In a different setting, for example a more Judean environment, Jesus was called the "Holy One of the Mighty One" (Mark 1:24).

False Attribution

Jesus as a *holy man* was regarded by his followers as a sage (see Borg 1991, 1994). It was general practice to attribute common wisdom to people who were deemed especially wise. This means that some of the sayings attributed to Jesus can also be found in secular sources. An example is the saying "it is better to give than to receive," which can be found in the wisdom of the moral philosophers of the time (see Acts 20:35; cf. Theissen 1999:90). By expanding Jesus' wisdom in this way, his authority was inflated. Therefore, in focusing on the phraseology of a particular gospel writer, it is possible to separate what is distinctive of Jesus' speech from the general wisdom attributed to him and from the narrative creations of the author. A general rule is that what can be expected to come from the culture and the traditional wisdom, has no claim to be from Jesus. On the other hand, that which is unexpected and goes against the grain, obviously did not originate from the traditional. The rules of evidence are the following (Funk and Hoover 1993:31):

- What Jesus said went against what would have been socially and religiously acceptable.
- Jesus' sayings often called for a reversal of roles.
- What Jesus said went against the ordinary and the expected.
- Exaggeration, humour and paradox are characteristic of Jesus sayings.
- Jesus used vivid images and often refrained from explaining his metaphors.

Examples of such images and metaphors can be found in the stories of the Good Samaritan (Luke 10:25–37) and the Prodigal Son (Luke 15:11–32). Samaritans were culturally unacceptable and therefore it is unusual for a Samaritan to be the hero of the story. The father of the prodigal son would have lost honour in his society if he responded positively to a son who treated him badly. His response to his younger son is therefore unusual.

Jesus' reticent manner is unusual in a culture where it is important for a man to increase his honour any way he can. Three generalizations about Jesus' manner are (Funk and Hoover 1993:32):

- Jesus does not take the initiative concerning conversations or healings.
- Jesus rarely speaks of himself in the first person.
- Jesus does not claim to be the *Messiah* (or, for that matter: *Son of Man*, *Kyrios*, or *Son of God*).

Another instance of false attribution is when scribes who became followers of Jesus, quoted from the Septuagint either presenting it as words of Jesus, or using prophesies to "prove" that an event in their time was the fulfillment of God's promises. A third example of false attribution is when statements of the followers of Jesus, influenced by their experiences of resurrection appearances, were attributed Jesus.

Difficult Sayings

Embarrassing or harsh sayings were sometimes modified in order to make them more acceptable. This can be seen in sayings that vary from evangelist to evangelist, especially when the saying could clearly have been cause for embarrassment. "Variations in difficult sayings often betray the struggle of the early Christian community to interpret or adapt sayings to its own situation" (Funk and Hoover 1993:23). An example is the saying that it is easier for a camel to go through the eye of a needle than for a rich man to enter the kingdom of God (Mark 10:24). The embarrassment is softened by Mark's addition of: "all things are possible with God" (Mark 10:27). By bringing God's infinite grace into the discussion, the harshness of the saying is toned down. A disputable saying could compromise Jesus' honour. By removing the embarrassment, Jesus' authority is protected.

Christianizing Jesus

Funk and Hoover (1993:24) state rather strongly that Jesus "is made to confess what Christians had come to believe" and elucidate this by explaining that "sayings and narratives that reflect knowledge of events that took place after Jesus' death are the creation of the evangelists or the oral tradition before them." This evidence of contextualization at a later level can, at the same time, be an indication of a process of institutionalization. "Features of stories that serve Christian convictions directly are likely to be the product of the Christian imagination" (Funk 1998:35). Signs of later "Christian" ideas attributed to the first followers of Jesus would indicate anachronism. The opposite is also true: data that, though embarrassing to the later Jesus factions, was nevertheless retained in the written text, could be an indication of authenticity. This means that the gospel writers included the material in spite of the embarrassment, because it could be traced back to Jesus. The baptism of Jesus by John is such an "embarrassing" incident. One can therefore be "skeptical of stories that undergirded the authority of particular leaders of the Christian movement" (Funk 1998:35). In order to uncover the layers of tradition *behind* the written text, the development of the oral tradition has to be investigated. In this endeavour scholars make use of "rules of attestation" (see Funk and Hoover 1993:26):

- Sayings of Jesus attested to in two or more independent *sources* are older than the sources in which they are embedded.
- Sayings attested to in two different *contexts* probably circulated independently at an earlier time.
- The same or similar content attested to in two or more different *forms* has had a life of its own and therefore may stem from an old tradition.

Research on the transmission of oral tradition shows how oral memory works. Rules of oral evidence (Funk and Hoover 1993:28; Funk 1998:27) are:

- The oral sayings and stories are short, concise, often repeated, have simple plots, few characters and are self-contained.

- The words of Jesus most often reproduced in writing have been transmitted as aphorisms and parables.
- The earliest layer consists of single aphorisms and parables that were transmitted orally.
- The gist of the stories are remembered, rather than the precise words.

These rules for oral evidence explain the variations of sayings and stories in the Jesus tradition. These were the sources used by those who eventually put the Jesus tradition into writing. The authors of the gospels did not have a unified source. They had to choose from different variations. This and how they utilized these sources, account for the differences in the final product, the written documents.

In order to tell the story, the narrator creates dialogue for the characters. Funk and Hoover (1993:29–30) call this "the storyteller's license." Though events and words may have come from sources containing the actual words of Jesus, the final dialogue would not be the "authentic words of Jesus." This can especially be seen in the controversy dialogues between Jesus and the Pharisees. These dialogues are often based on an authentic Jesus *logion*, but the controversy refers to the conflict between the "Christian" scribes and the post-70 CE Pharisaic scribes. In many cases the controversies are about the Pharisees questioning Jesus' authority. The final chapter will illustrate that these controversy dialogues were used by "Christian" scribes to defend their own authority against the Pharisaic scribes. Dialogue that had been created for Jesus could have had the following intent:

- To express what Jesus could have said in specific circumstances.
- To express Jesus' message as understood by his followers.
- To forecast what was still going to happen in the story.
- To express Jesus' message as understood by the community at that time.
- To express the evangelists' own views.
- To provide words for Jesus when no one was present to hear him speak.

The creation of dialogue contributes to the biographical nature of the narrative gospels. Dialogue reveals characterization, which sheds light on the ideologies of the characters and the narrator. The sayings and deeds of Jesus were changed considerably in the process of the transmission of the Jesus traditions. These changes took place in the oral phase and on the written level. Only the written texts, of course, are available for analysis.

Funk (1998:27) points out the difference between enactment of stories, which they call *showing*, and recounting or *telling*. *Showing* is when something in the story can be *seen* and *heard*. The senses are directly engaged by the story and the language of experience is used. These experiences come from the imagination of the gospel writer or could have been created by a post-Easter "Christian" community of which the writer would have been a member. In the process of institutionalization forms (*Gattungen*) were needed for rites. The stories of Jesus were recounted in the faith communities. The authors of the gospels who could have been members of these communities could have incorporated the enactments of the community in their "biographies" of Jesus. "For enacted scenes to be convincing historically, they must be dramatically plausible" (Funk 1998:28). A story is plausible when the elements, such as time, place, characters and actions are realistic. Anachronisms, for instance, detract from their plausibility and are an indication of a creation by the narrator. In other words, a story can consist of historically reliable information as well as embellishments by the author. This means that the story as a whole cannot simply be classified as "historical" or not. In order to distill the historical information a story could be analyzed in terms of its narrative components and each component be assessed separately (see Funk 1998:30–31).

During the phase of the "New Quest for the Historical Jesus" researchers called this the "criterion of coherency" (see Borg 1999a:8–9). Some of the characteristics of Jesus that have been identified, are that he was an itinerant, that conventional family ties did not mean much to him, that he was seen as demon-possessed, that he socialized with undesirable people, that he did not adhere to the purity regulations of his society, that he was a healer, that he was reticent. Discrepancies with these characteristics would raise suspicion concerning the authenticity of the words or deeds in a story. I will show that the use of titles for Jesus can be seen as such discrepancies.

A Synchronic Test Case: Q and the Synoptic Gospels

The Biographical Nature of the Gospel Genre

The interests of post-Easter "Christianity" clearly played a role in the transmission of the Jesus tradition from its oral to its written form. Ideological interests and conflicts are revealed when the *genre* of the written evidence is examined. The plot of the gospels as narratives is constituted by the ideologies of characters and of the narrator who employs the characters within a structure of time and space (see Brooks and Warren 1970:319). Emphasis on the *genre* represents a shift in gospel research. *Formgeschichtliche* research focused on micro elements (e.g., parables, miracles and pronouncement stories) in the gospels. The question as to the *genre* represented by the *gospels as a whole*, was not asked. Applying redaction criticism and narrative criticism to gospel research brought about a change. In the 1970s the Society of Biblical Literature began a Task Force on the Gospel Genre. This indicated a movement away from the previous consensus, which was mostly the result of the *formgeschichtliche* work of Rudolf Bultmann ([1921] 1931) and Martin Dibelius ([1919] 1971). According to them the *form* of the Gospel of Mark (the oldest gospel) cannot be compared with existing genres in Israelite and Graeco-Roman literature. The gospel genre was seen as *sui generis* (see Kloppenborg 2000:112). In the beginning of the new movement in the research of the gospel as genre, Norman Peterson (1978b) in his book, *Literary criticism for New Testament critics*, referred as follows to the influence of redaction criticism:

> Redaction critics are rarely conscious of the consequences of their conclusions from the historical-critical evolutionary theory . . . Nevertheless, *the evolutionary theory has collapsed because redaction criticism has pulled the plug on its source of power*. Whereas the theory saw the power of literary formation in a romantic symbiosis of tradition and environment, redaction criticism has relocated this power in authors on the one hand and in genres on the other, with genres now construed as cultural media of communication. Wittingly or not, therefore, redaction criticism has made possible the asking of literary questions about our non-literary writings. Indeed, I suspect that it has made it impossible not to ask them, since outside of biblical studies issues of authorship, composition, and genre are considered to be literary issues.

Institutionalization of Authority and the Naming of Jesus

This renewal was not only limited to the "final redactional stratum" of the synoptic gospels and John (the "biographical" gospels). The investigation was also extended to the forms represented in the earlier strata of the Jesus tradition and the sources behind for instance Mark and John. The work was first undertaken by Moses Hadas and Morton Smith (1965:3) who investigated the *aretology* (stories of heroes and gods) as "an ancient type of biographical writing... a formal account of the remarkable career of an impressive teacher that was used as a basis for moral instruction" (cf. Burridge [1992] 1999:17). This was taken further by Smith (1971:174-99) in his work, "Prolegomena to a discussion of aretologies, divine men, the gospels and Jesus"; Hans-Dieter Betz (1968:114-33) in his work, "Jesus as divine man'"; Otto Betz (1972:229-51) in his work, "The concept of the so-called 'divine man' in Mark's Christology"; Howard Clark Kee (1973:402-22) in his work, "Aretology and Gospel" and M. Eugene Boring (1984) in his work, *Truly Human/Truly Divine: Christological Language and the Gospel Form*.

Especially important is the contribution of James Robinson and Helmut Koester (1971) in their *Trajectories through Early Christianity* (see Koester 1971a:158-204; 1971b:187-93; Robinson 1971a:71-113; cf. also Robinson 1970:99-129). Robinson's (1971a:71-113) important contribution was the insight that not only the "kerygmatic tradition," but also the "sapiential tradition," found their written expression in the "biographical" form. According to Robinson ([1971] 1979:103-13), the genre "wisdom sayings" (*logoi sophoi*) is represented in the Q tradition (cf. Hodgon 1985:73-95; Burridge 1999:18, 248; Kloppenborg 2000:344). The "kerygmatic (apocalyptic) tradition" should therefore not be seen as totally irreconcilable with the "sapiential tradition." Robinson (1979:112) puts it as follows: "This movement [from an apocalyptic context to a wisdom context] is made all the more comprehensible in view of the apocalypticism and wisdom, rather than being at almost mutually exclusive extremes within the spectrum of Jewish alternatives, share certain affinities and congruencies that encourage a transition from one to the other." Kloppenborg (1986:443-62; 1987:279, 326) points out that the later recensions of Q also exhibit a "biographical" form. He puts it as follows: "Despite the fact that Q lacks a continuous narrative framework, it too contains various argumentative progressions that involve long blocks, in some cases encompassing the whole of Q" (Kloppenborg 2000:115). In another context, Kloppenborg (2000:202) says: "The development from an instruction to a *bios* is not unusual. At least part of the impetus for the introduction of biographical elements—a narrative introduction, for example—had to do with the inherent requirements of the instructional genre for legitimation for the sage's words."

The earlier point of view that the genre of the Gospel of Mark is *sui generis* did not exclude *genre* from the discussion when the *form* of Mark was examined. It is virtually impossible to explore the meaning of written evidence without taking the *form* in which it appears into account. Eliseo Vivas (1968:103) articulates it as follows: "Let me iterate the point: the plan is not *sui generis*. No artist, however talented, can make objects each of which is in a class by itself. If he [or she] could, his [or her] work would be totally idiotic, utterly private, each job would be a monad without windows or pre-established harmony. His [or her] work would say nothing to anyone but himself [or herself], the maker—if it did that much."

Richard Burridge (1999:52) concludes that "genre is a system of communication of *meaning*" (italics original). He adds: "Before we can understand the meaning of a text, we must master its genre." In making use of the insights of contemporary narratological research, one could be tempted to see the gospel genre as biography in the technical sense of modern novellas. The latter was described by Martin Dibelius ([1919] 1971:1–2) as *Hochliteratur*, that is literature which is the product of an individual artist who intentionally *creates* an independent work of art according to literary norms. This work of art is intended to be appreciated as literature. *Kleinliteratur*, however, is the product of folkloristic "art." Narratives belonging to this category will also exhibit narrative characteristics, such as a plot, characterization and space. The structure of the gospels as example of this kind of narrative, was created by a "redactor" who, operating within a specific *Sitz im Leben*, reorganized the material into a "biographical" structure. The source material consisted of traditions that only existed in oral form, as well as other micro-*Gattungen*. Therefore, "folkloristic biographies," such as the gospels, can also be analyzed by means of narrative techniques and the narrator's point of view (as described by narrative criticism). Folkloristic biographies are not void of formal characteristics.

The *Formgeschichtler*'s (e.g., Bultmann 1931:53–64) reticence to call the gospels "biographies," should be seen against the background that some exponents from the Romantic period studied folkloristic narratives anachronistically from the perspective of *Hochliteratur*. According to Bultmann (1931:7-8) there are similarities between folkloristic studies and investigating the *formal* characteristics of the Jesus tradition. Milan Kundera's ([1967] 1992:140-141) description of the birth and development of a folksong articulates the *function* of biographical *Kleinliteratur* rather effectively:

> The ancient countryside had lived a collective life. Communal rites marked off the village year. Folk art knew no life outside those rites. The romantics imagined that a girl cutting grass was struck by inspiration and immediately a song gushed from her like a stream from a rock. But a folk song is born differently from a formal poem. Poets create in order to express themselves, to say what it is that makes them unique [*Hochliteratur*]. In the folk song, one does not stand out from others but joins with them [*Kleinliteratur*]. The folk song grew like a stalactite. Drop by drop enveloping itself in new motifs, in new variants. It was passed from generation to generation, and everyone who sang it added something to it. Every song had many creators, and all of them modestly disappeared behind their creation. No folk song existed purely for its own sake. It had a function. There were songs sung at weddings, songs sung at harvesting, songs sung at Carnival, songs for Christmas, for haymaking. For dancing, for funerals. Even love songs did not exist outside certain customs. The rural evening promenade, the song under the maiden's window, courtship, all were part of a collective rite in which song had its established place.

With their emphasis on the gospels as *Kleinliteratur*, the form critic stressed the influence of the *cult* as *Sitz im Leben* on the transmission of the Jesus tradition. Talbert (1978), however, convincingly showed that examples of the Graeco-Roman βίος also fulfilled a *cultic* function (cf. the critical discussion of Talbert's work by David Aune 1981:9-60). Burridge (1999:204-5) argues that the traces of oral tradition in the gospels and the evangelists' use of sources, do not exclude the possibility that the gospels could exhibit the genre of "biography," though "much less sophisticated" (see Tolbert 1989:59-79). Burridge (1999:204-5) puts it as follows:

> This ability to select and edit a wide range of sources is similar to the use of sources by writers of βίοι. Redaction criticism has freed

us from seeing the evangelists as mere slaves of oral tradition; instead, they are creative theologians and literary artists who took their source material and turned it into the gospel *according* to their understandings . . . *Thus the freedom to select and edit sources to produce the desired picture of the subject is another feature shared by both the gospels and Graeco-Roman* βίοι. (italics original).

Burridge's "first conclusion," after having compared Graeco-Roman biographies that originated in a *cultic* setting with the gospel genre, is: *biography is a type of writing which occurs naturally among groups of people who have formed around a certain charismatic leader, seeking to follow after him* (Burridge 1999:80; italics original). In his study of the genre of the Gospel of Mark, Detlev Dormeyer's (1989:194) outcome is similar. According to him "Marcan Christology" shows a biographical tendency. The names *Son of God, Christ, Son of Man* and *Teacher* are the building blocks of "Marcan Christology" (see Tatum 1999:59). Dormeyer (1989:194) sees the Gospel of Mark as a "neugeschaffene biographische Untergattung 'Evangelium'" (cf. Burridge 1999:100). The names given for Jesus are, therefore, characteristic of the "biographical" genre. The names are also an indication of how followers of Jesus institutionalized the "Christian cult" around its "founder." The functions of the "founder" and the "officials" of the cult were expressed by the names given to them. For example, Jesus was called κύριος (a divine teacher) and the "officials" were admonished not to call themselves (πρῶτοι) (see Mark 10:44).

Naming can also reveal ideological conflict and polemic. Burridge's (1999:80) second conclusion is that "*a major purpose and function of* βίοι *is in a context of didactic or philosophical* [ideological] *polemic and conflict*" (italics original). Patricia Cox (1983:135; cf. also Berger 1984:1242) articulates it as follows: "Biography was from its inception a genre that found its home in controversy. Biographers . . . were self-conscious mediators of specific traditions, and their works had both apologetic and polemical aims, apologetic in defending, affirming, and sometimes correcting opinion about a hero; polemical in suggesting by the strength of the defense, and sometimes by outright attack, the unworthiness of other traditions by comparison."

So far four characteristics of a "biography" that are also applicable to the Sayings Gospel Q and the synoptic gospels have become evident:

- the use of *sources* in biography;
- a *cultic setting* as the context in which biography should be understood;
- *naming* the "hero" in a biography;
- *apologetic and polemical aims* of the biography.

Philo Judaeus' (circa 30/25 BCE—45 CE) work, *The Life of Moses*, is an example of a Graeco-Roman βίος in a Judean-Hellenistic milieu (more Hellenistic than Judean—see Goodenough 1962:75–90). In this work there is less allegorical interpretation than in his other work (see Burridge 1999:132). Al four of the above mentioned characteristics of a βίος are present in Philo's *The Life of Moses*. Just as Egyptian Ptolomaic influence can be seen in first-century Palestine (including Galilee and Syria), so a case can be made that Philo's work would have been known in the circles of Israelite and "Christian" scribes, or at least that they shared a tradition (see Runia 1988:48–75; 1993:63–86). No direct dependence on Philo can be indicated in the works of Qumran or in the canonical gospels. However, there are indications of common imagery. For example, Matthew's childhood narrative shows certain similarities with Pseudo-Philo's Moses story (see Crossan 1994c:59–81).

As far as the use of *sources* is concerned, *The Life of Moses* begins by relating how Philo made use of both oral and written traditions "and from the writings of the priests . . . and from what comes from the village leaders of the people" (*Moses* 1.4—cf. Burridge 1999:142). In Book I, the heroic deeds of Moses as king (1.5–334) are praised and in Book 2, his greatness as law-giver (2.8–65), priest (2.66–180) and prophet (II.187–287) (cf. Burridge 1999:137, 146). This *naming* is appropriate in a *cultic* context and the aim is to inform the *am ha'aretz* (the ignorant of the law) about Moses from the perspective of the educated ruling classes (1.1–4—cf. Burridge 1999:149). Moses is recommended to a larger audience as the supreme *law-giver* whose instructions should be accepted and obeyed (Burridge 1999:149). Goodenough (1962:118) points out the apologetic tendency in Philo's *The Life of Moses*. Burridge (1999:216) investigated the gospel with this in mind and came to the following conclusions:

> Probably the most common purpose of βίοι . . . was their use in debate and argument. The titles of Weeden's works on Mark [see

his *Mark: Traditions in conflict* (1971)] demonstrate this polemical purpose . . . Mark struggled against a false view of Jesus as a miracle/wonder worker. Bilezikian [see his *The liberated gospel: A comparison of the Gospel of Mark and Greek tragedy* (1977)] also sees polemic in Mark, directed against the Twelve and traditional Christianity in the struggle of the "Gentile-oriented church."

The structures of the three synoptic gospels and the Sayings Gospel Q will now be discussed against the background of the information gathered on the "biographical" nature of the gospels. The aim will be to investigate the evangelists' "narrative point of view," that is the *ideology* of the gospel narratives. As far as the Sayings Gospel Q is concerned, it will first be necessary to take a brief look at its tradition history before proceeding to the "narrative point of view."

The Sayings Gospel Q

A Tradition History in Phases

Historical critical research on the Sayings Gospel Q acknowledges an evolution of the Q tradition (cf. Bultmann 1931:354). Nowadays the evolution of the Q tradition is described in terms of three recensions (see Kloppenborg 2000:87–111). This approach is mainly found among historical Jesus researchers (see Miller 2000:1–18; Schmidt 2000:19–38). Although Arland Jacobson (1992:68) acknowledges a development within the Q tradition, he does not distinguish between three layers as such. He sees the development not as intentional expansions for specific reasons (theological and/or circumstantial), but as sayings added to and placed in juxtaposition to the existing ones. He does not deny that the Sayings Gospel Q as a literary unit has a "theology" of its own.

My investigation especially makes use of the insights of John Kloppenborg (1987, 1988, 1991, 2000). His work has increasingly convinced researchers that three strata can be distinguished in the development of the Sayings Gospel Q (see e.g., Allison 1997:3). Markus Cromhout (2007:257–85), who also builds heavily on Kloppenborg's insights, prefers to work only two stratified layers. For the purpose of this book the choice for two or three layers does not matter so much. The first is still called the "formative" stratum (Cromhout 2007:264) and the latter the "main redaction" (Cromhout 2007:268). The sapiential (wisdom) nature of Q^1 is characteristic of this layer (for criticism of this point of view, cf. Allison 1997:4-8). It is comparable to the book of Proverbs in the First Testament. The "formative" stratum (Q^1) underwent redactional changes. The next level in the development of the Q tradition, which is the result of redactional work, is indicated as Q^2. Dieter Lührmann (1969:15; cf. Tuckett 1996:52-57) distinguishes between "collection" (*Sammlung*) and "redaction" (*Redaktion*) (see also Tuckett 1996:54). Even earlier than Lührmann, Schulz (1971) realized that the later Q traditions display a developed Christology as well as the motif of the delayed parousia, which were absent in the formative stratum of Q (see also Tuckett 1996:59; Jacobson 1992:40-42). Schulz (1971:482) puts it as follows: "Aus enthusiastischen Prophetensprüchen, in denen sich ursprünglich der erhört-gegenwärtige Menschensohn Jesus meldete, werden jetzt Worte des irdischen Jesus als des Endzeitpropheten vor der nahen Menschensohn-Parusie." Bultmann (1931:73) refers to the redactional overlays in the Jesus tradition as *Herrenworte* (dominical sayings), because of the authoritative nature of Jesus' instructions as the *Kyrios*. He distinguishes three sub-categories of *Herrenworte*: wisdom teaching, prophetic and apocalyptic sayings, as well as legal sayings and church rules (Bulltmann 1931:73 n. 1, my italics).

According to Kloppenborg (1993:9) Q "represents a distinct theological vision and social configuration within early Christianity." Q^1 focuses on an early Christian believing community and its message. In Q^2 an elaboration of the Q tradition speaks to a changing situation. On this level the community began seeing itself as having a mission to reach out to Israel beyond Judea with its message. The origins of the Q community, its "geographical provenance" (see Kloppenborg 2000:171-78), can be located in North Galilee (see Tuckett 1996:102-3; Mack 1989:53ff). External circumstances prior to the destruction of the temple in 70 CE also had an impact on the development of the Q tradition (see Freyne 1980:311-18; Saldarini 1988:35-49; Kloppenborg 2000:175). The Jesus movement experienced opposition from the Judean élite. New circumstances necessitated additions to the Q tradition, resulting in what we today call Q^2. The Christological titles are found in the recension material. *Son of Man* appears in Q^2 and *Son of God* in Q^3 (see Mack 1993:137).

After the war and the destruction of the temple in 70 CE the Q community struggled to find a new identity. The Great Revolt had a devastating impact on the Galilean countryside (see Cromhout 2007:253-54). Before the war the Pharisees were tolerant of different viewpoints and schools of thought. This provided a fairly comfortable situation for the Christians. After the war, however, the tolerance disappeared and conformity to Pharisaic thinking was demanded, which presented a problem for the Christian communities. This is the world and circumstances of the formation of Q^3. Two developments can be seen in Q^3. Apocalyptic eschatology, the beginnings of which could already be seen in Q^2, was expanded in Q^3. The mission discourse found in Q^2 develops a "universal" perspective in Q^3 (cf. Mack 1989:4-7). Mark only made use of Q^2 (cf. Theissen [1989] 1992:206-21; 258-71; see, however, Kloppenborg 2000:80 note 37). Matthew and Luke made use of the third and "final" version of the Sayings Gospel Q (cf. Kloppenborg 1987:246-66). (Burton Mack [1993:172] is of the opinion that all the narrative canonical gospels are dependent on Q^3.) Luke remained closer to Q^3 than Matthew. The term "kingdom of God" occurs frequently in Q^1, but lacks an apocalyptic edge (cf. Mack 1989:124). In Q^1 the followers of Jesus are defined as people who obey the instructions of God as *paterfamilias*. The theme of discipleship is emphasized. God's kingdom is as near and as real as the "reign" of the father of a household. The disciples are depicted as the "sons of the high one"—Q 6:35) and God as "your father is the compassionate one" (Q 6:36b). Conventional wisdom taught that poverty and other forms of misery were the result of God's judgement. Q^1 changes this to the compassion according to an alternative wisdom, namely righteousness toward the destitute. A further change is discernable in Q^2 where compassion is treated in a way similar to the Deuteronomist (see Jacobson 1982:365-389; Kloppenborg 2000:121): God's compassion is not boundless. God expects Israel to realize the ethical ideal of compassion toward the lowly. The theme of poverty is reinterpreted. If Israel sins, God will send prophets to judge them and proclaim their punishment. God's people (the destitute) are likened to the persecuted prophets of old (see Q 6:26). The coming judgement is directed against the leaders of Israel (see Q 11:39b). In Q^1 the emphasis is on compassion and the ethical demand is obedience to Jesus' instruction (wisdom). In Q^2 authority becomes important (cf. Mack 1989:137-41). The style of rhetoric changes from aphorisms in Q^1 to narration, dialogue, controversy stories, example stories, extended parables, admonitions and apocalyptic announcements in Q^2.

According to Douglas Oakman (1999:147–148) it is important to have some idea as to the social origins of the Q recensions. He considers Kloppenborg's (1987, 1988, 1991, 1993) proposal most convincing. Q consists of proverbial sayings and is part of the broader category of wisdom instruction (see Kloppenborg 2000:143–153). Since wisdom instruction regulates the ordinary lives of people, it is to be expected in the settings of courts, towns and villages. Scribes regulated wisdom instruction in towns and villages. Egyptian evidence indicates that the instructional genre of wisdom literature was cultivated in these sectors (Kloppenborg 1991:85). Mettinger (1971:140; cf. Jamieson-Drake 1991:36) points out that "scribal schools" followed the Egyptian model as early as the monarchical period of Israel's history. "[I]n Egypt all education was essentially scribal education," Mettinger (1971:140) observes.

Regulation of the lives of people came from the top, from the rulers whose instructions in the form of codifications influenced the everyday lives of the people (*am ha-'aretz*). The "great tradition" and the "little tradition" merged (see Redfield 1956:68–84; Scott 1977:16–20; Fiensy 1991:2). John Kloppenborg (2000:207) comments as follows on the insights of Scott: "James Scott (1977) has emphasized not only the interdependence and symbiosis of the great and little traditions but also the strong potential for conflict. The great tradition, since it is the formulation of privileged social strata, is naturally configured to favor their interests. It does this by legitimizing hierarchy, cultic and political centers, kingship, the extraction of surpluses, and the use of force in preserving élite privileges."

The instructions of the great tradition were given by officials such as, for instance, royal administrative personnel. Harper (1928:27–38) states that "the religious cult of an ancient community played so important a part in the life of that community that there can have existed no sharp line of division between an official of the cult and an officer charged with ordinary municipal matters." The "officials of the cult" and the "officers charged with municipal matters" should not be confused with the scribal activity of *normative Judaism* (the later synagogue movement) after the Bar Kokhba revolt in 135 BCE when the rabbis constituted the *bene ha-knessett* (see Horsley 1996:151). This development of a rabbinical movement in the second and third centuries took place in centers such as Sepphoris, Tiberias, Capernaum and Chorazin. However, traces of such scribal activity during the period of *formative Judaism* (the time when the

A Synchronic Test Case: Q and the Synoptic Gospels

New Testament was written) in these same places can be found in textual references, for example in the Sayings Gospel Q, Mark and Matthew (see Hare 1967:103–14; Neusner 1991:157–163).

The Jesus movement in Galilee and the work of early post-70 CE rabbis, called the "earlier scribes and sages" by Horsley (1996:181–184) can be seen as a "revitalization of village communities." After the temple was destroyed, the Pharasaic scribes and sages reorganized themselves in places such as Jamnia (in Judea), Galilee and Syria. There they tried to duplicate the old value systems of the temple in the households of the villages, especially regulations concerning hierarchy in society and the purity ideology of the temple. A similar activity of revitalizing village communities was found among the Jesus groups. The value system they implemented was based on Jesus' alternative wisdom. L. Michel White (1986:256) states the following: "The Q stratum bearers are already localized leaders (*patres familias*) who look *back* to the earlier itinerant missionaries [the people of Q¹] as their 'source' for the words of Jesus." The difference in value systems and interests led to conflict between Pharisaic and "Christian" scribes. According to Arnal (2001:154), the "little tradition in fact is simply the popular reflection, appropriation, and distortion or subversion of high culture."

The polemic between Jesus' teaching and the Pharisees in the gospel tradition must not be seen anachronistically as two established institutes, a "church" and a "synagogue," in conflict with each other. The conflicting interests were the result of a process of institutionalization that took two directions in the village communities. In the gospel of Mark reports of Jesus teaching in the synagogues in Galilee mention that he was challenged by Pharisaic scribes (see Mk 1:21, 27; 2:1, 6). "It seems likely that the tradition of Jesus' teaching behind such literature as Mark, Q, and the Didache would have been cultivated in Galilean communities" (Horsley 1996:184). The context of this early scribal activity among Jesus followers and Pharisees was that of the *bet-midrash* (formative Judaism) rather than that of the *bene ha-knessett* (normative Judaism). From the second century onwards the synagogue began functioning separately from the village administration (see Cohen 1992:157–173; Levine 1992:201–222). This was not the case, however, in formative Judaism. (This distinction is not made by Sean Freyne 1988:202–210.) Jesus himself was not a *grammateus* (ὁ γραμματεύς), but he was a *sage* (ὁ ἅγιος). The title "Rabbi" (*grammateus*) pertains to formative Judaism and the concept "sage" to a charismatic setting independent of the "institutional authority" that belongs with synagogical activity.

According to David Orton (1989:52) γραμματεῖς in the Judean-Hellenistic period were persons of *high official rank* and *authority*: "They were overseers, instructors and judges; they bear Mosaic authority and are connected with Levites and the implementation of the Law." Neusner (1991:161) refers to the Judean scribe of this period as follows: "The union of the *scribe* and the *priest* yielded the *sage* who bore the honorific title *Rabbi*" (my italics). Such a "sage" fulfilled a scribal role and should be distinguished from the "charismatic sage" who could be illiterate. According to Kloppenborg (2000:200) it is "self-evident that insofar as Q represents a written document, it is the product of scribal technology." Kloppenborg (2000:201) describes the consequences of this as follows:

> [W]ho besides scribes had the ability to compose it this way and who would have chosen a typically scribal genre? ... Q does in fact betray a number of features characteristic of scribes ... : interest in the process of as well as the context of instruction ... [S]cribes did not uniformly serve the interests of the ruling élite. There is ample evidence from Egypt to indicate the presence of a variety of scribes, of varying educational levels, in towns and villages, some serving in the apparatus of the provincial administration and others functioning as free-lance professionals. The κωμογραμματεύς (village scribe) was concerned with tax and census matters. But the writing of loan and lease agreements presupposed the existence of private professionals prepared to assist in these transactions ... There is no reason at all to suppose that this sector was uniformly aligned with the ruling classes against the poor or that this sector functioned exclusively as retainers of the élite. Q^1 *reflects the technology and interests of these private professionals* (my italics).

Kloppenborg (2000:203–4) argues that Q^2 displays a "contrasting ethos" with "competitors" and suggests "that at this stage of Q, the rhetorical situation demanded a defense or legitimation of the Q people's existence" (cf. also Reed 1994). Kloppenborg (2000:204) describes the *Sitz im Leben* of Q^2 as follows:

> the Q people are associated with towns sufficiently large to have markets and a small scribal sector, and sufficiently proximate to the larger centers of Tiberias and Sepphoris to come into periodic contact with Pharisees and other representatives of the Judaean

hierocracy. Q's cultural allegiances, however, are with the Galilean countryside and against the city, which is regarded with distrust and suspicion. *In defense of the Jesus movement, the framers of Q construct a notion of Israel and its epic heroes which stands in opposition to Jerusalem, the Herodian dynasty, the Pharisees and lawyers, and the unbelief that is encountered in the market places* (my italics).

In other words, the scribes, responsible for the compilation of the Q tradition (contra to Horsley 1991:58), were in conflict with some scribes of the Galilean village administration. The Jesus faction in pre-70 CE Jerusalem came into conflict with the Jerusalem administration. Mark and Matthew, using the traditions of Q (sapiential) and the earlier Jerusalem Jesus faction (kerygmatic), report similar conflict in their post-70 CE Galilean/Syrian communities (cf. Orton 1989:49).

In the period 25-30 CE Jesus came into conflict with the Galilean village administration and the Jerusalem administration. The traditions of Jesus in conflict situations were taken over by Q and the gospels and reflected their own polemical situation—a situation described by Piper (1995a:63) as "suspicion about the institutions of power." They used Jesus' strong arguments to give meaning to their own struggle. By giving honorary titles to Jesus, their "founder," they gained honour in the eyes of their opponents. Mark describes the conflict between Jesus and his family in Nazareth (Mark 6:1-6) as a synagogical challenge-riposte about Jesus' honour. From Mark's point of view it was seen as: "Only in his hometown among his relatives and in his own house is a prophet without honour" (Mark 6:4). In Matthew's narrative structure this "Marcan-coloured" Jesus saying follows immediately after a "Matthean-colored" Jesus saying: "He [Jesus] said to them: 'Therefore every teacher of the law' (i.e., "scribe") who has been instructed about the kingdom of heaven is like the owner of a house who brings out of his storeroom new treasures as well as old [i.e., "old wisdom" redefined]" (Matt 13:52). In Mark (14:53-65) Jesus' trial takes place before the *bet-midrash/bene ha-knessett* (Mark 14:55; see Mk 14:65).

Regarding the conflict situation in which the Q tradition originated, Oakman (1999:147) goes a step beyond Kloppenborg when he suggests that Herod Antipas' administrative personnel around the Galilean Lake probably provided the first draft of Q. This would mean that Q^1 could be dated between the late twenties and 54 CE and Q^2 in the period 54-66

CE. Zahavy (1990:87) has worked out the "sociology of scribalism" in the Judean-Roman period. He considers it possible that similar circumstances could have prevailed twenty to thirty years previously when the Q tradition was formed. The result is that Q^1 would be the product of "Christian" scribes with some sort of a relation to the scribal activity of the Herodean court and Q^2 the product of "Christian" scribes with Judean ties. The wisdom sayings found in Q^1 were reinterpreted in Q^2 and Q^3 as well as in the later synoptic tradition (Oakman 1999:148). The conflict with the Pharisees and the post-temple "Judaic" movement becomes visible in Q^2 and especially Q^3 and these traditions were taken over by the synoptic gospels.

In Kloppenborg's works certain interesting possibilities for investigating the transition from Q^1 to Q^2 appear. Agrippa II took over control of Tiberias (the new capital of Galilee) in 54 CE (see Kloppenborg 1999:782). According to Horsley (1996:35), the term *hoi protoi*, the leading figures of Tiberias, in Josephus (Vita 64, 67; cf. Ant 18.273) refers to the "officials in Agrippa II's administration." They are the next generation after the "principal officials and councilors of the royal administration" of Herod Antipas in Tiberias, referred to by Mark 6:21. One of the radical changes on account of this transition of power was that the archives, earlier moved from Sepphoris (previously the capital of Galilee) to Tiberias by Herod Antipas, were now transferred back to Sepphoris. This brought about a change in scribal activity. The scribes either had to go from Tiberias to Sepphoris or would be replaced. Change brings about uncertainty, which often prompts the appearance of apocalyptical forms (cf. Mack 1989:24). These social and political changes can be a reason for the movement toward apocalyptic elements in prophetic form in Q^2. On account of the work of Coote and Coote (1990), Oakman supports these suggestions of Kloppenborg (see Oakman 1999:147).

The hypothetical Sayings Gospel Q, considered to be a source used by the writers of the synoptic gospels, consists of a collection of Jesus sayings which belong to the literary genre of sapiential instruction. The sayings were not merely put together at random, but were organized according to themes. "[T]here is also a measure of unity and coherence among several clusters as well as a logical and thematic development throughout the course of the entire collection" (Kloppenborg 1987:89; cf. Allison 1997:1–66).

A Synchronic Test Case: Q and the Synoptic Gospels

Some scholars, like Von Harnack (in Kloppenborg 1987:89-90), traced Q back to the historical Jesus. Such an unqualified view of Q leaves no room for redactional activity. Wellhausen (in Kloppenborg 1987:89-90) criticized this idealistic view. Yet, despite the criticism of Von Harnack, Q was still seen as containing the very earliest Jesus traditions. Q was considered to be an unsophisticated, "raw" version of the earliest Jesus tradition, transmitted by *anthropoi agrammatoi kai idiotai*. Kloppenborg (1987:90) disagrees and describes Q as a sophisticated example of its literary type and, being *written*, Q was clearly not just a "set of oral folk sayings of a pre-literate group."

Kloppenborg debates the structure and division of Q with Manson (1949:39-148), Crossan (1983:156, 342-345), Polag (1982:23-26) and Schenk (1981:5-9). He finds the divisions of both Manson and Crossan too inexact. Polag and Schenk provide a more detailed, thematically organized division. Kloppenborg (1987:92) proposes the following "heuristic division" of Q (see Kloppenborg 2000:100 for a more detailed analysis):

1	John's preaching of the Coming One	Q 3:7-9, 16-17
2	The temptation of Jesus	Q 4:1-13
3	Jesus' inaugural sermon	Q 6:20b-49
4	John, Jesus and "this generation"	Q 7:1-10, 18-28; (16:16); 7:31-35
5	Discipleship and mission	Q 9:57-62; 10:2-24
6	On prayer	Q 11:2-4; 9-13
7	Controversies with Israel	Q 11:14-52
8	On fearless preaching	Q 12:2-12
9	On anxiety over material needs	Q 12:(13-14, 16-21), 22-31, 33-34
10	Preparedness for the end	Q 12:39-59
11	Two parables of growth	Q 13:18-19, 20-21
12	The two ways	Q 13:24-30, 34-35; 14:16-24, 26-27; 17:33; 14:33-34
13	Various parables and sayings	Q 15:3-7; 16:13, 17-18; 17:1-6
14	The eschatological discourse	Q 17:23-37; 19:12-27; 22:28-30.

Q as a whole presents a thematic unity. Arland Jacobson (1982:384–385) argues that a strong strain of Deuteronomistic theology can be found in Q. Kloppenborg (1987:93) is of the opinion that, though Deuteronomistic influence (an emphasis on ethics) is certainly detectable in Q, it is not quite as strong as Jacobson suggests. Jacobson did, however, contribute to an increasing awareness that Deuteronomistic theology provided the perspective for a specific stage of Q redaction. "This redaction lends to the collection an important unity" (Kloppenborg 1987:93). Though Q was not written in narrative form, it does display logical and qualitative progressions, which are demonstrated by Kloppenborg (1987:94–95). These progressions contribute to the structural coherence of Q.

Q contains mainly sapiential but also prophetic forms. An analysis of the literary forms and theological motifs that provide a unifying element to the collection, sheds light on the relationship between these two forms. Neither the form-critical nor the tradition-historical method is deemed adequate for a redactional analysis of Q (Kloppenborg 1987:96). According to Kloppenborg, the models put forward by Dieter Lührmann (1969) and Arland Jacobson (1978) are more acceptable. Lührmann (1969:20–22) points out that redactional activity becomes visible when a specific theme appears frequently and in a variety of forms and contexts, for example in different clusters of sayings, in overlaps between Mark and Q, or in the Q *Gemeindebildungen*. In this regard, however, Kloppenborg (1987:97) is critical of the work of Lührmann and cautions that, "[i]n the Q materials, it is notoriously difficult to distinguish sayings which are the creation of the Q redactor from 'community constructions' . . . In most cases it is virtually impossible to determine whether a particular saying is a creation of a redactor or whether it is simply a piece of tradition which was deemed appropriate for inclusion because it resonated with the interests of the redactor and his community."

Jacobson (1978) calls his method for the redactional analysis of Q "compositional analysis." He sees signs of redactional activity in "grammatical shifts, breaks in the train of thought, shifts in audience, shifts in tradition or theology" (Jacobson 1978:9). He also analyzes the reasons for clustering independent units together in larger units. This sheds light on what is primary material and what constitutes later redactional additions. Jacobson identifies three "redactional" stages, each with its own characteristics: the compositional stage, an intermediate, and a final redaction. While essentially agreeing with Lührmann and Jacobson as far as method is concerned, Dieter Zeller (1982:395-409; 1992:389-411) adds a criterion for the detection of redactional activity in Q, namely sayings augmented by interpretations. Kloppenborg (1987:98) cautions that a distinction should be made between the expansions of the oral phase and those of the written phase. Only the additions made in the written stage provide valid information about the redactional development of Q. Kloppenborg's (1987:98-100) method for analyzing Q redaction consists of three phases (see also Kloppenborg 2000:118-128):

- determining the principles by which originally independent sayings and clusters of sayings were grouped together (building on the results of form criticism);
- analysis of insertions and glosses;
- comparing Q with other streams of the tradition, especially Mark.

The focus of this method is on the first two phases. Kloppenborg (1987:100) admits to a limitation concerning those sayings that have no place in one of the larger clusters. In such a case it is difficult to determine on *literary* grounds whether it should be placed in the formative stage or whether it is a redactional addition. Van Aarde (1999:815) demonstrates the problem with the example of the *mission* of the twelve disciples. He shows how difficult it is to ascertain whether it originated in the formative stratum or was a product of redaction. Organizing the sayings according to their content or themes can only be done after the redactional phases have been determined by means of an analysis of the larger groups of sayings.

Ideological Point of View

According to Kingsbury (1981:5), the theology of Q exhibits a very specific perspective on the "history of salvation" (see Fitzmyer's [1989:59-63] discussion on Luke's use of this theme). One aspect of this perspective comes from the sapiential tradition of Israel. A long line of Old Testament prophetic messengers were sent by God to call the people of Israel to repentance. In the light of the previous discussion the reference to "prophets" can be regarded as a result of the conflict among scribes about the legitimacy of sayings. According to Kingsbury (1981:6) figures like John the Baptist, Jesus and the disciples in the Q tradition represent a continuation of the line of prophetic messengers (Q 10:3). The prophets and their message were, however, not welcomed by Israel (Q 11:49–51; 13:34). John, Jesus and the disciples were also not welcomed. This opposition reveals the conflict between the "Christian" and the "Judean" scribes (see Kloppenborg 2000:203). The "history of salvation" as described by Q is, therefore, a history of judgment against Israel (Kingsbury 1981:6).

Another aspect of the perspective of Q comes from the apocalyptic tradition of Israel. The discussion of the tradition history of Q indicated that the apocalyptic tradition originated in the later recensions of the formative stratum. At this later stage Jesus was portrayed as an "apocalyptic/eschatological prophet." Jesus' teaching inaugurated the end-time and history was moving toward its conclusion. As far as the "history of salvation" is concerned, there was no time to lose. There was still hope that Israel (the opponents) would hear the message and repent, but there was a sense of urgency.

According to Q, the prophets belong to the old dispensation, "the time of the prophets." Jesus brought about the new dispensation, "the time of the eschatological harvest." John is the bridge between these two eras. John is a prophet, but he is more than the prophets of the Hebrew Scriptures. He is a special messenger sent to prepare the way for the One who is mightier than he and for the approach of the end-time (cf. Wink 1968; Ernst 1989; Tatum 1994). Such a messenger is in itself a fulfillment of Old Testament prophecy and, therefore, John is also an end-time figure (Q 7:27; Mal 3:1) (Kingsbury 1981:7). John signifies the end of one era and the beginning of the next. Jesus introduces the new era. He is "mightier" than John (Q 3:16; 7:18–19; 22–23). In the later recensions of the Q tradition Jesus is the Son of Man (Q 7:33–35) (Kloppenborg 2000:186) and Son of God (Q 4:1–13). According to Q the "history of salvation" reaches its culmination at the end-time. Q expects history to come to an end and that end is imminent. The Son of Man will appear at the end and carry out the eschatological judgment. On the other hand, the imminent expectation of the end must not give the impression that Q's eschatology is without nuance. There are some indications that, though the end-time is considered to be close, it may not be instant. A summary of Q's perspective could be: the end is imminent, but there is still time

A Synchronic Test Case: Q and the Synoptic Gospels

(Kingsbury 1981:7). In the final chapter it will be shown that Q's *ideological point of view* that Jesus is Son of Man should be seen as a product of the *institutionalization of charismatic authority*.

Q and the Naming of Jesus

Q begins with John the Baptist calling Jesus the "Mightier One." According to Mark (1:1, 7) the "Mightier One" is the royal Messiah, the Christ. However, Q never refers to Jesus as Messiah. Yet, in Q Jesus remains the decisive figure in the "history of salvation" (Kingsbury 1981:7). In Q Jesus was elevated from a wisdom sage to the authoritative Son of Man who, though killed by the opposition, conquered death and was vindicated as the "Mightier One." Q sees Jesus as the Son of Man who will come at the end of time, but also as the one who has already been sent by God to fulfill a specific mission in this world (cf. Vaage 1991:103-29). Jesus as the Son of Man symbolizes that the end has come and that the "Christian" community is still experiencing the consequences of this coming (see Q 3:16; 7:17; 13:35). John's description of Jesus as the "Mightier One" (Q 3:16) indicates that Jesus acted with authority. His followers acknowledged him, the Son of Man, as *Kyrios* (Q 12:42-46; 13:25-27; 19:12-26). The parousia of the Son of Man is described in detail by Q (cf. Hoffmann [1992] 1994:159-98; Vaage 1991:103-29; Tuckett 1996:239-82). He comes from heaven and appears for all to see (Q 17:26-30). His appearance is unexpected and people who are not prepared and ready to give themselves completely, are in trouble (Q 17:31-33). People are separated when the end comes: some are saved and others not (Q 17:34-35). The Son of Man comes to judge. Those who have heard and accepted the message of salvation will be part of the glory of God's kingdom (Q 13:18-19; 20-21; 28-29; 22:20). Those who refused to listen to Jesus' message and repent (11:25-32) and those who persecuted his followers (Q 13:34-35) are condemned and punished (cf. Schürmann 1975:133-35; Higgins 1980:90-92; Zeller 1985:526-28; Kloppenborg 1987:130-31; Jacobson 1992:166-68; Tuckett 1996:258). Being ready for the coming of Jesus means being prepared to confess Jesus publicly (Q 12:8) and to serve him (Q 12:42-44; 19:12-26) (Kingsbury 1981:9). Jesus is not only the one who comes at the end of time. He was sent by God to fulfill a mission in this world (cf. Tuckett 1996:393-404;

Lührmann 1969:58, 86–87; Uro 1987:210–23). The title Son of Man is an indication of what his task and mission comprise (Q 7:34; 9:58; 12:10).

Jesus is also designated by Q as the Son or the Son of God (Q 4:1–13; 10:22) when reference is made to his relationship with the Father (see Mack 1993:137). The story of the baptism of Jesus in Mark (1:9–11) has the function of establishing Jesus as the royal Messiah, the Son of God who acts with divine authority on account of the empowerment of God's Spirit. Since Q does not refer to Jesus as Messiah, the story of his baptism is not told (Kingsbury 1981:9). Tuckett (1996:214) comments as follows on this "silence at the level of Christology":

> The Jewish term Messiah is never used in Q. This is rather surprising given the evidently very early use of the term to refer to Jesus ... and the way in which the term then apparently became so firmly attached to Jesus, both inside and outside Jewish Christianity, that it became almost just another proper name ... There is also the fact that "Messiah" is a very Jewish term, and ... Q represents a very "Jewish" stratum of the tradition, so that the absence of the term from Q is all the more striking ... [N]evertheless, the non-appearance of the term serves to distinguish Q from Paul and all the evangelists and makes Q's profile rather distinctive in terms of Christology.

As far as Christology in Q is concerned, Allison (1997:34) puts it as follows: "Q^3 is characterized by a very rich Christology ... [b]ut there is no elaboration of christological topics in either Q^1 or Q^2." Whereas Mark uses the title Son of God to further expand his understanding of the Messiah, Q does not connect either Son of God or the Son with the Messiah. However, Q does contain a pericope that functions in the same manner as the baptism does in Mark (Kingsbury 1981:9). It is the pericope of Jesus' thanksgiving to the Father (Q 10:21–22). It is about the relationship between the Father and the Son. The Son was sent by the Father to bring God's salvation to the world. In Q the story of the temptation functions as a commentary on the thanksgiving to the Father. This very close relationship between the Son and the Father is tested by the temptations. In all three cases Israel succumbed to their own will and disobeyed the will of God. Jesus, however, "knows" the will of God and remains perfectly in tune with it (see Kingsbury 1981:10). The very close relationship between the Father and the Son prevails. Satan does not succeed in finding a flaw in the relationship. Then, in Q too, Jesus sets out to fulfill his mission with

Israel and does so with full divine authority (Kingsbury 1981:11). Since Jesus knows and does the will of God perfectly, he is the one through whom the Father and the Father's will are made known to the people.

In Q Jesus is also portrayed as "wisdom's envoy" (see Tuckett 1996:218-21; cf. Christ 1970). "Wisdom appears as the agent who sends out the prophets, all of whom suffer rejection and violence . . . [It] represents a highly distinctive coming together of two themes in Judaism, that of rejected Wisdom and that of the violent fate suffered by the prophets" (Tuckett 1996:219). Chapter 4 will elaborate on this theme. It will be shown that the suffering of Jesus as wisdom sage was compared to the conflict that the Jesus followers experienced. By attributing the honorary title *Son of Man* to Jesus, his followers portrayed him as conqueror and, by doing so, defended their own honor.

The Gospel of Mark

Narrative Point of View

Central to Mark's gospel is the death of Jesus on the cross. This Jesus is also the one who is to come. The author of the Gospel of Mark expects the final coming of Jesus (Mark 13:24-27). However, the cross is more important to Mark than the parousia and this emphasis shapes his ideas about Jesus and salvation (Kingsbury 1981:28). Ernest Best (1983:66) refers as follows to Mark's emphasis on the death of Jesus:

> The death of Jesus broods over the entire Gospel. It first becomes explicit at 3.6 where, after a series of controversies between Jesus and the Jewish leaders, the Pharisees and the Herodians take counsel together how they may eliminate him. It was however already probably implicit in the very first incident in which Jesus is involved, his baptism. Whether we take the words, "You are my beloved Son; with you I am well pleased," as based on the words of the suffering servant in Isaiah or on the words of Abraham to Isaac when he took him away to sacrifice him the thought of death is present. In any case, the Christian community for whom Mark was writing knew that Jesus' life ended with his execution at Jerusalem. The first readers of the Gospel before they heard it knew its content, not only the individual paragraphs but also its end, the death and resurrection of Jesus.

We have seen that Mark was one of the first authors to compile a gospel out of a large body of material. This material included sayings of Jesus as well as narrative commentary on his sayings and deeds (cf. Vorster [1987] 1995:269-88). "That Mark's Gospel is a narrative, cannot be doubted ... The story he created is Mark's image and the narrative world is his narrative world. He selected and arranged his material in terms of order and space and it is he who decided on what each character will do or say and when. Even if Mark closely followed tradition and 'historical events', it was still he who created the image ... Jesus ... " (Vorster 1995:272). The pre-Marcan stories were transmitted orally throughout the Jesus communities. Some of them were clustered together in the written evidence of the early Q tradition. Examples of such larger sections are the debates (Mark 2:1-3:6), the parables (4), the miracle stories (4:35—6:52) and the teaching of Jesus (14-15) (Kingsbury 1981:28).

Since the pioneering work of William Wrede ([1901] 1971; 1904:169-77) Marcan scholars have become convinced that, in reworking the material, the author of the Gospel of Mark transformed it into a work of literature and into a work of theology. In the first part of the Marcan story (1:14-8:26) the narrator tells of Jesus gathering disciples (see Tannehill [1977] 1995:169-96; Best 1983:83-92), teaching and preaching, healing and exorcising demons (see Kingsbury 1981:29). In the second part (8:27—16:8) the author portrays Jesus on a journey from Galilee to Jerusalem (see Malbon [1982] 1995:253-68; cf. Van Eck 1995:11-70). There he undergoes a terrible suffering which ends in his death. But Jesus does not remain dead—he is raised from death and lives again.

> A diachronic investigation of Galilee and Jerusalem in the Gospel of Mark focuses attention on the journeys of the Marcan Jesus and on the various ways in which these journeys are anticipated. A close chronological reading brings out narrative patterns of foreshadowing or echoing—to suggest both a visual and an auditory metaphor.
>
> Jesus' initial journey from Nazareth of Galilee to Judea, near Jerusalem (1:9), foreshadows Jesus' final journey to Judea, to Jerusalem. In the beginning Jesus journeys to Judea to be baptized by John into a ministry that leads, in the end, to a journey to Jerusalem to be crucified. But Jesus' initial return to Galilee from the wilderness in Judea (1:14) also foreshadows Jesus' final return to Galilee "as he told you" from the tomb in Judea (16:7). The ministry of the Marcan Jesus opens with Jesus' return to Galilee

A Synchronic Test Case: Q and the Synoptic Gospels

from Judea; the Marcan closing anticipates a like return. (Malbon 1995:258)

The author of Mark places the story of Jesus against the background of the Old Testament story of God and God's people. What happens to Jesus is interpreted by Mark as a fulfillment of Old Testament prophecy (see Vorster 1981:62–72; Sanders and Davies 1996:270–71). As "theologian," Mark interprets the life of Jesus as the fulfillment of Old Testament promises and, therefore, the focal point of God's interaction with human beings. The figures of both John the Baptist and Jesus of Nazareth are a clear indication that the eschatological time has dawned. This is the era that begins with John and will end with the final triumphant coming of Jesus. Though his eschatological time includes the ministries of John, Jesus and the early followers of Jesus (before and after Easter), for the author of Mark the emphasis is clearly on the ministry of Jesus.

> The reason Mark wrote the story of Jesus in this way had little to do with the historical Jesus, much however, with the recent history of the Jesus movement to which Mark belonged. A failure to reform the diaspora synagogue [see McKay 1998:106], from which this group or groups had finally found it necessary to withdraw, resulted in confusion about the group's purposes, hostility against Judaism, and withdrawal into a sectarian mentality and enclave. Mark associated the death of Jesus with the group's rejection by the synagogue and then linked both to the destruction of the temple. The end of the temple was, according to Mark, a righteous judgment, a vindication of the rightness of the cause and kingdom for which the group stood ... When Mark did make that connection the Christian myth of succession or substitution was born. Jesus had been the rightful heir to the kingdom in conflict with Second Temple Judaism ... *Jesus, the once and future king, now was to reign in the place of the vanquished high priests* (Mack 1988:355, 356, my italics).

In order to understand Mark's portrayal of Jesus as the "crucified Christ" (Tatum 1999:59), several related themes should be taken into account. Mark does not often use the expression Son of God to refer to Jesus, but when he does a specific function is intended. For instance, Mark's very first description of Jesus is that he is Son of God (1:1). (Some scholars, however, see this title as "additional," since it "is missing in several important mss and in quotations cited in a number of early Christian authors" [Schmidt 1990:42]). God calls Jesus Son of God at his baptism and transfiguration (1:11; 9:7) and so do the unclean spirits (3:11). When Jesus is dying the Roman centurion who is present at the cross makes the statement: "Truly this man was God's Son" (15:39). "For the cross, Jesus made his way to Jerusalem. By the cross, he is revealed to be Son of God (Tatum 1999:59). This "high Christology" is found in the story of Mark from the beginning to the end. Mark 1:21–45 develops the theme of Jesus the Son of God (1:1, 11; cf. "the Holy One of God"—1:24). Here Jesus exemplifies authority in word and deed (1:21–22, 27, 29–31, 41). Osborne (1994:162–163) puts is as follows:

> This new authority "astounds" (v 22) and "overwhelms" (v 27) the people, who see the hand of God in Jesus but cannot understand the true meaning of his actions . . . This authority is especially evident in Jesus' teaching. Even his deeds are called "a new teaching with authority" (v 27), and Jesus' priorities clearly center on preaching the kingdom message (vv 38–39) . . . Yet Jesus' miracles at the same time exemplify his authority and are a focus of his messianic activity. He is a "healer" of "all" (vv 32, 34), one whose hand is at all times stretched out to the sick (1:29–31, 32, 34, 40–42) . . . In addition to his healing ministry, Jesus engages in combat against the demonic forces. This cosmic war is seen in two exorcism stories (vv 23–26, 32–34) . . . The startling aspect of these stories (indeed, of all exorcism miracles) is that there is never any actual battle. Jesus expels the demons with hardly a conflict, and the battle is over virtually before it can begin . . . As a result of his "authority in word and deed," Jesus' fame grows geometrically . . . throughout Galilee (v 28) . . . the whole city of Capernaum (v 33) . . . in synagogues throughout Galilee (v 39) . . . "from every quarter" (v 45).

The theme of the "messianic secret" pervades Mark (Tatum 1999:59; cf. Tuckett 1983). Throughout the Gospel of Mark Jesus is portrayed as trying to keep his identity and task a secret. "Jesus orders demons, witnesses to his healings, and even his own disciples not to make him known (1:34; 3:12; 5:43; 7:24, 36; 8:36; 9:9, 30). In Mark, the evangelist appears to be using the secrecy motif to show that Jesus has de-emphasized the more spectacular aspects of his ministry in favor of *his vocation as the suffering 'Son of Man'* (8:31; 9:31; 10:32–34) *and suffering 'Son of God'* (15:39)" (Tatum 1999:59, my italics.)

A Synchronic Test Case: Q and the Synoptic Gospels

Mark's presentation of the story of Jesus is from a specific point of view and with a specific intention. The direction of his thought can be seen from early on in his narrative (cf. Matera [1988] 1995:289-306). Throughout the story he gives clues as to what is going to happen to Jesus. One such clue is the fate of John the Baptist (see Matera 1995:293-94). Since his role is linked to that of Jesus, what happens to him gives the reader an indication of where Jesus is heading (cf. 14:43-46). Another clue is Jesus' interaction with the Galilean and Judean élite. Jesus teaches "as one who had authority, and not as the scribes" (1:22). How this relates to the institutionalization of charismatic authority, will be worked out later. The controversy stories give evidence of conflict between Jesus and the élite (see Dewey [1973] 1995:141-52). These stories concern cultic regulations and the controversies are settled by appeals to "Christological" arguments (cf. Kuhn 1971:82-83). According to Jerome Neyrey (1998:675), "Mark's narrative consists of a constant testing of Jesus' claim to be a reforming prophet or an authorized son of God and a constant refusal to acknowledge the claim." According to Dewey (1995:149), the controversy stories "serve the needs of the [Judean] community against Jewish Christians who accept the full power of the earthly Son of Man." Mark portrays the elite plotting against Jesus (3:6) en Jesus alluding to his fate (2:20). When Jesus chooses his disciples, Judas is directly pointed out as "the one who also betrayed him" (3:19) (see Kingsbury 1981:30).

Jesus comes into conflict not only with "the enemies" such as the élite and the Judean crowd (Mark 4:1-2), but also with those who are supposed to be his "friends," his family (3:20-21, 31-35) and fellow villagers (6:1-5) (see Kingsbury 1981:31). Alienation is reported throughout the story and leads to Jesus' suffering and eventual death on the cross (15:25-41). The passion of Jesus is the focal point of Mark's narrative. Almost everything in the story (previews, e.g. the passion predictions, and flashbacks, e.g. the resurrection) points to the cross. In the scene of Jesus' resurrection he is still called "the one from Nazareth" (16:6), indicating that he remains the crucified one even though he has risen.

The way in which Mark tells his kerygmatic story indicates that he sees the cross as the key to understanding the work and person of Jesus. This has narrative implications (Kingsbury 1981:32). It is to be expected that the various narrative lines will come together at this point (see Via

1975:128–130). According to Kingsbury (1981:32) at least three such narrative lines can be indicated:

- the line of the story as revealed by the summary passages Mark selects;
- the secret of Jesus' identity as the royal Son of God;
- the incomprehension of the disciples to understand the mission of Jesus before his death and resurrection.

Via (1975:128–30) sees the line of the incomprehension of the disciples intersecting with the line of the rejection of Jesus by his opponents at the cross. Tannehill (1995:188) puts it as follows:

> In one sense the story of the disciples is over, for nothing further is recorded of the actions of the twelve who have been the central figures in this story. The disciples' story has come to a disastrous conclusion, and the author has spared nothing in emphasizing the disaster. This ending sent reverberations back through the whole preceding story. The reader who was at first content to view the disciples as reflections of his [or her] own faith and who may have continued to hope for a happy ending to their story must now try to disentangle him[- or her]self from them, which will mean choosing a path contrary to their path. The possibility of this other path is recognized within the story, for there is a sense in which the disciples' story is *not* over. There are features of the story which hold the future open . . . So the Gospel holds open the possibility that those who deserted Jesus will again become his followers, reinstating the relationship established by Jesus' call.

Characterization and Naming

In the prologue (Mark 1:1–13 [15]) Jesus is introduced as the main character and John the Baptist as his predecessor (1:2, 7). The story of John the Baptist is told (1:2–8) to anticipate the tragedy of Jesus' life-story. John predicts that someone will come who is mightier than he (1:7) and then Jesus comes onto the scene (1:9–13) (Kingsbury 1981:33). Jesus is empowered by the Holy Spirit (1:10) and is declared to be God's beloved Son (1:11) by a voice from heaven. Mark quotes from the Hebrew Scriptures: Gen 22:2; Ps 2:7; and Isa 42:1 (cf. Sanders and Davies 1996:270–71). By applying these words to Jesus he depicts Jesus as the one chosen and sent by God to inaugurate the eschatological kingdom for Israel. The reference to Psalm 2:7 indicates that Jesus is also the king of Judah from the line of David. Mark's picture of Jesus is that he is the Davidic Messiah expected by Israel. Sanders and Davies (1996:271) formulate it as follows: "In Mark, Jesus is the *Messiah*, the *Son of David*, understood to be predicted in Scriptural passages like Ps. 118.25f. (Mk 11.9f. and 10.47f.) . . . In the Passion narrative, 'the king of the Jews' (Mk 15.2, 9, 12, 18, 26; cf. 15.32) is . . . a key term in the trial before Pilate and the crucifixion."

This Messiah is, at the same time, the Son of God: "The beginning of the gospel of Jesus Messiah, the Son of God" (Mk 1:1). The term "messiah" is a derivative of the Hebrew *ha-mashiaḥ* ("the Anointed"). The term was a later development and refers to Israel's end-time savior. According to Cohn-Sherbock (1997:2–3), textual references in the Torah such as the promise to Abraham (Gen 12:2–3), the promise to Isaac (Gen 26:3–4) and the Jacob covenant (Gen 28:12–14), are implicit reverse projections of a messianic expectation. This expectation becomes explicit in texts such as 2 Samuel 23:1, 3, 5 and 2 Samuel 7:8–10 where the messianic idea is connected with the Davidic dynasty. David is seen as the "anointed" (*messiah*) of God. God's provision and protection will become manifest in the actions of the long line of successors to the Davidic throne. At the same time the messianic idea began functioning as the symbol of the ideal of a unified Israel, no longer divided by the interests of the North and the South (see Amos 9:11–12). Richard Horsley (1996:19) refers as follows to this ideal: "According to the histories of the monarchy written or edited by royal scribes, the representative 'elders' of all the tribes participated in the popular acclamation or 'anointing' (*messiah*) of David as king over all Israel (2 Sam. 5:1–3)." The prophet Amos (see 5:16–17; 6:7; 7:17; 8:10), however, was certain that destruction and exile would occur before this ideal could be attained (see Cohn-Sherbock 1997:4–5). The prophet Hosea (6:1–2) seemed to have had a similar thought:

Come, let us return to the LORD;
> for [God] has stricken, and [God] will bind us up.
> After two days [God] will revive us;
> > and on the third day [God] will raise us up,
> > that we may live before [God]. (RSV)

In his book, *Jewish Messianism and the Cult of Christ*, William Horbury (1998:66-67) describes the *Wirkungsgeschichte* of the "messianic unity ideal" as follows:

> Towards the end of the first century AD the interpretation of the cloud vision in the Syriac Apocalypse of Baruch makes the messiah sit on the throne of his kingdom (chapters 70-73) at the climax of the series of good rulers—David, Solomon, Hezekiah and Josiah (61; 63; 66). The connection of the messiah not just with David, but with the line of good kings, emerges in a different way in the famous last words ascribed to Johannan b. Zaccai . . . The more straightforward presentation of a royal succession leading up to the messiah, as in Gen. 49.10, reappears in Pseudo-Philo's *Biblical Antiquities*, where Kenaz is presented as one of the kings and rulers . . . The pattern is repeated in a Christian source at the end of the first century, with recollection of the priestly as well as the royal line, when Jacob's blessings of all the tribes are summarized in 1 Clement 32.2.

When Peter addresses Jesus as "the Anointed" (ὁ Χριστος) (Mark 8:29), Mark lets Jesus react with the "messianic secret" formula (8:30), keeping Peter from making this confession public. In the context of the Gospel of Mark (also taken over by Matt 16:22-23) it is clear that Peter did not see "destruction" as a necessary prerequisite for the coming of messianic redemption. The Marcan Jesus (as continued by Matt 16:21), however, declares that the triumphant *Son of Man* will be raised to life after three days (Mark 8:31; 9:31; 10:33-34—cf. Hos 6:1-2). Mark shows that Peter (8:29-30), the Twelve (9:33) and the sons of Zebedee (James and John) (10:35-45), the "pillars" of the post-Easter Jesus movement in Jerusalem (Gal 2:9), did not understand what God intended with the messianic ideal. Peter wants the "healing" without the preceding "destruction." The disciples yearn for greatness and the sons of Zebedee for royal honour. The Markan Jesus is the realization of the prophetic word (Isa 11:1-2, 3-4, 6) about a messianic ideal of *service* and being present for the poor:

> There shall come forth a shoot from the stump of Jesse,
> and a branch shall grow out of his roots.
> And the Spirit of the Lord shall rest upon him . . .
> He shall not judge by what his eyes see,
> or decide by what is ears hear;

> But with righteousness he shall judge the poor,
> and decide with equity for the meek of the earth. (RSV)

The messianic ideal reaches a climax in the third prediction of Jesus' suffering at the turning point of the plot in Mark's narrative. The sons of Zebedee (John and James) are admonished by Jesus (10:42-45) not to desire to be like those who rule over the nations, or like those "great men" who exercise authority over them (the nations). The person who wants to be *first*, must be everyone's *slave*. The Son of Man (i.e., the triumphant messiah) came to *serve* and not to be *served*. According to Mark (10:46-52) it was the blind Bartimaeus of Jericho, and not the "pillars" of the Jesus faction in Jerusalem, who had insight into the role of the serving and healing Son of David (Messiah). Mark narrates that Bartimaeus, when he heard that Jesus who was moving through the streets of Jericho on his way to Jerusalem, shouted: "Son of David [Messiah], have mercy on me." In the following pericope (11:1-11) Mark tells the story (by adapting Ps 118:25-26) of how the followers of Jesus in general and not the Twelve in particular, were the ones who honored Jesus when he entered Jerusalem on a donkey. The followers used expressions such as the "blessed" of the *Kyrios* (11:9) and as "the blessed coming of the kingdom of our father David" (11:10). In the Gospel of Mark this is followed by the story of Jesus cleansing the Jerusalem temple. Here, too, the messianic ideal of God's righteousness and justice for those who are deprived of provision and protection by the patrons of the people, can be seen (see Ps 72:112-114). In the Gospel of Mark (11:17) Jesus cites Jeremiah (7:11), where the Second Temple ideology is compared with a "den of bandits." According to the messianic ideal of a united Israel, the temple in Jerusalem is "God's house," and this house "will be called a place of prayer for all nations" (Mark 11:17). This ideal of unity can also be found in, among others, Isa 26:1-4; Mic 2:12; 4:2-4; Zeph 3:19-20; Jer 23:5-6; 31:31-33; 33:14-16; Ezek 37:24:25 (see Cohn-Sherbock 1997:8-16).

Jesus' teaching in the temple in Mark 12:35-37 provides a key to understanding why the later faction of the Jesus movement in Jerusalem failed to grasp the meaning of Jesus' messianic role. It also shows that Mark considers the title Messiah not to be an adequate symbol in itself with which to evaluate Jesus' work. In order to express adequately both the defeat (crucifixion) and the victory over defeat (resurrection), Mark adds the title *Son of God*, taken from the Graeco-Hellenistic background, to that of Messiah of Israel. Matthew concurs with Mark and expands the confession of Peter (Matt 16:16) that Jesus is "the Christ, the Son of the living God." According to Mark 8:29, Peter simply calls Jesus "Messiah." In 15:37 the dying moment of Jesus is described metaphorically as the triumphant call of a herout: "Jesus called in a loud voice" and "died." The Roman centurion (15:39) reacted to this with an extended acknowledgement of the "truth" about Jesus, namely that he was truly the "Son of God." For Mark, Jesus' claim to authority lies not only within the *Würdeprädikation* "Messiah of Israel," but more specifically in the value judgment that Jesus as *Messiah*, is also the suffering and triumphant Son of God.

An emphasis only on the messiahship of Jesus could lead to the desire to be "high officials," without taking into account what it really means to follow Jesus: suffering, dying and being triumphant servants. The latter goes together with Jesus being "Messiah" *and* "Son of God." Mark 12:35–37 recounts the controversy between Jesus and the Jerusalem scribes. They want to understand "Son of David" only in the sense of might and power. According to Mark, Jesus quotes from Ps 110:1 where "messiah" is understood as a subordinate to the *Kyrios* (cf. Cohn-Sherbock 1997:17): "*The Lord* says to *my lord*: 'Sit at my right hand . . . '" (Ps 110:1, RSV). According to the Markan Jesus, it is David, as an instrument of the Spirit of God (12:36), who is speaking here. Jesus then asks: if David calls the addressee *Kyrios*, how can David be the *son of the Kyrios* (God) (12:37). The meaning is clear: the "truth" about the authority of Jesus is that he is more than just "son of David" (= "messiah"). As Messiah he does not have authority, because the "messiah" is subordinate to the *Kyrios*. Jesus as Son of God has authority. His authority is confirmed by his victory over suffering and death (see also Rom 1:3–4).

Jesus' words and deeds are presented in a way which affirms that he is indeed the royal Son of God and Messiah enabled by the Spirit of God to fulfill his function. He speaks and acts with divine authority, he declares that the time of God's kingdom has arrived (Mark 1:14–15), he calls his followers (1:16–20), does exorcisms and performs healings in order to restore the broken lives of people. Mark, however, keeps this identity of Jesus as Son of God a secret from the people, though of course God and the demons know who Jesus is (see Sanders and Davies 1996:272). As the story unfolds only certain aspects of the secret are revealed (Kingsbury 1981:34). From time to time Mark has people asking questions as to Jesus' identity. Characters in the story answer these questions with their ideas of who he is. But the answers are all incorrect. This contrasts with assertions about Jesus that are only partially correct. In this way the secret of Jesus' identity as Son of God remains in tact. Only at the end of the story, at Jesus' death and resurrection, is the secret revealed. By telling the story in this way the author indicates that Jesus' identity as the royal Son of God is crucial to his destiny. As the obedient Son of God he is willing to go the way of the cross (see Mark 14:35-36) (Kingsbury 1981:34). "[T]he phrase 'Son of God' indicates his importance, but by picturing him as a truly obedient Israel, not as the Second Person of the Trinity. The synoptic gospels did not formulate questions about Jesus' nature in the terms which were exercised by later generations of Christians and hence had no need to use 'Son' in the sense found in the Creeds" (Sanders and Davies 1996:272).

The Gospel of Matthew

Narrative Point of View

The emphasis in the Gospel of Matthew is that the "eschatological" rule of God (see Sanders and Davies 1996:264) has come near in the person of God's *Son*, Jesus who is Emmanuel (1:23; 18:20; 28:20). "Does Jesus, by being Emmanuel, bring an eschatological expectation to fulfillment? According to Jewish tradition, while God had been 'with' his people in the past (e.g. Num 23.21; Deut 2.7), he would, it was hoped, be especially 'with' them in messianic times (Isa 43.5; Ezek 34.30; 37.27; Zech 8.23; 11QTemple 29.7-10; Jub 1.17, 26; Rev 21.3)" (Davies and Allison [1988] 1997:217-218).

In order to tell his story Matthew makes use of traditions transmitted by Mark and the Sayings Gospel Q. Except for the material taken over from these sources, Matthew also has material unique to his gospel, namely the *Sondergut* of Matthew. The way in which Matthew arranged the material from the sources and added his own, tells a story. The Marcan tradition served as the framework (see Bauer 1988:23-24) to which he added material from Q (see Davies and Allison 1997:97-127). The speech-complexes in Matthew (5-7; 10; 13; 18; 23; 24-25) mainly contain material from Q. These speech-complexes lead to the climax of the story, the passion, death and resurrection of Jesus (26-28). The passion story features prominently and Matthew's narrative can also be called a "gospel" or "kerygmatic story" (see Kingsbury 1981:61).

Matthew' story about the life of Jesus contains much more material than Mark's. Where Mark begins with the baptism of Jesus, Matthew goes further back to his genealogy, birth and infancy (1-2). The end of the story in Matthew also goes beyond that of Mark. In Mark a prediction is given that Jesus would be seen again in Galilee. Matthew reports such an appearance (8:16-20). According to Kingsbury (1975:7-25; cf. Howell 1990:81-85), Matthew's story is told in three phases. Matthew first introduces the reader to Jesus *Messiah* (1:1-4:16). In the second phase he describes the public ministry of Jesus Messiah (4:17—16:20). The last phase of the story is about the suffering, death and resurrection of Jesus *Messiah* (16:21—28:20). The transition from one section to the next is marked by a typically Matthean formula: "From that time on Jesus began to . . ." (4:17; 16:21).

Davies and Allison (1997:58-72) discuss other possibilities for structuring the Matthean narrative. The structure of C. A. Lohr (1961:403-35), which divides Matthew into five parts is one such a possibility. He uses the five speeches in Matthew as point of departure and uncovers a concentric chiastic structure (cf. Combrink 1983:61-90). The typically Matthean formula he uses as point of departure is a different formula than the one used by Kingsbury. Lohr uses the formula in Matt 7:28-29; 11:1; 13:53; 19:1; 26:1: "And when Jesus finished these sayings . . ." According to the concentric chiastic structure the parable discourse in Matthew 13 forms the central section of the Gospel of Matthew. This discourse ends with a reference that "he" (possibly the author) is a *grammateus*. The emphases of both divisions of Matthew are important to my thesis. With regard to the fivefold division, the relevance of scribal activity for understanding the relationship between the pre-Easter and the post-Easter Jesus followers can been pointed out. Kingsbury, known for the three part division of Matthew, sees the plan of the gospel as a salvation history which unfolds in these three phases (see Bauer 1988). The narrative pattern that Kingsbury follows in his division is useful for the synchronic description of the life of Jesus as narrated by Matthew (see Kingsbury 1986).

The theme of Matthew's story, namely God's nearness to people in Jesus, is reiterated by 1:23 at the beginning and 28:20 at the end of the gospel. Matthew 1:23 is a quotation from Isaiah: "Emmanuel . . . God with us." In 28:20 Jesus says to his disciples: "I am with you always, to the close of the age." According to Matthew the nearness of God in Jesus is an indication that the end-time, the time of Gods salvation, has come. Matthew places Jesus within history (Kingsbury 1981:63). Jesus' story spans the period from Abraham, the father of Israel (1:2) to the end of time (28:20). Within this broad history Matthew distinguishes between the "time of Israel" (the First Testament) and the "time of Jesus." The first is the age of prophecy and expectation. The second is the time of fulfillment. The time of Jesus can be pinpointed as from his birth as Son of Abraham, Son of David (1:1–25) to his parousia as the Son of Man (28:16–20) Theologically speaking the Gospel of Matthew sees the prophecy of the coming of the "Emmanuel," the Son of God, fulfilled in Jesus. The end-time has come and in Jesus God is present to all people. This Jesus is the Son of God and, as such, as important to Gentiles as he is to Israelites.

Characterization and Naming

The first part of Matthew's story (1:1–4:16) introduces the reader to Jesus. Initially Matthew portrays Jesus as the Messiah, the Son of David, the Son of Abraham (1:1). The most important title, namely Son of God is not mentioned here yet, but, because of its importance, it is placed in the mouth of God at the baptism of Jesus (3:17). Matthew largely took over Mark's Christology of Jesus as the Davidic Messiah and the royal Son of God, and adapted it to suit his own intention and situation (Kingsbury 1981:65). Matthew uses titles for Jesus in order to reveal Jesus' mission to the reader. The name "Jesus" means "God is salvation," and this is what Jesus' mission is all about: "you shall call his name 'Jesus,' for he shall save his people from their sins" (1:21). Because Matthew attaches such significance to the name "Jesus," he does not allow the name to be used by everyone merely as a common appellation for Jesus. In Mark people such as Bartimaeus and the two men possessed by evil spirits called him "Jesus" (Mark 1:24, 5:7; 10:47), but not in Matthew (Matt 8:29; 20:30).

Matthew follows Mark in depicting Jesus as the long-awaited *Messiah* from the house of David who comes with the authority of God. Matthew deviates from Mark by also calling Jesus Son of Abraham. The significance of this name is to indicate that Jesus was part of the history of Israel from the beginning and that Jesus was the fulfillment of what God had promised Israel. On the other hand "Abraham" was also connected with the Gentiles: "Many will come from east and west and sit at table with Abraham, Isaac, and Jacob in the kingdom of heaven" (Matt 8:10-11). So God's promise of salvation will not only be fulfilled to Israel but also to the Gentiles.

Jesus' *Davidic sonship* is more important to Matthew than to the other gospels. He uses the title more often (cf. Duling 1991). Matthew makes it clear that Jesus is a descendant of David. The connection between David and Jesus runs through Joseph who, according to Matthew, is a "son of David" (1:16). Joseph is not presented as the biological father of Jesus, since Jesus was conceived of the Holy Spirit (1:18, 20), but he did receive his name from Joseph (1:25). This means that Jesus was adopted into the line of Joseph. In the Gospel of Matthew Jesus heals and helps people who are of no account in Israel (outcasts such as the sick, crippled, women and Gentiles) and these are the people who, in turn, acknowledge Jesus and believe in him as the Son of David. "The irony is that they 'see' and 'confess' what the leaders of Israel and the crowds do not" (Kingsbury 1981:66–67). To Matthew, as to Mark, Jesus is much more than the Son of David. Jesus is the Son of God. Matthew's emphasis, however, differs from that of Mark. Davies and Allison ([1991] 1998:686) compare the use of the title Son of God in Mark and Matthew as it appears in the scenes of the transfiguration (Matt 17:1–8) and baptism (Matt 3:13–17) and reach the following conclusion:

> In Mark the heavenly voice declares to the disciples, "This is my beloved Son." In Luke this becomes, "This is my Son, my Chosen." In Matthew we find this: "This is my beloved Son with whom I am well pleased." These variants are interesting, especially that in our gospel [Matthew]. "With whom I am well pleased" also occurs in the narrative of Jesus' baptism, but originally it is from Isa 42.1, where it refers to the suffering servant of Deutero-Isaiah. Matthew appears to have added the phrase in order to signify Jesus as the one who is destined to bring his law to the nations (Isa 42.4). Such a suggestion is supported by this, that the following words "listen to him," in their broader Matthean context point to Jesus as an ethical teacher, like Moses.

The story of the temptation of Jesus (Matt 4:1–11) also shows Jesus as the Son of God (4:3, 6). Jesus accepts his vocation by resisting the temptations of Satan. The Christology of Matthew can, therefore, be summarized as follows: Jesus, in the line of David (1:21), is the Son of God (2:15; 3:17) who has his origin in God (1:20) and is chosen to shepherd the end-time people of God (2:6); empowered by God's Spirit for his messianic ministry (3: 16-17), he remains obedient to God in confrontation with Satan (4:1-12) and saves God's people from their sins (1:21) (see Kingsbury 1981:70).

The title Son of Man is used by Q, Mark and Matthew. In Q Jesus is called Son of Man and this titular use of the name refers back to Jesus' use of "son of man" in its generic form to indicate humanity in general. As Son of Man Jesus is the end-time judge. Mark's Son of Man is the one who works in this world, suffers, dies and comes again (Kingsbury 1981:71). Matthew takes Mark over, but places the emphasis where Q does: on the parousia of the Son of Man.

> Jesus' identity as the Son of God depends on his generation by the Holy Spirit and his Adamlike origin as a new human being . . . To say it in another way, he is the Son of God because he is the Son of Man. His identity as the Son of Man, however, does not refer only to his human nature, as is all to frequently assumed. For "the Son of Man" is a designation that is derived from the millenialism of Jewish apocalypticism, specifically the figure of "one like a human being" of Daniel 7:13. By identifying Jesus with this divine being whose coming was anticipated in the imminent future, the earliest Christians stipulated him to be an Adamlike personage who came out of the future in order to constitute a new humanity. To entitle Jesus as the Son of Man is to confer on him the distinction of being the first final human being and attendantly the progenitor of a new human race. (Waetjen 1999:29)

In Matthew people only use the title Son of God for Jesus in the form of a confession, and then only after this knowledge has been revealed to them by God. For example, after Peter's confession, "You are the Messiah, the Son of the living God!" (16:16), is added: "flesh and blood has not revealed this to you, but my Father who is in heaven!" (16:17). In Mark people do not comprehend Jesus' true identity of *Son of God* before he dies on the cross, but in Matthew they do (cf. 14:33; 16:15-16). In Matthew the secret of Jesus' divine sonship is "given" to the disciples (11:25-27; 13:11, 16-17) (Kingsbury 1981:72). Matthew's use of the title Son of Man can be understood against this background. Herman Waetjen (1999:35-36), referring to the last recorded interaction between Jesus and the disciples (28:16-20), describes the "sharing of sonship" as follows:

> [H]is disciples, the community of the new Human Being ["the Son of Man"] that he constitutes, are co-enthroned with him and deputized to universalize the actualized reality of God's rule. After presenting himself to the two women ... he subsequently appears to eleven of the twelve representatives of the new Israel he had chosen before his death. He addresses them in terms of his identity as the new Human Being and the fulfillment of Daniel 7:13–14 that his resurrection has effected: "All authority in heaven and on earth was given to me" (Matt 28:18) ... Eleven ascended into the mountain; twelve descended. [Read Matt 28:16 and 28:20 in relation to each other.] This is not explicitly stated by the narrator, but it is implied by the final verse of the Gospel, 28:20. Jesus does not remain behind on the mountain, nor does he ascend into heaven. He joins himself to the company of the Eleven: "See, *I* with you *am* even to the consummation of the age." As the twelfth, therefore, he reconstitutes Israel and imparts to its representatives both his identity and his empowerment as the new Human Being.

According to Kingsbury (1981:72–73) Matthew uses the title Son of Man to indicate Jesus' interaction with the "world." It becomes his "public title" as it were. Before the world Jesus is Son of Man, but for his followers he is Son of God. As far as the parousia of Jesus is concerned, the two merge: the future Son of Man and the Messiah, Son of God become one. Both figures become "king," know God as "my Father," and call the disciples "my brothers." The relationship between Jesus and the disciples is a prominent theme in the plot of the Matthean narrative. "Matthew uses the same terms to describe both Jesus' life and ministry on the one hand, and the disciple's life and mission on the other. Verbal and thematic redundancy or repetition reinforces the links ... " (Howell 1990:256).

The Gospel of Luke

Narrative Point of View

The Gospel of Luke is the only one that begins with a prologue (1:1–4) as was customary for the literature of the time (see Alexander 1986:48–74; Bonz 2000:129–32). The prologue contains the intention of the author and the characteristics of his writing (see Goulder 1989a:198–204). Luke indicates that this will be a narrative (Kingsbury 1981:94) in a series of two parts (see Schneider 1977:129–311). He calls this narrative one of several

A Synchronic Test Case: Q and the Synoptic Gospels

existing stories regarding "the things which have been fulfilled among us" (1:1). It shows that he was aware of the existence of these documents and could have used them as sources. The documents could, therefore, have included Q, Mark and other sources for the material found only in Luke.

The way in which Luke organized the material is significant. The infancy narratives and the resurrection stories are material only used by Luke. These stories form the beginning and the ending of his narrative (1–2; 24). The structure of the gospel comes from Mark, whereas Q can be seen mainly in two sections (6:20–7:35; 9:51–18:14). The gospel is structured in such a way that the passion and exaltation form the climax of the story. Luke, Mark and Matthew share the tradition of the "passion kerygma" of the early church (see also 1 Cor 15:3–5) (Kingsbury 1981:94).

Luke's story begins with the birth of John the Baptist and ends with the resurrection and ascension of Jesus. The Gospels of Mark, Matthew and Luke were not factual accounts about the life of Jesus, but "kerygmatic stories" (see Marshall [1970] 1992:21–52; Green 1997:14–20). Luke presents his story (see Esler 1996:224 n. 2; Green 1997:1–6) as the correct way to understand the life of Jesus, the one who was sent by God. The gospel is addressed to a specific person, Theophilus (1:3), but also to the believing community of which Luke himself is part (see Esler [1987] 1996:24–45)—hence the pronoun "us" (1:2) (see Fitzmyer 1989:16–22; Robbins 1975:5–18; 1978:215–242; Bonz 2000:170–173). The purpose of writing his story is: "in order that you might know the truth concerning the things about which you have been instructed" (1:4). In other words, the story wants to "inform" the believers of "accurate knowledge" about God's work in Jesus that has been "taught" to them.

Luke's gospel is even more extensive than Matthew's (Kingsbury 1981:96). Luke begins with the birth of John the Baptist before Jesus' birth (1:5–25), whereas Matthew begins with Jesus. At the end of his story Luke also goes beyond the resurrection to the ascension of Jesus (24:50–53). After the preface Luke introduces the reader to John the Baptist, the one who foretells the coming of the Messiah of God (see Goulder 1989a:270–281; Fitzmyer 1989:86–116; Geyser 1956:70–75; Robinson 1957–1958:263–81; Allison 1984:256–58), and then Luke introduces Jesus, the Messiah. After the introduction the story continues with the public life of Jesus. He journeys from Galilee (4:14–9:50) to Jerusalem (9:51–19:44) (see Goulder 1989b:453–483; 1983:561–568; Grundmann

1958:252-270; Reicke 1959:206-216; Sellin 1978:100-135). In Jerusalem Jesus teaches in the temple after which follow his suffering, death on the cross, resurrection and ascension (22:1-24:53). The journey to Jerusalem forms the line of the story.

Since Jerusalem and the temple are of the utmost importance to Israel's social, economic, judicial and religious life (see Baltzer 1965:264), the message of this journey to Jerusalem is that God's salvation is coming to Israel (Kingsbury 1981:97). The context in which Luke places his story is even broader than that of Mark and Matthew: from the very beginning of history, namely creation, to the very end, the final fulfillment. Jesus' genealogy, therefore, is taken back to Adam (3:38) (Abel 1974:203-210; Goulder 1989a:281-291; Brown [1977] 1978:76, 90-94) and he is the Son of Man, who will come at the end of time (21:25-27) (Kingsbury 1981:97). The story of Jesus is not only pertinent to Israel, but also to the whole world. However, Luke's particular interest is how God will save Israel, the people of God (see Tannehill 1985:69-85; 1986:130-41; Jervell 1962:41-74). The "time of prophesy" (1:70; 24:25-27, 44-45) is when God's salvation is foretold and then, in Jesus "the time of salvation" (2:30-32) arrives. Hans Conzelmann (1954:117) is known for his words, "er [Luke] bestimmt ihre heilsgeschichtliche Stellung und leitet daraus die Regeln des Verhaltens zur Welt ab," in his book, *Die Mitte der Zeit: Studien zur Theologie des Lukas*.

According to Kingbury (1981:97) the coming of Jesus, the presence of the Holy Spirit (Luke 1:41, 67; 2:25; 3:22) and God's eschatological kingdom (17:21) indicate that "the time of salvation" has come. Jesus is the focal point of this time. He alone is the Savior (σωτήρ) of all people, of Israel and the Gentiles (see Bovon 1983:125-126; Green 1997:134-135; Bonz 2000:182): "there is salvation in no one else, for there is no other name under heaven given among human beings by which we must be saved" (4:12). The figure who forms the bridge between the time of prophecy and the time of salvation, is John the Baptist. John is not only the "prophet" (1:76; 7:26) from the old dispensation, he is also the one who prepares the way for the Lord (1:16-17; 3:3; 7:27). This task places him in "the time of salvation" and so the bridge between the two dispensations is built. In the Gospel of Luke the theological claim is made that Jesus is the Savior of Israel. In Acts this message is extended to the Gentiles (Kingsbury 1981:98).

Characterization and Naming

The name Jesus means: "Yahweh is salvation," but Luke takes it further than Mark and Matthew and calls Jesus Savior. In the Old Testament this term refers to God as the "Savior" of the people of Israel (Kingsbury 1981:99). God saves them from a variety of misfortunes. In the Gospel of Luke the name Saviour (σωρήρ) is attributed to Jesus. Bock (1987:78) describes the referential meaning of this title as follows:

> *Sōtēr* in the Old Testament refers, where it refers to men, to a deliverer from enemies. It is used of the judges whom God raised up to deliver Israel (Judg. 3.9, 15; Neh. 9.27). However it is a rare title for kings. Only Jehoahaz is called a deliverer, when he leads the nation against Syria (2 Kgs 13.5). Its primary use involves the description of God as Saviour, e.g. the LXX rendering "the God of my salvation" as "Saviour" . . . In the Old Testament, the Messiah is never referred to as *sōtēr*. Rabbinical material also uses the term once . . . In Greek circles, the term is used with reference to either gods or men who save from danger. It is used of doctors, rulers, and philosophers. It was not an official title for the Roman ruler, though it was used popularly.

By transferring this name to Jesus, Luke shows that in "the time of salvation" which has dawned, God will deliver people in a very specific way: through the person of Jesus. It remains an act of God, the "Savior," and is executed by Jesus who then becomes the *Savior* sent by God. This act of deliverance in Jesus is an indication that God's kingdom has become a reality in the world.

Luke also refers to Jesus by means of the title *Kyrios*. In the Septuagint God's name, "Yahweh," is translated into Greek with the word *Kyrios*. God's "lordship" is an indication of God's rule over all of creation: "Shout to God with loud songs of joy! For the Lord, the Most High, is terrible, a great king over all the earth" (Ps 47:1-2). Luke endows Jesus with these characteristics of God by referring to Jesus as the "*Kyrios* of heaven and earth" (Luke 10:21). Jesus' rule is announced before his birth: "you shall call his name Jesus . . . and the Lord God will give to him the throne of his father David, and he will reign over the house of Jacob for ever" (Luke 1:33-35). God will rule through Jesus who then becomes ruler like God. Therefore Jesus is *Kyrios* as God is *Kyrios*. Jesus acts with divine authority. Sanders and Davies (1996:293) point out that Jesus is referred to as *Kyrios* in the Gospel of Luke, not only by characters in the story (see 5:8, 12), but also by the narrator (see 7:13, 19):

> The title draws attention to Jesus' dignity but does not attribute divinity to him. Elsewhere in the gospel, *kyrios* refers either to human beings with authority (e.g. 12.37, 47; 13.25) or to God, following the Septuagint (e.g. 2.23, 26; 3.4; 4.8, 12, 18, 19). God is also called *Despotes* "Lord" (Luke 2.22; Acts 4.24), a title used both in the Septuagint and in Graeco-Roman literature.
> Again, like Matthew and Mark, Luke presents Jesus as the *Son of God*, giving him the same metaphorical relationship to God which Scripture gives to Adam (3:28), to Israel and to Davidic kings (Ex 4.22; Hos 11.1; Ps 2.7 quoted in Acts 13.33).

Luke also sees Jesus as Messiah-King (23:2) from the line of David, as Son of God (see Luke 2:49) and as Servant (2:43)/Holy Child (Acts 4:27). Luke connects Jesus as *pais* with David as *pais* in Acts 4:25, but he also expands on the title Messiah or Christ. He portrays Jesus as the ultimate *Savior* of humankind. As Messiah and Davidic King, his coming is the fulfillment of the prophecies of the Hebrew Scriptures (Kingsbury 1981:101). God's promises become reality. These titles also indicate that he inaugurates the new dispensation, "the time of salvation." Luke does not take the messianic secret over from Mark. All people should know that the *Messiah* has indeed come and should rejoice. Esler (1996:34) puts it as follows: "[The] evidence suggests an openness to non-Jews within the scheme of salvation, although not, it should be noted, to the exclusion of the Jews (Luke 2.31–2; 14.15–24)."

Jesus, as the royal Messiah could be called "the King of the Jews" (Luke 23:38). This king, however, is not the revolutionary king accused of posing a threat to the Roman government. His kingship is of a different kind and Luke gives the correct perspective on this matter (see Schmithals 1987:373). The political apology is reflected in Luke-Acts by the picture of the founder of the church, his apostles and the servants of the Word, as people who struggled against the representation of the Jesus-movement as a political movement (e.g., Luke 7:1–10; 19:38; 20:20–26; 23:2–7; Acts 17:7; 25:8). The image of the founder of the church as well as the church's 'managers' is that of servant and victim of persecution (e.g. Acts 3:18; 4:27; 4:30 and 4:29; 13:35, respectively). In Luke-Acts God's kingdom is proclaimed as opposing Caesar's kingdom. Yet, in Luke's mind-set there is also a similarity: as Roman power depended on the approval of Jupiter, so Jesus' authority depended on God's approval. Marianne Bonz formulates the similarity *and* opposition between God's rule and Caesar's power as follows:

> The last point—that Rome's eternal rule has been granted in accordance with divine will only if one accepts the divine legitimacy of . . . Jupiter—brings one directly to a consideration of the motives behind the composition of Luke-Acts in a narrative epic style . . . Luke-Acts presents a rival vision of empire, with a rival deity issuing an alternative plan for universal human salvation. Furthermore, Luke-Acts names a very different sort of hero as the primary instrument for the implementation of that plan, a different concept of the chosen people, and a very different means by which conquest leads to inevitable victory. (Bonz 2000:182)

Though Luke does portray Jesus as *Son of David*, this name is not as important here as it is in Matthew (see Kingsbury 1981:102). For Luke Jesus' Davidic lineage points to the fulfillment of God's promise to David that there will always be someone of Davidic descent on the throne of Israel (cf. Luke 1:32–33; 2 Sam 7:12–13). In the context of the accusations that Jesus posed a threat to Rome (Scheffler 1993:164), Luke shows what his Davidic authority means: it does not mean revolution, but it means that he would fulfill his mission of messianic ministry (Kingsbury 1981:103). Jesus, as Son of David, had the task of healing en restoring those who were rejected and alienated from the community (Luke 4:18–19).

More important to Luke than Son of David and as important as Messiah, is the title Son of God. The title Son of God is used to add to the meaning of royal Messiah (see Kingsbury 1981:103–4). The child conceived by the power of the Holy Spirit has his origin in God and is therefore the Son of God (Luke 1:27, 32, 35). Jesus is "more" than Son of David; he is Son of God and *Kyrios*. Luke's portrait of Jesus as Son of God begins with his miraculous conception by the Holy Spirit of God who "overshadows" (ἐπισκιάζω) Mary (1:27, 35). Jesus is "holy" (1:35), which means that he is to perform a special function for God. Having been given this special task in the service of God, the Son of God (1:35) receives the strength he needs to fulfill his task by the Spirit of God. Then he is tempted by Satan as a test to ascertain whether he would be worthy of this task: absolutely obedient to the Father (see Goulder 1989a:291–98). His absolute obedience brings the *Son* in a very close relationship with the Father. This is clearly reported in the mission discourse: "All things have been delivered to me by my Father; and no one knows who the Son is except the Father, or who the Father is except the Son and any one to whom the Son chooses to reveal him" (10:22). The Son of God is the one who brings God's kingdom into this world and who defeats Satan who was thought to have been the ruler of the world (see Fitzmyer 1989:146-74). As παῖς (2:43; Acts 4:27) Jesus is both "son" and "servant." Son of God points to the personal relationship between the Father and the Son. If, however, the context is that of the task or mission of Jesus, then the title Servant of God is used (see Kingsbury 1981:105). Luke expands on Mark's use of the title Son of Man for Jesus (see Kingsbury 1981:108). When Jesus informs his disciples of his impending suffering the title Son of Man is used in the Gospel of Luke (9:22; 18:33; 24:7) to imply Jesus' victory. The Son of Man will be vindicated and glorified. Firstly he will ascend into heaven where the "Son of man shall be seated at the right hand of the power of God" (22:69). After that the parousia will occur and the Son of Man will be "coming in a cloud with power and great glory" (21:27). Whereas Matthew sketches the parousia in an apocalyptic fashion, Luke uses the theme to encourage the believers to cling to their faith in the face of difficult circumstances and temptations (21:40; 17:22; 18:8; 21:36). The followers of Jesus will not only see the Son of Man glorified. They, who have also known suffering, will experience the benefits of his vindication too (21:27-28) (Kingsbury 1981:109). An example of this is the story of Stephen's death as a parallel to the death of Jesus (Acts 7:54-60; see Bonz 2000:177).

The suffering Son of Man becomes an example for his followers (see again the we-passages) who will also suffer much in this world (see Fitzmyer 1989:117-45). Fitzmyer (1989:135) formulates it as follows:

> The Christian disciple is so to live as to bear witness to the risen Christ and his teaching. Such testimony becomes a major motif in Acts:
>
> > "We are witnesses of all that he did in the country of the Jews and in Jerusalem. Him whom they did away with, in hanging him on a tree, God raised up on the third day and made manifest, not to all the people, but to witnesses fore-ordained by God, to us who ate with him and drank with him after he rose from the dead. He commissioned us to preach to the people

and to bear witness that he is the one appointed by God to be the judge of the living and the dead" (Acts 10:39-42).

To suffer along with Jesus, the Messiah, the Savior, the *Kyrios* and Son of God means to be certain of one's own vindication just as God has vindicated Jesus. This "certainty" (Luke 1:4) is seen in the Petrine confession that he and the other apostles in Jerusalem are God's "fore-ordained witnesses" ("chosen in advance"; see Newman 1971:156 by God (Acts 10:41a). They are the witnesses of Jesus' resurrection. After the resurrection they ate and drank with him (Acts 10:41b). Jesus sent them to bring a message to the people (Acts 10:42a). The content of this message is that Jesus was appointed as Judge also of those still living (Acts 10:42). All the prophets witness that they (the witnesses of his resurrection), in his name, in other words *for him*, have the *authority* that Jesus and the prophets had (John the Baptist is the last of the prophets) to forgive the sins of the people. Above all, he is the *judge*, the one who is appointed *for you* as (Acts 3:20): the *deliverer Messiah*.

Synopsis

In this chapter it has been shown that titular names given to a character by other characters in a narrative or by the narrator, are expression of their relationship with and perspective on the character. This "character" in the gospel narratives who received titular names from other characters, is Jesus. At an early stage of the evolution of the Jesus tradition his sayings were clustered together and the process of clustering was "actively controlled." Clusters were expanded and narrative contexts were created in order to convey a particular ideological narrative point of view. "Creating" presupposes editing of the tradition and clusters of tradition. The consequence was that Jesus' wisdom was inflated. His wisdom went against the order of society and therefore necessitated a reversal of roles. As "laconic sage" Jesus spoke little of himself. Most of the "illocutionary" statements made about him as though he spoke them himself, are phrases derived from the Septuagint.

These statements indicate that those who "spoke" them were very much under the impression of their experience, or the experience of others reported to them, of having seen the crucified, resurrected *Son of*

Man, *Kyrios* and *Son of God*. From the perspective of the resurrection the character of Jesus was made to confess or say and do what the followers of Jesus had come to believe. Such "confessions" that supported his authority were most probably also intended to confirm the authority of his followers.

Jesus' sayings and deeds are often concise and have simple plots, but in the Sayings Gospel Q and the gospels they appear in more expanded "biographical" structures. Narrators created the dialogue, often based on an early aphorism. Dialogue presupposes characterization. Characters are named and within the narrative structures of the gospels, the names used for Jesus begin to unfold in structural interrelationships. The genre of biography generates meaning since reasons are given for events, such as, for example, the death of Jesus. So also reasons are given for the belief that Jesus was vindicated. As biographies the gospels are not *Hochliteratur*. Q, Mark, and Matthew can be seen as the products of cultic activity. Cults are groups of people who assemble around a charismatic leader (the founder of the cult) and seek to follow him—after his death as well. The plots of βίοι function in contexts of polemic and conflict. In such context defensive and offensive polemic respectively defend, validate or even correct the opinions of the "founder" (or hero). The ignorant are informed about the wisdom and saving acts of the "cult leader" (a Moses, an Asclepios or a Jesus) by means of naming.

The early Jesus traditions found in the Sayings Gospel Q reflect opposition to the Jerusalem oriented scribes in the period before and after the destruction of the temple in 70 CE. The Q tradition originated in the context of the revitalization of village communities. "Jesus groups" and other Israelite groups were in the process of finding a new identity. A new identity goes hand in hand with the redefinition of societal structures and social values. The Q tradition is witness of a process where the wisdom teaching of Jesus about compassion for the destitute and God's alternate kingdom (in terms of which God is seen as the *paterfamilias* of a village household to whom unconditional loyalty is due) develops in dialogue and polemic about values. In this process the "little tradition" of a sage merges with the "great tradition" of the scribes. The process can also be described as the "sociology of scribalism": "*The union of the scribe and the priest yielded the sage who bore the honorific title Rabbi*" (Neusner

A Synchronic Test Case: Q and the Synoptic Gospels

1991:161, my italics). In Q Jesus is not a messianic figure, but he is the *Judge* with a mission (Son of Man). As Son of God Jesus knows the will of God. Jesus is God's wisdom envoy. The follower who confesses Jesus as Son of Man, Judge and Son of God is ready for his coming.

When Mark tells the story of Jesus, the history of Israel is reflected in his story. However, in Mark Jesus' teaching is a new teaching with authority. The more spectacular aspects of his deeds are de-emphasized in favor of his vocation as the suffering Son of Man and the suffering Son of God: the Messiah is at the same time the Son of God. Therefore the disciples should not want to be like "first men" or "great men" who enjoy having authority over others. Mark distinguishes between the twelve disciples who want powerful positions and the other followers (disciples) of Jesus. According to Mark it is not the Twelve but some of the other followers who praise Jesus with the title of the Blessed One who comes in the name of the Kyrios. Messiah is the title the disciples give to Jesus, but the "narrated Jesus" subordinates the title Messiah to the title *Kyrios*. Mark as narrator treats Messiah as a description of Jesus' identity, but it alone does not suffice: the title Son of God is added in order to describe Jesus' identity more fully.

In the Gospel of Matthew Jesus fulfills a role of being part of Israel's history. At his birth he becomes known as the Son of Abraham and the Son of David and at his parousia it will become clear that he is the Son of Man. For both Israelites and Gentiles he is the Son of God, which is a confessional title. Jesus' identity as the Son of God depends on his being Son of Man. To call Jesus Son of Man means to acknowledge him as the new Human Being who constituted a new humanity, the reconstituted and empowered Israel.

In the Gospel of Luke Jesus' journey from Galilee to Jerusalem forms the *Mitte der Zeit*, preceded by the "journey" of the prophets and followed by the "journey" of the *ekklēsia*. From this perspective on *God's story* (*diēgēsas*), and the central role Jesus plays in it, the *Regeln des Verhaltens zur Welt* (Conzelmann 1954:117) are inferred. The story wants to provide accurate information about Jesus. He is the Messiah of Israel, and Savior like other prominent philosophers, rulers or teachers. Jesus is *Kyrios* of heaven and earth, the Messiah-King. Jesus is Son of God and is holy: the Spirit of God enables him to fulfill his special function. As Son of God he is *pais*: obedient son and suffering servant. As Son of Man he ascended with power (*dynamis*) and glory (*doxa*). Those who witnessed all these thing are the ones who received his authority (see Luke 24:36–53).

CHAPTER 3

The Institutionalization of Charismatic Authority

Authority within Ancient Israel and Early Christianity

IT HAS BEEN ARGUED that the followers of Jesus acknowledged and expressed his authority naming him. These "names" developed into "titles" when the post-Easter followers of Jesus allocated power to Jesus. This was further explored when the naming of Jesus was investigated from a diachronic perspective and from a synchronic perspective. The synchronic study showed that the various "titles" function within structural relationships in the gospel narratives. These relationships illustrate how the titles express different facets of the *authority* or *power* of Jesus. The diachronic study (as well as the investigation of the tradition history of the Sayings Gospel Q that was included in the "synchronic" inquiry) illustrated the various levels or degrees of *authority* or *power* attributed to Jesus by means of the different titles. Some titles were used at certain stages of the history of early Christianity, whereas the use of other titles was restricted to certain regions. The investigation showed that Jesus did not use these titles of himself. One can conclude that there was a *historical development* of the use of the titles for Jesus. There was also a *historical development* from the *authority* Jesus had among his followers to the *position of power* that was given to him later by means of the titles.

It was argued that, in the pre-industrial agrarian society of Israel and early Christianity, naming was done primarily in the sphere of *scribal activity*. The argument was concluded with a discussion on *demystification,* which aimed to clarify the *ideological* interests behind the use of titles for authority figures by scribes. The objective of this chapter is to continue the discussion on demystification by viewing it from the perspective of the sociological process of the development from *authority* to *power*. Since *ideology* is often an indication of the presence of conflicting interests, *conflict theory* will be relevant to the discussion. Firstly, the use of terms and concepts will be clarified. Secondly, a general and broad investigation of *authority* in the ancient Middle-East, ancient Israel, the Hellenistic period and early Christianity will be undertaken. Thirdly, the focus will be on the development from *authority* to *power* and the argument will conclude with a brief look at conflict theory. In this section I will make use of the research of Gunneweg and Schmithals (1982), Holmberg (1978) and Vledder (1997).

In order to clarify what is understood by "dominating" institutions, the concept of "rule" or "authority" will be briefly discussed. Some related terms in English are: dominion, rule, command, power, authority. In Latin the terms *dominium, potestas, auctoritas* and *imperium*, and in Greek *archē, kuriotēs, despoteia* and *exousia* describe the concept of rule. The rule of the paterfamilias, however, be it the father of the household, the monarch or God, was supposed to be a benevolent rule aimed at protecting the subjects and contributing to their wellbeing (see Gunneweg and Schmithals [1980] 1982:9). In different times authority and power were gained in different ways. In an industrial society power and authority are acquired by those who possess capital or skills. In agrarian pre-industrial societies people who possessed land had authority. They were organized in collective units such as families, extended families, clans, tribes and dynasties. In industrial societies, on the other hand, power is often centered in individuals. However, in these societies authority is not only in the hands of individuals, but is also exercised by more abstract entities such as, for example, power structures, the mass media, technical, political and social processes. People also often submit to the abstract power and authority of custom and tradition. On an intra-personal level people can be controlled by, for instance, needs, past experience, instincts, as well as reasonable self-control. This constitutes a broad perspective on power and authority (Gunneweg and Schmithals 1982:10–11; cf. Wrong 1979).

Max Weber (1968a:15–16), however, defines "authority" within narrower confines. He sees authority as "the probability that a command with a given specific content will be obeyed by a given group or persons." He poses the question as to when the authority of the ruler over the ruled is legitimate. Is it ever acceptable and legitimate for some to rule over others, for some people to exert power over others? Weber identifies three types of legitimate authority.

- The first type is *traditionalist* authority, which pertains to the authority of the paterfamilias, the patron or royal figure who sees to it that order is maintained.
- The second type is *charismatic* authority, which appears when the given order is changed by revolution. This happens when a charismatic leader (such as a sage or a prophet figure) opposes the traditional order and finds a following among people who become convinced that his vision and ideas promise a better life for them. The acts and deeds of such a charismatic leader can, in time, become traditionalized and normative.
- *Legal* authority is the third type of legitimate authority and it is exerted by means of the codification and enforcement of laws by power structures.

In order to distinguish between the more nurturing and the more official aspects of authority (with the innate possibility of the abuse of power), Latin, rather than Western languages, provides the most useful terminology. In Roman thought a distinction was made between the terms *potestas* and *auctoritas*. *Potestas* meant the power of officials who were legally invested in their office. Their authority and limits were determined by law. *Auctoritas*, on the other hand, was not based on an office or a given position. It was acquired on account of a person's attributes and capabilities, as well as the recognition of others (see Gunneweg and Schmithals 1982:16–17). *Auctoritas* could be a quality of a person with insight, wisdom and charisma, with the power to influence and convince, and it could also be a quality of tradition, holy scriptures and accepted rules of wisdom. *Auctoritas* can, therefore, be a great asset to someone with *potestas* (an official position of authority such as a priest or a scribe), but it does not automatically come with the position. A person with *potestas* can be someone without *auctoritas*. For example, according to Seneca, the Emperor Claudius was not someone with authority, though he was the emperor of Rome. In his satire *Apocolocyntosis* (13:12), Seneca calls the emperor a "pumpkin" and states that it would be ridiculous to revere him as a god (see Eden 1984:1; Schönberger 1990:54). "(I)t also follows that in principle *potestas* has to do with compulsion, while *auctoritas* always has to do with freedom. Authority exists only where there is free acceptance" (Gunneweg and Schmithals 1982:17; cf Van Gennep 1989).

Auctoritas provides the safe space in which a person can grow, whereas legal authority provides the order and safety for people to live together. In this sense authority is necessary for human life, while anarchy (a total rejection of all forms of authority) would be detrimental to life. On the other hand, to turn away from authority in order not to remain dependent, is also a natural and normal phenomenon. An irrational and harmful protest against authority is often brought on by a situation where *auctoritas* has been supplanted by *potestas* (see Gunneweg and Schmithals 1982:20). This means that force has taken the place of persuasion and coercion has destroyed freedom. In English this negative aspect of authority could be indicated by the term "authoritarian," whereas the positive, nurturing form of authority can be described as "authoritative."

Max Weber (1968b:53) distinguishes between the terms "power" and "domination." "Power" is the ability to execute one's will regardless of whether the other party or parties agree or resist. The relationship is coercive. "Domination," on the other hand, is when the other party or parties have at least some interest in obeying the person or institution with power. They therefore do so voluntarily (see Weber 1968b:53, 212). One of the reasons for compliance is when the leader's authority is accepted as legitimate. In such a relationship power plays a role and authority is legitimate and becomes institutionalized (Holmberg 1978:125). It is therefore necessary to distinguish between "power, "domination" and "authority" (see Hennen and Prigge 1977:9–32). "Domination" and "authority" are on the same level, whereas "power" functions in a different sphere. The term "domination" is used for the authority of a social system, whereas "authority" pertains to people (cf. Bochenski 1974:35). In a relationship where there is authority, the ruler's behavior is such that the ruled obey willingly because the authority is accepted as right and good (Holmberg 1978:131). The reason (rationality) for obeying authority is not because it is mandatory, but because the ruled agrees (Friedrich 1960:5). "Authority rests upon the ability to issue communications capable of reasoned elaboration . . . which relates actions to opinions and beliefs, and opinions and beliefs to values" (Holmberg 1978:131). On the level of authority and domination obedience is, therefore, given voluntarily because the authority is regarded as legitimate. When people obey for reasons other than the legitimacy of the authority, for instance under threat of physical harm, it can then be seen as "power" rather than authority. Coercion is termed "violence" and this use of "power" is a perversion of authority and domination (Hennen and Prigge 1977:27–29). As far as the legitimacy of authority is concerned, a distinction should be made between "legality" which means "being in accordance with the law" and "legitimacy" which is the quality of the "rightness" of something (see Holmberg 1978:128).[1]

According to Holmberg (1978:130; cf. also Bendix 1960:295) the following components make up a relationship of authority:

- the ruler;
- the ruled;
- an expression of the ruler's will to influence the behavior of the ruled;
- the compliance of the ruled;
- the subjective acceptance of this by the ruled.

The first four components are also to be found in the realm of exerting power, but the last point is distinctive of authority, over against power. Authority is a social relationship based on domination where the ruled comply with the ruler's wishes on the grounds of conviction. The authority is accepted because the insights of the ruler are trusted and therefore the commands of the ruler regarded as legitimate. This kind of relationship requires "transparency," in other words the ruled must be able to see reasons for regarding the domination as legitimate. If the ruled should come to the realization that the beliefs and values of the ruler are no longer valid in society, the authority of the ruler will cease to exist (see Holmberg 1978:132–35).

---

1. Cf. also Friedrich (1963:234; 1972:92); Schelsky (1975:23); Schutz (1975:15).

It has been indicated that Max Weber (1968a:215; cf Holmberg 1978:136–150) distinguishes between three types of legitimate authority (*legitime Herrschaft*):

- rational-legal authority—the ruled believe that the rules and the persons who have authority under these rules, are legitimate;
- traditional authority—the ruled believe that the traditions are sacred and the authority of persons acting under these traditions, is legitimate;
- charismatic authority—people accept the authority of an exceptionally holy or heroic person of exemplary character and consider the normative instructions of this person to be legitimate.

Though there are other typologies (cf. Blau 1963:313–14; Eschenburg 1976), Holmberg (1978:136) chooses Weber's as his basic point of departure. This book is interested in how Holmberg applies Weber's theory to biblical interpretation, therefore Weber's typology will feature prominently as well. Criticism against Weber's typology is that it does not include some modern forms of legitimate authority (see Hartmann 1964:4; Sternberger 1968:247), that the three types overlap since all three types build on tradition to some extent (see Winch 1958:238; Friedrich 1963:235; Sternberger 1968:247), that all authority has charismatic elements, in other words that it has something to do with the value system and the social order of society (see Shils 1965; Eisenstadt 1968). Weber (1968a:262–64) admits that it is not likely that "pure" types could ever exist, but that his typology is a classification meant to assist the process of analysis. Holmberg (1978:137; cf. also Blau 1963:309–11) points out that this debate illustrates how difficult it is to construct "ideal types" since elements overlap or are dependent on elements in other types. He considers Weber's classification to be of analytical value "especially in non-modern historical situations." These are the situations relevant to this investigation.

Holmberg (1978:137–50) proceeds to describe charismatic authority, starting with the insights of Max Weber. David Horrell ([1997] 1999b:313), cites from Weber's work and describes the concept "charismatic authority" as follows:

The Institutionalization of Charismatic Authority

Charismatic authority . . . resides not in a person's occupation of a particular role, office, or social position, but in his or her individual qualities, "by virtue of which he is considered extraordinary and treated and endowed with . . . exceptional powers or qualities. These are such as are not accessible to the ordinary person, but are regarded as of divine origin . . ." [Weber 1968b:241]. Charismatic authority is, for Weber, a "revolutionary force" (1968[a]:244). However, it cannot remain stable, but becomes "routinised": "traditionalised or rationalised" (1968:246ff; further Eisenstadt 1968).

Holmberg's description and the application of his findings on the Bible are of interest to my investigation. Weber (1968a:241) expresses his view of "charismatic" as follows: "The term 'charisma' will be applied to a certain quality of an individual personality by virtue of which he is considered extraordinary and treated as endowed with supernatural, superhuman, or at least specifically exceptional powers or qualities. These are such as are not accessible to the ordinary person, but are regarded as of divine origin or treated as a 'leader'" (cf. Lemmen 1990:135-45). He points out that this assessment is value-free because the "superhuman abilities" of the charismatic are not evaluated. The acceptance of others that the charismatic person has these powers, is taken as the point of departure. "Charisma is not an individual psychological trait but a strictly *social* phenomenon; without acknowledgement from a group of believers charisma simply does not exist. Thus it is a quality characterizing some authority relations thereby distinguishing them from other types of authority relations" (Holmberg 1978:138; cf. Lemmen 1990:135-37).

In pre-modern societies some form of magical (religious) activity would attract followers to the charismatic leader. Some followers would be closer to the leader, also on account of their "charisma," and would become the "disciples." There is no system of organization or set of formal rules governing the group. Eventualities are treated in a charismatic way. They are often regarded as having a divine origin, be it judgments or revelations. According to Holmberg (1978:139) charismatic authority is *extra-ordinary* (*außer-alltäglich*) and are contrary to the rational and *traditional authority* which are everyday forms of authority. The wisdom instruction of a charismatic teacher is therefore inclined to subvert *conventional wisdom*. Charismatic groups tend to reject forms of traditional authority and establish a new way of life. Charismatic change is revolutionary and comes from within.[2] It is a totally new orientation towards life, the world, values and norms. It is "foreign to everyday routine structures, it is anti-economic, anti-organizational and highly personal. And that is why charisma in its pure form is an unstable, short-lived type of authority which very soon becomes either traditionalized or rationalized or both" (Holmberg 1978:139). This is the process of institutionalization.

Different types of charisma that Weber, nonetheless, also acknowledges as *charisma*, are not personal, but can be found in objects and institutional roles. He calls them "hereditary charisma" (e.g., that of royal families) and "office charisma" (e.g., the priesthood). They are still seen as "charismatic" even though impersonal, on account of their quality of extra-ordinariness.

Holmberg (1978:140) goes further than Weber and develops a "modified and complemented version" of Weber's work. He first examines charisma from a psychological and sociological perspective. He distinguishes between the psychology of charismatic leadership and how charismatic authority functions socially. Holmberg then expands on Weber's idea that charismatic authority emerges within social situations that are distressful and intolerable. People yearn for change. The charismatic leader brings a new vision and directly or indirectly promises change. Such a leader is seen as a savior figure.

Holmberg (1978:141-42) criticizes Weber for not distinguishing sufficiently between *charismatic leadership* and *charismatic authority*. Charismatic leadership focuses on the relationship between the leader and the followers. It is an intensely personal and emotional relationship: "affection becomes devotion, admiration becomes awe, respect turns into reverence, and the feeling of trust approaches blind faith. The leader can do nothing wrong, everything he says, wishes or prescribes is absolutely true and right as he is considered to be a source of goodness, truth and strength in himself" (Holmberg 1978:142). Charismatic authority is not as intense or emotional. "It rests upon the group's shared belief that it is *legitimate* for the superior to impose his will upon them and that it is illegitimate for them to refuse obedience. In a religious context the inevitable conceptualization of this attitude to the leader is the belief that he is more

2. In the words of Weber (1968a:245): ". . . kann Charisma eine Umformung von innen her sein, die, aus Not oder Begeisterung geboren, eine Wandlung der zentralen Gesinnungs- und Tatenrichtung unter völliger Neuorientierung aller Einstellungen zu allen einzelnen Lebensformen und zur 'Welt' überhaupt bedeutet."

than an ordinary human being, that he has a divine gift and calling and is consequently closer to God than the rest of [hu]mankind" (Holmberg 1978:142).

A charismatic leader brings a new message that is radical and can be revolutionary.

> Such a change in the religious sign system is brought about above all by *charismatics*—i.e. by the influence which individuals exert on others on the basis of an irrational power of emanation—independently of pre-existing authority roles and traditions, often in the face of the vigorous hostility of the world in which they live. The stigmatizing of the charismatic by the world around can even increase his influence: if he survives rejection by social an moral contempt and negative sanctions, he puts the "system" which repudiates him in question all the more tenaciously. This *connection between stigma and charisma* emerges in a pure form in primitive Christianity: in particular the crucified Jesus . . . In addition to the connection between charisma and stigma there is a *second connection: between charisma and crisis*. Charismatics who have an innovative effect develop in times of upheaval, when many people were ready to forsake traditional convictions and adopt new orientations . . . Furthermore, crises are not just experienced by the lower strata. They embrace all social strata—and here opposition between strata or classes is almost always an element in the crisis. (Theissen 1999:6–7).

"Supernatural" abilities place the charismatic leader closer to the sacred. Therefore, when the charismatic brings a "new message" to the people, existing institutions and traditions can be left behind or expressly rejected. The message has to be relevant and acceptable to the specific culture for it to have authority. The intention of the message is that a new society will be constructed. The mission of the leader also becomes the task of the group. Their task is to transform reality. From this self-understanding a group identity develops and the group is seen as "an anticipation or prototype of the new society or Kingdom to come, and in intense missionary zeal" (Holmberg 1978:147–48). The group now generates a charisma which ensures its existence after the death of the leader.

What "rule" meant in the ancient Middle-East and what it means today in the modern West are vastly different. Though people have always, and probably will always exercise authority over others, the way in which this has been done through the ages has greatly changed. In order to better understand biblical narratives, it is essential to know how power structures worked in the cultures of the Bible. Ancient Israel formed part of the ancient Orient and, therefore, authority in this setting will be examined. It was believed that the ruler was called to his task by the gods or a specific god. The city from which he ruled was the centre of the world and his kingdom would not come to an end. The ruler had to obey the god(s) who called him, and his task was to bring prosperity and justice to his people. "Justice" was viewed as a state of goodness that included prosperity. The ruler, thus seen a benefactor, was often regarded as the shepherd of his people, the one who would provide for them. He was responsible for the well-being of the flock entrusted to him by the god(s). In this concept of rule, divine lordship and human-political government converged (see Gunneweg and Schmithals 1982:23-26).

The ruler had to keep enemy forces and threats to the stability of society at bay. In this capacity he was seen as a savior-figure. The state would deliver people from their enemies and the ruler was their savior (Gunneweg and Schmithals 1982:26). The divine-human ruler had a broad responsibility which included the entire creation and the order of the cosmos. He performed the rituals necessary to promote natural prosperity and fertility. In this respect he fulfilled the function of priest. Hunting was regarded as controlling wild animals. This contributed to the order of the cosmos, combating chaos. The ruler was the supreme hunter. Hunting wild animals was, therefore, similar to subduing human enemies. Both were acts of preserving the order.

In Egypt the pharaoh was regarded as a god-like figure whose rule brought salvation to the people. Salvation by means of the rule of the divine representative was universal, therefore no salvation was possible beyond the limits of this rule. Beyond the order of this rule there was only chaos. "Precisely therein consists the religious character of the rule, and one could just as correctly say, therein consists the universal-political character of this religion (Holmberg 1982:30). When the government in Egypt collapsed circa 2200 BCE new power structures came into being. Now not only the pharaoh, but also members of the élite classes and in principle all men, became part of the saving event. In the mystery cults, which came later, the initiate would partake in the divinity of the mystery-god and could, therefore, bestow salvation onto others (see Mylonas

1961:224–86). Holmberg (1982:31) regards this as an after-effect and transformation of the god-king rule and authority.

Israel, as a small nation inhabiting a strategic spot in the ancient world, was not untouched by the surrounding nations' ideas about authority and rule. The question would then be what the extent of this influence was. Some scholars propose that Israel adopted the god-king ideology of the surrounding world and find evidence for this view in certain Psalms, for example. Others dispute such an influence (see Thompson 1999:168–78). Gunneweg and Schmithals (1982:32–33) find both these alternatives unacceptable and take a middle road. On the one hand, Israel's view on authority and rule cannot be summarily equated with that of the ancient Orient, but on the other hand a definite influence cannot be denied.

The Hebrew Scriptures abound with references to "king" and "rule," that mostly denote earthly rulers and do not refer to God (see Weisman 1984:21–26). Some of the Psalms are lyrical about the king and his rule. In these songs traces can be seen of the "universalism typical of the thinking about authority and rule in the ancient Orient . . . This is also in harmony with the view . . . that all kings and indeed the very ends of the earth are subject to the great Davidic king" (Gunneweg and Schmithals 1982:34–35). This is not expressed on historical grounds, since Israel was never that impressive a kingdom, even in the time of David and Solomon. Much rather it is an expression of the oriental ideas previously mentioned. The authority that a "son of God" receives from God when commissioned, is essentially limitless and therefore extends to "the ends of the earth." In the Hebrew Scriptures there is evidence that the king was, indeed, seen as "son of God." In Psalm 2:7b God says to the king: "You are my Son; today I have become your Father'" and continues in v. 9 with the commission to rule: "You will rule them [the nations] with an iron scepter; you will dash them to pieces like pottery." On the one hand this does not refer to a physical father-son relationship, while on the other hand it cannot be seen as only figurative language. It is probably an adoption formula, examples of which can be found in Egyptian and First Testament documents (see Wulfing von Martitz 1969:401; Gunneweg and Schmithals 1982:35–37). By means of this formula a man was acknowledged as legitimate son, whether there was a physical relationship with the "father" or not. In this respect the Israelite view differed from the Egyptian where the king was physically the son of the god. What was similar, however, was that the king ruled as God's son, in contrast with for example Hammurabi, who was only *called* by the gods (see Gunneweg and Schmithals 1982:36).

One can conclude, therefore, that "the idea—the ideology—of the God-king rule and authority can be documented clearly as found in Israel . . . Psalm 2 is not alone; it is one of many comparable testimonies of ancient Israel that conceive of rule and authority as salvific divine governance and occurrence" (Gunneweg and Schmithals 1982:38). The king was responsible for just and righteous rule. Righteousness refers to more than merely earthly justice, it refers to the total order of salvation, the order among people in the world and the order of God becoming a reality in the world. It includes salvation, peace, prosperity, blessings and the wellbeing of the people.

Though unknown to Egypt, the kings of Israel were anointed (see *inter alia* Ps 45:7; 1 Sam 10:1; 16:13; 1 Ki 1:39; Ps 2:2; 18:50; 20:6; 89:20) and were specifically known as the *anointed ones of God*. This is an honorary title which was bestowed upon kings as part of the enthronement ritual. The ritual of anointment (see Collins 1995:11–14) gave the anointed one a part in the splendour, glory and power of the one in whose name he was anointed (see Gunneweg and Schmithals 1982:41–42). The Davidic king is said to have had enormous power, also creative power, but it is emphasized that this power comes from God (see Ps 89). The Davidic king lived in his palace on Mount Zion next to the temple where God lived. "Living next door to God, so to speak, he sits upon his throne at the very right hand of God. This place of honor is assigned to him by his God . . . . The king who rules at the right hand of God is also at the same time a high priest 'after the order of Melchizedek'" (Gunneweg and Schmithals 1982:44). The fact that the Romans erected their fortress next to the temple in Jerusalem was not an innocent move.

The general ideology of authority and rule in the Ancient Near-East is prevalent in Israel as well: the king as "son of God" who was called by God, given power by God and functioned as saviour and protector of the wellbeing of the people. God remained the all powerful one and the king was God's obedient servant. In the eyes of the people, however, the king, the anointed one, was the representative of God.

In Hellenistic thinking the ideology of the god-king took a new turn. After having conquered Egypt, Alexander the Great visited the oracle of the god Zeus Ammon at the oasis of Siwa and was addressed as "son of God," the successor of the Egyptian god-kings. For the first time a Greek ruler entered the realm of the divine (Gunneweg and Schmithals 1982:49). Greek gods were, however, much closer to mortals than the God of Israel. They were not all-mighty creators. Though immortal, they were also subject to the whims of fate.

> For this reason the boundary between the deified supermen and the anthropomorphic gods was not an insuperable barrier. Hence, human heroes, whether they were of mythical origin (e.g., Heracles) or were historical figures (lawgivers, physicians, artists), were cultically venerated after their death, because it was believed that they, the benefactors of humanity, had been received into the circle of the immortals. The Hellenistic ruler-cult is connected with this tradition (Gunneweg and Schmithals 1982:51).

An example of a deified king was Julius Caesar who was hailed by an inscription found in Ephesus (48 BCE) as: "high priest, emperor and twice consul, the god born of Ares and Aphrodite and visibly manifest and universal savior of human life" (in Gunneweg and Schmithals 1982:51–52; cf Dittenberger 1960:760–767). After his death he was called the divine Julius and his son, the later Caesar Augustus, was known as *Divi filius*, the son of God. He was given the title *savior* (σωτήρ) during his lifetime. After Augustus and his successor, Tiberius, this cult expanded and developed (see Taylor 1981) as later rulers demanded to be worshipped and abandoned any pretense of being there for the wellbeing of the people. They simply used their power (*potestas*) to their own glorification and advantage. This led to negative reactions from Roman and Israelite subjects alike. "Such claims had to lead to protest and to a collision" (Gunneweg and Schmithals 1982:53).

The attitude toward kingship in Israel differed from that of the surrounding nations. In Israel God was seen as the one who ruled. A human ruler could be commissioned by God in a time of crisis. But when the crisis had passed the position of authority would no longer be filled (cf Judges). The judges were charismatic figures who functioned as leaders during such times. The title "judge" as highest position in Israel during this period, indicates that they were responsible for bringing about God's justice and conveying God's blessings and salvation to the people.

In the book of Judges the attitude of Abimelech who aspired after power and authority is shown to be wrong, whereas Gideon's words attest to the desired attitude towards power and authority in Israel: "But Gideon told them, 'I will not rule over you, nor will my son rule over you; the Lord will rule over you'" (Judg 8:23 – NIV). Some First Testament texts portray Israel's desire for a king as negative. The royal texts and especially the royal psalms, on the other hand, sing the praises of the king. However, is can be stated that in general "in Israel the criticism of the kingship is as ancient as the kingdom itself" (Gunneweg and Schmithals 1982:57).

The time of the judges was, however, not a period of justice and order. In Judges 17:6 it is described as a time of chaos: "In those days Israel had no king; everyone did as he saw fit." The kingdom which followed would then put an end to this disorder, but not necessarily to God's rule. A theological problem ensued:

> God, as the true and sole ruler, now is, as it were, entangled in the thickets of worldly struggles for power . . . So in place of the deification of the human ruler, there appears the humanization of God as an earthly ruler and soldier. A God who is understood thus, who leads his followers into bloody battles and commands them to "devote" all booty, that is, to kill and to transfer to him, as to the true victor in the gruesome battle, the prey (cf 1 Sam. 15:2ff), is not at all different from the other pagan war-gods . . . (Gunneweg and Schmithals 1982:59–60)

The problem is that, when the human and the divine are mixed, both lose their authenticity. "The mingling of these makes men into gods and therefore falsifies true humanness, or it makes God into a man of war and therefore falsifies divine salvation, which cannot be identical with visible victory and even less with a bloodbath" (Gunneweg and Schmithals 1982:60).

Israel did, however, receive its first kings. People of humble origins were commissioned by God and were to rule in obedience to God. Though the royal texts are positive about kingship the critical voices can still be heard. There were those who did not respond well to Saul's kingship. 1 Samuel refers to them in a derogatory fashion as "troublemakers" (1 Sam 10:27 – NIV). Though kingship is not what God intended for the people, it would not have been possible against God's will. God does "allow" Israel to have kings, though the prophet Samuel warns that when kings depart from the ways of God the result could be oppression of the people. In the stories of the kings, kingship is not an undisputed blessing from God.

In the God-king ideology the king's place was at the right hand of God and he was the instrument of God's rule and mediator of God's salvation. The prophets, however, refuted this and became the critics of the kings. They confronted the kings in order to persuade them to return to God and restore the order and blessings that had disappeared on account of their disobedience. Though kings such as Omri and Ahab were politically and economically successful, they were severely criticized by the prophets for having abandoned God, not allowing God to rule over the people but usurping the power for themselves. "The prophetic books . . . bear witness to the conflict between prophecy and policy, between God's rule and the earthly rule of the king" (Gunneweg and Schmithals 1982:71). If the king does not rule "by God's grace" alone, but by his own power, he does not fulfill the function of saviour anymore, but incurs the wrath of God.

Prophets such as Jeremiah predicted the end of the Davidic dynasty and a catastrophe which would bring to an end the politically understood rule of God. In Isaiah, too, a different perspective on the matter of rule and kingship emerged: "[T]he criticism of the kingship and of the royal exercise of power is transformed into the hope of a rule and a kingdom 'not of this world' and of one anointed by God who, though indeed upon the earth, yet represents God's own and true lordship over the true Israel" (Gunneweg and Schmithals 1982:81). In the First Testament evidence of a positive attitude toward the God-king ideology can be found, but critical voices are also heard. On the positive side Israel functioned much like the surrounding nations within the God-king ideology. But in the criticism of royal rule and authority the identity of Israel as God's people under the rule of God came to the fore. This distinguished Israel from the ideology of the surrounding nations.

In the ancient Middle-East a royal title was given to gods such as Marduk, El or Baal in order to express their supreme authority over other gods and heavenly beings. This title was also given to God and Jerusalem, the home of the king, became the city of God (Ps 46:48). Since "other gods" did not function in Israel, God was seen as the ruler of God's people and of the universe (Ps 47:8). God as true king restricted the power of the earthly king. God exercised authority and ruled, whereas the king did God's bidding. The problem is to assess the function of human rule in the world if it can have no power, since the power belonged to God alone.

Institutionalization of Authority and the Naming of Jesus

The Babylonian conquest of 587–586 BCE signaled the end of the Davidic dynasty and this crisis changed Israel's understanding of rule and authority. The disaster was seen as God's judgment, predicted by the prophets. The predicament was attributed to Israel's sins, not because there was anything wrong with the rule of God. Even so, questions arose concerning the promise that there would always be a king on the throne of David, and the promise of salvation that went hand in hand with God's rule. The texts designated as "messianic" do not speak directly of a *mashiach* but refer to a future ruler from the house of David. These texts "represent a modification, intensification, and projection into the future of all those royal titles, dignities, rights and duties that had previously been spoken about the reigning king, promised to him or praised in him" (Gunneweg and Schmithals 1982:93). Isaiah 9:6–7 (NIV) speaks of the new king and his kingdom (my italics):

> For to us a child is born, to us a son is given,
> and the government will be on his shoulders,
> and he will be called *Wonderful Counsellor, Mighty God,*
> *everlasting Father, Prince of Peace.*
> Of the increase of his government and peace
> there will be no end.
> He will reign on David's throne and over his kingdom,
> establishing and upholding it
> with justice and righteousness
> from that time on and for ever.

The honorific names given to the new king are "throne-names" commonly known in Egypt as descriptions of the Pharaoh, but are not known in Israel as titles for a king (Gunneweg and Schmithals 1982:93). The titles point to the salvation that will be brought about by the promised new ruler. God provides for all who belong to God's kingdom. Not warfare and weapons, but peace and justice will be characteristic of this kingdom where the new king will rule with the word. The themes of the God-king ideology can be clearly seen. The *future* king will, however, be able to accomplish much more than even the best of the god-kings in the past. The old world will be replaced by a new one and this descendant from the house of David will establish a whole new era. Even the wild animals will be peaceful among themselves (cf. Isa 9:6–9). The rule of this king is no longer an earthly rule, it is completely new and different. It is *rule*, nonetheless. In Zechariah 9:9–10 the king is portrayed as gentle and humble, yet still a king whose rule will extend "from sea to sea and from the River to the ends of the earth" (Gunneweg and Schmithals 1982:96).

> In the reduction of the power of the royal *messiah* . . . there is expressed the expectation and hope that one day God would establish [God's] own kingdom, that '[God's] kingdom might come'. Just as the old idea of rule, transformed and even heightened, becomes the expectation of a future Messiah, so also the ancient, once mythical conception of God's kingship is purified to become the hope of God's coming kingdom. (Gunneweg and Schmithals 1982:97)

When this ruler and his new dispensation failed to come, however, the question remained how God's rule and human rule should be seen in the meantime. The prophet Haggai saw Zerubbabel, a descendant of David, as the present messiah (see Hag 2:20–23). This expectation led to disappointment. The two directions characteristically taken during the post-exilic period are *eschatology* (the expectation of the future rule of God – see Preuss 1978; Gowan 1986) and *theocracy* (the belief that God is already ruling in the present) (Gunneweg and Schmithals 1982:101–2). These two ideas are not necessarily mutually exclusive and can be found together in various forms and mixtures. In the work of the Chronicler, however, the line of theocracy is taken. The fulfillment of the prophets' message occurred when the Persian king (as "God's anointed," Isa 45:1; cf. 44:28) freed the people from Babylonian exile. God's salvation had come, was present and no future event would be needed.

Ezra and Nehemiah also attested to an "actualized rule of God." The relationship of this rule with the actual rule of worldly authorities affected the organization of Israel and also influenced the understanding of authority and rule in the early Jesus community. An example is Ezra, who reorganized the legal relationship between Israel and the Persian authority. Both the law of God and Persian law would apply to the people. The law of God was seen as the law of the king: "Its [the law's] *auctoritas* is divine, but it is protected by the royal *potestas*, which can even impose harsh punishments to enforce its provisions (Ezra 7:26b). Therewith Judaism becomes a licensed cultic community on an ethnic basis. It lives, ruled by the high priest and the priestly hierarchy and instructed by the scribes in the law of God—and of the king—as a constituted theocracy" (Gunneweg and Schmithals 1982:104–5).

God judged the people for their sins and sent them into exile. God's salvation now came through the Persian king, an instrument in God's hand. God's salvation was bound up with the rebuilding of the temple. If God, once again, lived with Israel, God's presence and salvation would be experienced. A problem arose, however, when the ruling authority was no longer friendly, as happened in the Hellenistic and Roman periods. How should the rule of God be seen and the salvation of God experienced in such circumstances, and how should God's people act toward hostile authorities? In such circumstances "the cultically and legally constituted theocracy, which sought to gain verification in reality itself and to insure itself organizationally, ran aground on its own inner contradiction" (Gunneweg and Schmithals 1982:107). This problem could only be solved when salvation would no longer be sought in present conditions, but in the "now already" and the "not yet" contradiction. Salvation could then be free from all that enslaves rather than seen concretely as being freed from the powers that be.

The prophecies in the First Testament of a new king and a new dispensation kindled the hope of a new rule by God and salvation through the new ruler appointed by God. The problems with the rule of human god-kings and their supposed salvation would then be a thing of the past. The hope of a coming *messiah* escalated in the period between the two Testaments. Different honorific titles were used to refer to this expected figure. For instance, a messianic prophet (see Deut 18:15) and a messianic high priest (see Zechariah 3–4) were expected. People spoke of the "Son of David," the "Servant of God," the "King," the "Son of Man." Some saw Jesus, whom they confessed to be the Christ, as the fulfillment of these expectations. This confession of Jesus as the Christ is attributed to Peter by Matthew. "An utterance handed down by Matthew and connected with Peter's original confession accordingly reads, 'You are Peter, and upon this rock I will build my church . . .'" (Matt 16:18) (Gunneweg and Schmithals 1982:110). Other titles such as, *Son of God, Kyrios* and *Saviour* soon became widely used for Jesus and *Christ* became part of his proper name: *Jesus Christ*.

Gunneweg and Schmithals (1982:110–11) argue that Jesus was confessed as Christ rather than as Son of David or King in order to steer

The Institutionalization of Charismatic Authority

clear of the Hebrew Scriptures and the later dilemma of the expectation of political salvation. In Mark 12:35-37 Son of David is rejected as a title for Jesus, the argument being, if David calls the Christ "my Lord," he cannot be the Son of David. In Matthew 21:9 Jesus is hailed as the Son of David, noticeably not in the sense of warrior ruler, but riding a donkey and bringing peace. Romans 1:3-4 portrays Jesus as the Son of David, but does so in the sense that David was Jesus' ancestor, not implying titular meaning (see Bultmann [1976] 1985:155 n. 154).

In the gospels the title *King* is also stripped of all political connotations and placed firmly within the religious realm. In Luke 19:38 Jesus rides a donkey on his way to the temple when he is hailed as king. The council of the elders, however, accuse him of having *political* aspirations: "He opposes payment of taxes to Caesar and claims to be Christ, a king" (Luke 23:2b). Jesus was regarded as a king by his followers, but not a political king.

"The christological titles were not newly created by the early Christian community, but were taken over from the environment and transferred to Jesus" (Gunneweg and Schmithals 1982:114). The honorific title most used for Jesus is *Kyrios*. In the environment in which Jesus lived this word was used in different ways. People of high rank were addressed as *kyrios*, a slave called his or her owner *kyrios*, the military commander, the king and emperor and various gods (e.g. Osiris, Serapis, Hermes) were called *kyrios*. The Greek translation of the First Testament used *Kyrios* in order to avoid God's name. Jesus as *Kyrios* in the New Testament has the meaning that he is *Kyrios* over the powers of sin (Rom 7:24-25), of death (1 Cor 15:56-57), and of the law (Mark 2:28) and therefore is the reason for and giver of freedom for people. "Early Christianity made many different attempts to render the event of the Cross and the Resurrection comprehensible in its salvation-bringing significance with respect to lordship and rule" (Gunneweg and Schmithals 1982:123-24). Jesus' salvific work is articulated in the language of ransom, which is mythological language borrowed from the slave trade. Slaves could be freed by someone paying a ransom for them. So Jesus is seen to have paid the ransom (his own life) in order to free people from cruel slave-masters such as sin and the law. Those freed in this way are no longer slaves to various masters, but call Jesus *Kyrios*. The rule of Jesus is also articulated in mythological language. Jesus conquered the enemies (sin and death), took away their power and dominion and became the ruler: "insofar as his rule must be described as *potestas* over the evil powers, his lordship is over 'all rule and authority and power and dominion' (Eph 1:21) that could dispute him. In relation to them, sitting at the right hand of God (v 20) is a symbol of Jesus' irresistible, compelling authority and power" (Gunneweg and Schmithals 1982:125). Jesus' authority did not lie in coercive power. His lordship did not manifest in *potestas*, but in *auctoritas*.

Jesus is the *Kyrios* who rules over the Kingdom of God (*basilea*). This refers to the rule of God or the new dispensation of God where everything will be different. Jesus was exalted by God in order to rule over God's kingdom. In the rule of Jesus, the *Kyrios*, the rule of God becomes manifest. Whereas God rules over all of creation, Jesus rules over the community of God. Jesus' rule is present, but God's rule will also be expected in future. Judgment belongs to the domain of God's rule. Believers hope to inherit the future rule of God (see 1 Cor 6:9; 15–50; Gal 5:21).

In the gospels God's kingdom and glory, as well as the lordship of Jesus, are contrasted with the *potestas* of worldly rulers (see Bonz 2000:182). An example can be found in the Lucan version of the birth narrative. The mighty emperor Augustus who issued decrees, is contrasted with the humble subjects who had to travel from Nazareth to Bethlehem in order to obey this decree (see Crossan 1994c; Cain 1999:13). There is also a marked contrast between the humble scene of shepherds and a baby in a manger with the glory of God's domain expressed in the angels' announcement and singing, and the light in the dead of night. But the main contrast is that between the command of the emperor and the message of the angel, between the powers of the earth and the powers of heaven, between civil dominion and divine promise (Gunneweg and Schmithals 1982:146). Under Roman rule the taxes became increasingly heavy and the people increasingly poor (cf. Cain 1999:16). The imperial census was aimed at making sure that there was an effective system in place for the maximum possible tax to be collected. The command "to enroll" would fill people with trepidation. In contrast, the angels brought the "good news of great joy." The *peace on earth* of which the angels sang, contrasts sharply with the *pax Romana* or *pax Augusta*.

> In the middle of the civil war, in 42 or 41 BC, Virgil penned his Fourth Eclogue, which announced the birth of the ruler and savior of the world, and nourished the utopian hope of the dawn-

The Institutionalization of Charismatic Authority

ing kingdom of peace . . . in the hope of Augustus and his house. When Augustus returned to Rome in 29 BC, after the civil war had ended, his first action . . . was to close the temple of Janus, the god of war. In the year 17 BC he revived a forgotten custom and instituted a secular festival with which the old *saeculum* was supposed to be buried and a new age of salvation to be introduced. In the year 13 BC the *ara pacis Augustae*, the peace-altar of Augustus, was established, and it was consecrated in 9 BC. (Gunneweg and Schmithals 1982:147)

This peace was not very stable since there were often bouts of unrest, and it cost a huge amount in taxes since large armies had to be constantly on the alert and ready. This was a peace that relied on *potestas*. The deification of Augustus in terms of the Hellenistic ruler-cult indicated that salvation was expected from his rule, power and authority. World peace was the important political theme at the time and it was theologically grounded in the deification of the emperor who was seen as the savior of the world. In this mind-set the *pax Augusta* and the salvation of the world were the same thing (see Gunneweg and Schmithals 1982:151). The true savior of whom Luke tells, is quite the opposite of the mighty Augustus. He was humble, came as a servant, and gave all glory to God, not to human rulers and their "power." Whereas the *pax Romana* was about the absence of war, the true peace of the real savior is not brought about by the abilities of human beings. It exists where God is present.

Also in the birth narrative of Matthew (2:1–12) the contrast between the baby and the king, in this instance Herod, is emphasized (see Cain 1999:13–14). Herod, born an Idumean, received the royal title from Rome and became ruler of Palestine. He remained loyal to Rome throughout his life in order to retain its favor. He had various beautiful buildings, water systems, and theatres constructed, and did much for the economic prosperity of the territory over which he ruled. Herod's kingdom was the size of that of David. He restored the temple to the glory of the time of Solomon. "In understanding his work as ruler in this sense as a messianic work of salvation, he combined the Roman-Hellenistic idea of salvation with the Jewish people's expectation of salvation that was grounded in the Old Testament promise" (Gunneweg and Schmithals 1982:164). The birth narrative in Matthew exposes Herod's ambitions and his brutal nature as a ruler who tolerated no competition or threat, but simply eliminated those who got in his way. No salvation can be found in earthly rule and a self-styled political "messiah" such as Herod, is the message of Matthew. Matthew points away from human lordship to that of God. God's lordship does not depend on what humans do. The lordship of God must be acknowledged to the ends of the earth.

When the point of view and use of the Christological titles of Matthew (or any other evangelist, for that matter) are "demystified," the juxtaposition of God's "lordship" and the "lordship" of people can possibly be seen as the product of conflict between Matthew as scribe and other Judean scribes about the "correct understanding" of Jesus. It is also possible that Matthew's naming of Jesus as *Messiah* is an elevation of his *authority* to *power*. The use of other Christological titles can be explained in a similar way. My intention is to argue that this process of the elevation of Jesus to a position of power, means power as *potestas*. Power as *potestas* was attributed to Jesus after Easter and especially in post-Constantine period (see Crossan 1994d). For example, in the post-Constantine period Jesus was often portrayed as *pantokrator* in literature and art. This title was previously only attributed to God (cf Rev 1:8). The sociological process of the development from *authority* to *power* will now be discussed by means of the social theory of the "institutionalization of charismatic authority."

Institutionalization and Defining Conflict

The process of the development from a charismatic group to a body with an organization such as a church, is called the *Veralltäglichung des Charisma* by Weber (1968a:246–54, 1121–48; cf. Lemmen 1990:137–45; Mödritzer 1994:277–84) and the *institutionalization of charismatic authority* by Holmberg (1978:162–95). In my opinion these terms pertain to what was called *demystification* earlier in the book. According to Weber (1968a:246) charismatic authority cannot remain as it is for a longer period of time, but must become either traditionalized or rationalized. People have the desire that the charismatic blessing should be available on a permanent basis in everyday life. The "staff" of the charismatic leader must also make the transition to an administration suited to everyday life.

The process of development and change from charismatic to something more permanent is influenced by different forces, especially economic interests. Holmberg (1978:162) describes the process as follows: "The ordinary adherents become paying members in an organization, the

The Institutionalization of Charismatic Authority

message develops into dogma and law, the staff into a paid hierarchy. So are gradually united the utterly antagonistic forces of charisma and tradition." However, in a pre-industrial agrarian society economic interests did not function independently in society. If this general development toward "officialdom" was applied to an agrarian situation and to the founding of a cult, the emphasis would not be on officials receiving a salary, but rather on the honorable positions the officials (priests and scribes) would occupy. According to Weber the death of the leader often provides the impetus for the process to begin, because decisions have to be made about the future of the group. It cannot just continue as it was.

> The staff needs and develops a consistent administrative practice, with rules for making decisions, the limitation of spheres of competence, and some sort of hierarchy within the staff itself. Moreover it is necessary to develop a fiscal organization for the financial support of the staff and for the movement as such. This type of motive can be called the community's systemic needs, i.e. needs that must be met if the movement is not to disintegrate. The real driving force of the routinization process is the staff and its strong ideal and material interest in the continuation of the community" (in Holmberg 1978:163).

The group that depended totally on the leader and lived in a spontaneous community life with the leader now had to become ideologically, socially and economically independent. In order to achieve this the staff "appropriate positions of power and economic advantage to themselves, and regulate recruitment to the stratum of the group that alone may exercise authority. Charisma now belongs to the staff only, the office-holders, and serves to legitimate their acquired rights" (in Holmberg 1978:163).

Holmberg (1978:164–66) criticizes Weber's view as too one-sided and negative. He does not believe that only the death of the leader and the material interests of the staff should be seen as the motivation for institutionalization. He would also include an investigation of the leader's possible interest in creating a lasting community, as well social forces such as "the traditionalization and rationalization of the community's doctrine, cult, ethical behaviour, and order of common life" (Holmberg 1978:165). He sees the charisma and charismatic message as compelling in itself. The aim to establish a new society could also provide a strong motivation for continuing the charismatic movement and could contribute to setting the process of institutionalization in motion.

Holmberg (1978:167–75) examines institutionalization from a general sociological point of view. He chooses the perspective of an anthropological analysis of human interaction as worked out by scholars such as Helmut Schelsky (1965a, 1965b, 1970) and especially Peter Berger and Thomas Luckmann (1975).

The Beginning of the Institutionalization Process

Human beings are creatures of habit, in other words their behavior follows certain repetitive patterns. Habit provides the impetus for institutionalization. Another human trait is typification, the mental activity of classifying according to typical acts or characteristics. When the typification is done collectively rather than individually, it can be referred to as roles. An institution is represented in and by roles. Role expectations are formed when people come to expect typical behaviors. "And the longer one participates without opposition and without proposing another course of action, the firmer becomes the consensus on what is demanded of the actors by the interaction. Institutionalization . . . expands and confirms actual consensus" (Holmberg 1978:168; cf also Luhmann 1970:30–31). An institution exercises social control. This means that it has no formal control, but its power lies in how difficult it is for individuals to go against the system. On the one hand this social control has the effect of limiting an individual's freedom. But on the other hand institutionalization also has the effect of creating a structured world for individuals. Not having to invest an enormous amount of energy in structuring their world, increases the freedom of individuals. This dual effect of institutionalization can be experienced on different levels of life, among others in marriage and religion.

As long as only two parties are involved, changes can still be made to the system with mutual agreement. When more people become involved, this flexibility changes. "The next 'generation' . . . experiences the institution as much more massive and opaque, part of the solid, factual structure of the outer world. And then, by means of a mirror-effect, the given patterns or institutions become more of a solid, unchangeable fact for the creators themselves—the product acts back on the producers" (Holmberg 1978:170). Those contributing to institutionalization become increasingly anonymous, are vaguely referred to as "they" and the more anonymous the authors of institutionalization become the more difficult it is to question the system, since nobody is responsible.

Legitimation

Legitimation occurs when the fundamental belief- and value-systems that function within the institutionalized world are used to explain and validate the system. The new generation receives these explanations and in the process they are socialized into the system. According to Holmberg (1978:171; cf. also Berger and Luckmann 1967:92–104), legitimation happens on different levels. The first level of legitimation is part of the vocabulary. The second level consists of simple wisdom, often in the form of proverbs, moral maxims, legends and songs. The third level displays theories that validate the institution. This knowledge is often preserved and imparted by "experts." The fourth level consists of symbolic universes, in other words traditions that provide a unifying frame of reference. When it is forgotten that human beings create their social world, systematize and institutionalize, then institutions are *reified*. They are seen as a given reality beyond human control. The result is that power interests become camouflaged and ideology "naturalized." A process of demystification, that is a deconstructive reading or "denaturalization," can expose these power interests. Insight in how ideology operates is helpful. Elisabeth Schüssler Fiorenza (1999:64) refers to Thompson (1984:254) in this regard:

> John B Thompson has pointed to three major modes or strategies that are involved in how ideology operates: legitimization, dissimulation, and reification (literally: to make into a thing) . . . The first strategy is an appeal for legitimacy on traditional grounds, whereas the second conceals relations of domination in ways that are themselves often structurally excluded from thought . . . The third form of ideological operation is a reification or naturalization, which represents a transitory, culturally, historically, and socially engendered state of affairs as if it were permanent, natural, outside of time, or directly revealed by God.

Cumulative Institutionalization

Cumulative institutionalization refers to the process of an institution growing and changing, becoming increasingly complex as a system. If this does not happen, the institution will deteriorate. A particular example of this cumulative effect can be seen in what Holmberg (1978:173) calls "the institutionalization of the institutionalization process" or double institutionalization. The first part of the process can be seen in institutionalized interpretations, offices and official procedures in, for example, the church. The other part is invisible and "takes place in the elementary processes of socialization and forming of public opinion. The latter part of the institutionalization process legitimates the former" (Holmberg 1978:173; cf. Luhmann 1970:34). Law is an example of double institutionalization. Custom consists of norms and rules to which people adhere in everyday life, in other words they regulate already institutionalized behaviour. Law is custom that has been "re-institutionalized at another level" (Holmberg 1978:73). Another example is "the authority of church leaders in doctrinal, cultic and disciplinary matters, or even the existence of specific rules for how to treat those who deviate from a given norm of belief or conduct" (Holmberg 1978:173).

The Role of the Elite in Institutionalization

The first level of institutionalization is a natural result of the interaction among people who are social creatures and creatures of habit. This, however, is not the case when it comes to higher levels of institutionalization. Eisenstadt (1968b:413) puts it as follows: "[T]he development and institutionalization of new types of political or economic organizations or enterprises is greatly dependent on the emergence of various entrepreneurs who are able to articulate new goals, set up new organizations, and mobilize the resources necessary for their continuous functioning." Holmberg (1978:174) calls these "entrepreneurs" an "active élite able to offer solutions to the new range of problems by verbalizing the collective goals and norms, establishing organizational frameworks and leading this process of innovation (political entrepreneurs, if successful, become new emperors and their entourage)." He sees charismatic leaders and their staff in the role of the entrepreneurial élite, in other words as those who create the new institutional structures (Holmberg 1978:175; cf. Eisenstadt 1965:55). Even if their idea is not to create a new structure, but rather to create a new way of living, an institutionalized structure is the outcome nonetheless.

Some of Holmberg's (1978) conclusions can be summarized as follows:

- Institutionalization is not a process that begins later, but starts when human interaction begins .
- The process of institutionalization is not controlled by the conscious efforts of people, but rather by forces inherent in human interaction.
- Group life necessitates a measure of systematization and rationalization irrespective of personal interests.
- Institutionalization serves the systemic needs of the group.

"The charismatic person is a creator of a new order as well as the breaker of routine order. Since charisma is constituted by the belief that its bearer is effectively in contact with what is most vital, most powerful, and most authoritative in the universe or in society, those to whom charisma is attributed are, by virtue of that fact, authoritative" (Shils 1968:387). The charismatic leader's authority goes against the prevailing social system and is revolutionary. Gradually the charismatic group develops its own social system with its own customs, rituals, doctrine, tradition, ethos and order. The intensity of the charisma is "diffused into the group." Holmberg (1978:179) describes institutionalization as a gradual process that can be traced right back to the leader. Initially the authority and control reside with the leader. This remains the case as long as he lives. After his death authority transfers to a social construct: the leader's words, message, example, rituals and institutions that previously had some authority now become the main bearers of the absent leader's authority. These elements are organized and unified for the benefit of the group (secondary institutionalization) and the verbal tradition develops into normative texts, ways of living become normative codes of behavior and the teaching tradition transforms into worship. The former disciples (staff/assistants) of the leader now become the leaders who take responsibility for the group, its policies, decisions and direction of growth (cf. Lemmen 1990:139).

Holmberg (1978:180) does not agree with Weber that the interests of the staff are the main motivation for the direction institutionalization takes. He does concede, however, that the actions of the elite constitute the decisive influence in the process of transforming charisma. The élite are the ones who consolidate the organization begun by the leader. They do not come up with a totally new direction but "conserve, expound, develop and systematize what has already been given ... [T]heir authority is of necessity traditional and rational and can by no means be purely charismatic, resting within themselves only" (Holmberg 1978:180). During the process of institutionalization of charismatic authority the charisma loses its direct force. It can now only be accessed indirectly, by means of representatives, offices, traditions and rituals.

According to Holmberg (1978:181) the primary institutionalization of the Jesus movement began when Jesus was still there. The group would have developed its own dynamic and social structure. The authority of Jesus would have been diffused and retained in his teaching, his ways of doing things, his outlook on life and in the people with whom he lived and worked. Secondary institutionalization would have begun after his death and in this more active phase the people who were closest to him would have played the greatest role. They can be regarded as the "entrepreneurial elite" of second order institutionalization. "They are simply the leaders of the 'church' in Jerusalem during its early days, recognized as such both within the group and outside of it" (Holmberg 1978:182). In a short time a system of doctrine was formed, a cult organized, missionary zeal exhibited and a sense of an own identity developed.

This was the group that Paul encountered when he arrived in Jerusalem. "Very early the kerygma was given typical patterns, and different kerygmatic formulas such as we find in 1 Cor 15:3–7 were formulated. The church had a christologically determined tradition concerning their interpretation of the Scriptures..." (Holmberg 1978:182; cf. also Hengel 1972). The missionary activity of this group led to Jesus communities that developed in Damascus and Antioch in Syria. The Gentiles converted by those Israelite/Judean Jesus followers who were ousted from Jerusalem, first had to become "Israelites" and be circumcized before they were accepted into the community. The first Jesus followers saw themselves as the beginning of the new dispensation brought by Jesus *Messiah* which they then established further and expanded. Though the Jerusalem faction of

The Institutionalization of Charismatic Authority

Jesus followers participated in temple worship, they also had their own initiation rite, namely baptism, their own ritual communal meal and their own cultic traditions.

> As the uniting and governing factor in this élite-conscious, charismatic group, which, while awaiting the parousia of Christ Jesus, shared a *koinōnia* that may have included a common central fund and a communistic sharing of incomes, Paul knew that he would find the apostles, with Cephas at their head. From the beginning of the Church's existence after Easter this collegium of plenipotentiaries had enjoyed an undisputed role of leadership, both in the mission directed outwards and in the inwardly directed functions of teaching and governing. (Holmberg 1978:183)

The Jesus faction in Jerusalem had by this time clearly been institutionalized. Though development still took place, the community settled into a basic pattern of life and worship. The authority of the leaders in Jerusalem was seemingly undisputed because it was believed that the risen Lord himself had commissioned them and that their authority was derived directly from him. Other early Jesus communities that developed in Antioch and Damascus remained dependent of the authority of Jerusalem (see Acts 13:1; Gal 2:11–14). The reason for this Holmberg (1978:184) sees in the greater charismatic authority of the Jerusalem faction because they were closer to the origin. The changes in the greater Jesus community and the dissolution of the Jerusalem faction of Jesus followers on account of the war and the destruction of the temple in 70 CE effectively ended the supremacy of this group. Holmberg (1978:185) concludes: "Therefore, the supremacy of Jerusalem and its apostles over the Gentile churches and their apostles (notably Paul) . . . is not merely a theological idea or a moral obligation but an institutionalization of its charismatic authority. And its institutionalization makes it a solid fact in the social life of the Church."

Gerd Theissen (1999:26) refers to this process as "the millenarian interpretation of the Jesus movement." He compares it with similar "millenarian movements" in the "Third World" and also with "millenarian movements of modern time." The following quotation explains the first comparison:

> The rise of an eschatological expectation according to which the world is soon to be changed in a miraculous way has many parallels in the so-called "millenarian movements" in the Third World.

> A comparison with them is illuminating. We keep finding ourselves in the field of conflict between two cultures, one of which advances imperialistic claims and makes an indigenous culture dependent on politics. Charismatic figures keep appearing in this situation of conflict who proclaim a change in everything and mobilize supporters for this change. There are always tensions with the political authorities. But whereas in the Third World cultures encounter one another which are in quite different stages of development, at that time in Palestine there was a clash between two highly-differentiated, equal cultures, Romans and the Jews. Each was aware of a historical calling and each had a marked sense of history, a great tradition of law, writings and a financial economy. That explains some differences from the other millenarian movements of modern time.
>
> 1. Certainly the Jesus movement begins as a movement of revitalization within Judaism . . .
>
> 2. In keeping with this, the Jesus movement differed from "nativistic" reactions against foreigners by being open to them – at first in eschatological dreams of a meal shared by the Gentiles with Abraham, Isaac and Jacob, and soon also by the acceptance of Gentiles in reality. (Theissen 1999:26–27)

The leading position of the Jesus faction in Jerusalem resulted in conflict with both the "official" temple and synagogue authorities, and with other early Jesus movements. The conflict with the temple oriented Judeans resulted in the institutionalization of the "charismatic authority" of Jesus, and the conflict with other Jesus movements can be seen in the implicit accusation that the Jesus faction in Jerusalem acquired power for themselves by attributing titles to Jesus (see *inter alia* Mk 10:35–45—esp v 43). In order to gain some insights into this process of conflict, the following will be discussed, making use of the research of Evert-Jan Vledder (1997):

- a definition of conflict;
- causes of conflict;
- the "units" of conflict;
- the functions of conflict.

In conclusion an overview will be given of some of the ideological undercurrents in the early Jesus communities and the nature of the

The Institutionalization of Charismatic Authority

conflict that resulted when the Easter event led to the "false attribution" of power to Jesus by means of honorary titles. The process of how this happened will be illustrated by focusing on the use of the title *Son of Man*. This conclusion will utilize the results of the investigation so far.

Bruce Malina (1988:3) describes conflict theory as follows: "Conflict theory is one of a number of social science theories that are to explain how and why human beings interact the way they do." The presupposition underlying a conflict theory approach is that people act primarily out of self-interest. The various interests are bound to come into conflict. Conflict is expressed by means of harmful epithets, derogatory names and negative labels against outsiders, and honorable titles, laudatory names and positive labels for acclaimed insiders (Malina and Neyrey 1988:35). Dahrendorf (1968a:108-11) makes a strong case that utopian societies do not exist. Conflict is not only a normal part of human societies, but Dahrendorf (1965:125; 1968a:127) sees it as stimulating creative change. His presuppositions are that change constantly occurs in societies, that social conflict is inevitable and always present, and that there is always coercion of some members by others in society (Dahrendorf 1959:162; see also 1958:174; 1965:210). Conflict theory asks questions about power and change.

In attempting to define conflict a decision must be made as to what should be included in the term "conflict." Will everything from petty squabbles to severe violence be seen as conflict, or will the term only be used when referring to explicit forms of hostility among people (see Fink 1968:431; Turner 1978:180)? If the broader and more inclusive view is taken, conflict can be defined as: "the permanent presence of antagonism (conscious or unconscious), opposition and incompatibility between two or more persons or groups. This antagonism, opposition and incompatibility lies on the level of interests, goals, values and expectations, and may or may not escalate to the point of violent coercion" (Vledder 1997:67; cf. Fink 1968:456; Dahrendorf 1959:135).

The basic cause of conflict is seen by Nader and Todd (1978:14-15) as "grievance," after which conflict follows. Dahrendorf (1968b; cf. Turner 1978:185) considers inequality among people to be the reason for ensuing conflict. Another possibility is that limited goods could be a source of conflict (see Coser 1968:233; Galtung 1990:307). There are no clear-cut causes of conflict, since it is a rather complex matter. The categories of incompatible interests, goals, values and expectations seem to be useful points of departure (Vledder 1997:69). According to Dahrendorf (1959:136, 138; see also Rohrbaugh 1984:529, 531) different interests account for the relationship of conflict among classes. The fact that some classes possess the power to further their own interests at the expense of others, only adds to the conflict. Especially important for me is when authority is used to dominate and, therefore, subject those who do not have authority and cannot exercise power (cf. Dahrendorf 1959:237; Lenski 1966:75; Wright 1979:5; Rohrbaugh 1984:534). In other words, *inequality*, be it on account of a difference in the possession of property, income, prestige or power, is characteristic of human societies through the ages and this inequality causes conflict.

Another potential source of conflict is "limited goods" or a scarcity of resources. These resources may be income, status, power, dominion over territory and women (see Coser 1968:233), as well as more abstract desirable assets such as honour, prestige, pride and valour (see Nader and Todd 1978:19; Darendorf 1959:209; Galtung 1990:307; Vledder 1997:80–81). In agrarian societies produce was limited and taxes high. This means that people were poor. In Mediterranean societies intangible assets such as honour, status, power and position can also be regarded as "limited goods." A fierce competitive attitude was prevalent in these societies. People competed for everything and, of course such incessant competition necessarily fostered conflict. Dahrendorf (1959:165; see also Van Gennep 1989:389–415), however, views the inequality of people and the resulting conflict as the main reason for the cohesion of societies, rather than the demand that people work together for the good of all. He sees authority as follows:

- There are always relations of domination and subordination.
- The dominant one or group controls the behavior of the subordinates by orders, commands, prohibitions.
- Dominance and subordination are social positions and therefore legitimized.
- Authority is exerted within limited confines and does not consist of unlimited power over others.
- Since authority is legitimized, disobedience can (and should) be punished. (Dahrendorf 1959:166–67, 237)

The potential social conflict in every society erupts when three elements are present:

- The group has a well-defined group identity (a sense of knowing who they are as a group, what the boundaries are, who is included and excluded).
- The people are unhappy with the conditions and circumstances of their lives.
- They believe that, if the attitude and behavior of the other group change in some way, things will be better for them. (see Kriesberg 1973:61–66)

Yet a further potential source of social conflict lies in the values to which people adhere. Values are the beliefs about what is right, good and true. The system of values provides legitimation to the society and is called ideology (Vledder 1997:87–88). In order to uphold their beliefs people often will not shy away from conflict. In situations of conflict these values form the manifest interests of a group and represent the conscious goals for which they strive and which they will defend (see Dahrendorf 1959:178).

The conflicting parties in any given situation can be individuals, groups, organizations, classes, nations or communities. Subordinate people with similar interests and grievances have the potential to become a group, though they may not yet be one. If these people organize themselves in order to address their grievances together, they become a group. Interest groups have some form of organization and members have regular contact.

Agrarian societies consisted of subordinate people. Agrarian communities were conquest states, societies that were formed on account of being subjugated by other groups (Vledder 1997:99; see also Lenski and Lenski 1966:195). The gap between the small élite class of rulers and the common people was enormous. The latter were regarded as only existing to serve the interests of the upper classes while their own interests were not taken into account.

Wherever there are people there will be conflict. Conflict is, more often than not, the way in which change is brought about. Dahrendorf (1958:178; 1959:208; 1965:125; 1968a:127) sees conflict as the creative force of change in society. In this sense conflict is functional in order for change to take place in the structures and ideologies of society (cf Coser 1956:80). Conflict can also have the function of strengthening group cohesion and clearly defining the boundaries of the group and of who belongs to the in-group and who to the out-group (see Coser1956:35). Conflict can also stimulate the group to develop new rules, norms and values and individuals to participate more actively in social life (see Coser 1956:121–28).

The most basic cause of conflict is when individuals or groups strive to maximize their own interests (Vledder 1997:111). It is often in the interest of the powerful to maintain the status quo and for the subordinates to change the circumstances of their lives. In order to survive, a measure of control over one's environment is necessary. Power and authority provide the means to control one's surroundings and make possible the provision of the desired scarce and necessary commodities. Those with power have what they want and strive to keep it, whereas those without power strive for what they do not yet have, and the scene is set for conflict. Not only are the interests motivated by survival and acquiring a position of privilege potential causes for conflict, but also interests motivated by ideology, in other words the value system of a group or society.

Conflict employed to maintain a social system, can have the effect of disrupting the society or of stimulating changes to the system or can even result in an entirely new system. As far as relationships are concerned, conflict can have the negative effect of disrupting the relationship or the positive effect of strengthening bonds. Within the process of conflict inner values and identity are adjusted (Vledder 1997:114). The changes brought about by conflict, will, in turn, lead to conflict over a different set of interests and issues. And so the process continues. This is called the spiral of conflict (see Kriesberg 1973:274).

CHAPTER 4

From Names to Political Titles: Jesus the Son of Man as Test Case

Reading the Jesus Tradition Politically

THE ORIENTATION OF THE previous chapters can be summarized as follows:

- in the context of an advanced agrarian society power centered around money and writing as the instruments of groups with political power;
- scribal activity made use of, for example, honorary titles—a writing technique that is an indication of polemic and conflict;
- names used for Jesus have a tradition history that can be studied on different levels of contextualization;
- the biographical genre and the narrative structure of the gospels are evidence that Christians applied the words and deeds of Jesus to their own post-Easter context in new ways;
- names used for Jesus within the narrative structure of the various gospels reveal the evangelists' points of view;
- the tradition history of the names used for Jesus as well as the function of these names in the plot of the narrative can be explained by means of demystification from a postmodern perspective on conflict and the social theory of the institutionalization of charismatic authority.

Such an interpretation can be defined as an ideological-critical or political exegesis. In this process the role of a charismatic figure is significant. His words and deeds were believed to be relevant and meaningful to others even after his death. The "charismatic leader" had a new vision for the redefinition of the existing reality. The followers verbalized this wisdom and transformed the "new order" into collective goals and norms. The articulated and codified norms were seen as vital, powerful and authoritative. This transformation, articulation and codification went hand in hand with the institutionalization of rites and ceremonies. Such a social universe was supported by a symbolic universe which, as a "sacred canopy," legitimated the articulation and codification. The legitimation benefited people in a pre-industrial agrarian society who lived together in dyadic relationships, supporting or rejecting one another. Verbal tradition developed into normative texts. "Institutionalization" strengthened the identity of a group in opposition to other groups. "Authors of institutionalization" remained anonymous and writings became normative. "Authors" often referred back to authoritative figures such as "apostles," "representatives of apostles" or "missionaries" by means of pseudonyms. In the process of legitimation, "value-systems" were constructed on the basis of proverbial sayings and teachings for which the "founder of the cult" was known. The scribal experts were the "legitimators" and in their scribal activity the "little tradition" merged with the "great tradition." Antagonism among groups, opposition and incompatibility were expressed in terms of interests, goals, values and expectations. Power was acquired and maintained to the benefit or at the expense of others. Authority was used to dominate. Positively seen, conflict functioned to strengthen cohesion and to develop new rules, norms and values.

The aim of this final chapter is to indicate that a "political" interpretation of the Jesus tradition is an illustration of the above-mentioned social theory. Utilizing the insights of Gerd Theissen (1999), aspects of such a "political" interpretation are explained. Secondly, Easter faith is seen as legitimation of authority. Thirdly, by focusing on the title Son of Man, it is demonstrated that titles used for Jesus are expression of the process of institutionalization of charismatic authority in the Jesus groups during the first century CE.

The basic values of a group reflect its deepest convictions. Formally these values are articulated in the texts of the community. Theissen

From Names to Political Titles: Jesus the son of Man as Test Case

(1999:81) states in this regard that "basic values prove to be *basic* values by shaping other values and norms. They serve as meta-values and meta-norms for other ethical statements" (Theissen's italics). He considers humility (the renunciation of status) and love, for example, to be basic values of the early Jesus groups. These basic values shape all relationships. As far as the relationship with the neighbor is concerned, the boundaries between in-group and out-group (horizontal boundaries) and those between higher and lower status positions (vertical boundaries) are crossed. In Theissen's (1999:81) view "this twofold crossing of boundaries can be demonstrated throughout the primitive Christian ethic, even where there is no direct mention of either love or humility." The crossing of the vertical boundaries (of position and status) take an interesting turn in the Christian ethic. The ideas of neighborliness and humility come from the lower echelons of society. But in the Jesus movements people who live according to these values are given high status by God. So a value from below makes it to the sphere of status and position. The opposite also happens. The values of the ethic of rule found among the upper classes are made accessible to the common people. Theissen (1999:82) calls it the "'democratization' of an ancient aristocratic ethic."

It is understandable that the values of the religion of Yahweh would also appear in the early Christian ethic. These values and norms were universalized by the followers of Jesus and became available and accessible to all people. But another stream of influence is visible in the Christian system of values. That is what Theissen (1999:82) calls "a partial acculturation to pagan values and norms (cf. Phil 4:8). This leads to an exchange between Judaism and the pagan world."

Whether one follows a social theory of conflict (cf. Coser 1964) or a social theory of integration (cf. Parsons 1937; 1977:24–50, 100–114; and Toby 1977:1–23), the social reality that remains is the struggle for "limited goods." According to the theory of integration societies manifest an inherent willingness to cooperate and come to consensus. These noble efforts are, however, continually frustrated by the conflict on account of opposing interests. In any struggle all available power will be used in order to attain what is needed or wanted. It could be coercive and economic power, or persuasive and normative power (cf. Etzioni 1961:3–67). "Normative power is applied first; only when this is or seems to be ineffective is there a resort to coercive power" (Etzioni 1961:57). In the former case those with power (military or economic) are able to force the weak to serve their interests. It is not only physical force, however, that can be utilized in the struggle: "The *ideological weapons* they use to do this include the *normative power of religion* and the *persuasive power of the educated*. But we also find these as weapons on the other side: time and time again oppressed groups and classes rebel against the rulers and the 'ruling system' which they manipulate—and also use the weapons of religion and education as legitimation. The struggle over distribution is notoriously accompanied by a struggle over *legitimation*" (Theissen 1999:83, my italics).

Normative power is also extremely important in the theory of integration where conflict, though acknowledged, is not the focus as it is in conflict theory. In the theory of integration the consensus relies heavily on the validity of normative power. Normative power is the power on which religion is based, whereas political power rather tends to make use of force. Scribes were mostly found in religious systems and were the representatives of wisdom (Theissen 1999:83). Jesus, as portrayed in the synoptic gospels, came into conflict with both the religious and the political systems: he questioned the prevailing purity system and openly opposed it at times. He was executed as the "king of the Jews."

The god-king ideology of the ancient Middle East represented a mixture of the religious and the political spheres (cf. Elsas 1993; Wlosok 1978). The pharaohs and other kings saw themselves as "sons of god" and in Greek cities rulers were venerated as gods (Theissen 1999:84). In Israel, too, kings were seen as legitimate rulers because they were the sons of God. After the decline of the monarchy in Israel the hope of a king was projected onto the future: the messiah would come from God. The expected Davidic messiah would have three characteristics:

- He will be a charismatic ruler over the twelve tribes and will create a theocracy, God's *basileia*.
- He will bring peace in stead of military force.
- He will drive the enemies from the land and conquer them.
  (Theissen 1999:85)

Jesus was seen by his followers as the fulfillment of these three expectations. His followers would carry the ideals further (cf. Windisch 1925:240–60). The Kingdom of God was central to the new society of Jesus followers. God's kingdom would differ from human kingdoms.

Whereas human kings were supposed to provide for the people but were not successful and the people continued to suffer, God would provide perfectly. Whereas human kings oppressed the people, God would give the people the power to reign alongside God. Therefore the followers of Jesus would not be "subjects," but "king's sons" (see Matt 17:24–27), worth even more than King Solomon (Matt 6:29; 12:42) and the Twelve would obtain judgment to the twelve tribes of Israel (Matt 19:28 par.). The *royal Messiah* would bring about all of this (see PsSol 17:26). Paul also used imagery of believers ruling and judging and being persons of high rank (see Theissen 1999:85–86).

The Jesus saying that it is better to give than to receive (Acts 20:35) was a "general *maxim of benefactors* in antiquity and . . . it can first be demonstrated as a maxim for royal disposition and behaviour" (Theissen 1999:90; cf. also 1995a:195–215). It was an aristocratic value to be a benefactor to the people and to use one's wealth for the benefit of the community (cf. Bolkestein [1939] 1967). Patrons did good works for those whose loyalty they wanted to secure and as a means to demonstrate their position and status in society. The fame their good works brought them, would ensure that they would be remembered and praised even after their death. Their benevolence did, however, not extend to the poor. In the Christian ethic this value from above, an aristocratic value, met with the value of neighborliness, a value from below, a value of the little people, and the fusion of the two became a Christian value. "However, this changes the purpose of the benefaction which is no longer to safeguard rule or to increase public prestige. It is now to provide for all in a communitarian fellowship in which all support one another" (Theissen 1999:91; cf. Hengel 1974b:60–73; Theissen 1995b:689–711). In the Jesus group those who suffered and those who served, not those who ruled, became the persons with high status. This early Christian perspective is articulated in Luke 22:25–26:

> And Jesus said to them,
> "The kings of the Gentiles lord it over them;
> and those who exercise authority over them
> call themselves Benefactors (εὐεργέται).
> But you are not like that.
> Instead, the greatest among you should be like the youngest,
> and the one who rules like the one who serves.

Institutionalization of Authority and the Naming of Jesus

As charismatic authority became more institutionalized in the early Jesus movement the ethic underwent some changes, namely from a radical to a more moderate ethic (see Theissen 1999:97–98). The itinerant charismatic lifestyle of the very earliest Jesus followers means that, because they dissociated themselves from the more mundane concerns of everyday family life, their ethic could be rather radical. "They lived a life detached from power, possession, work and family." The person of Jesus was the centre of their existence. He was an itinerant charismatic who continued to live this way even after Easter. The charismatic followers of Jesus became the first leaders of the groups of Jesus followers that began to form. The process of institutionalization of charismatic authority had begun.

> The development of primitive Christianity is then governed by a shift in the authority structures in the local communities. These gain in independence, orientate themselves on their own community leaders, the bishops, deacons and presbyters, and increasingly shield themselves from the itinerant charismatics who are travelling around.
>
> However, the moderate and increasingly conservative ethic of the domestic state establishes itself with ever greater weight. Criticism of the family is replaced with an ethic which supports the family, the renunciation of possessions with a social way of dealing with possessions, *the criticism of power with selective adaptation to the power structures of the world* ... (Theissen 1999:97–98; my italics).

There is evidence that some of the radical tendencies were not lost in the ethic of the increasingly institutionalized Jesus movement. Rather, the radical strains had a specific impact on the development of the Christ kerygma. "Christ himself becomes the primal model of a renunciation of power and a criticism of the powerful. He is the power of God which revealed itself in the cross as 'weakness.'" And so also "Christ himself becomes the primal model for the renunciation of possessions" (Theissen 1999:98). The idea of wisdom changed in the Christ kerygma when Christ himself became the Wisdom of God which is foolishness in the eyes of the world and the "wisdom of the wise" (the wisdom of the world) is made foolish by God (1 Cor 1:18–25).

It has been argued that conflict in societies is mainly about limited goods and conflicting interests among groups or individuals. Limited goods are, however, not necessarily of a material, economical or political nature. Conflict can result from conflicting abstract or religious ideas and philosophies such as wisdom, purity, holiness or education. In other words if normative power is desired, the result could be conflict and power struggles. "Wise men and priests have the power to define and legitimate. They define what is good and evil, clean and unclean, what is salvation and what is not. And they use their power to remove legitimation from what they regard as evil, unclean and unholy . . . Their influence and their power is based on belief in a legitimate order" (Theissen 1999:100). From this perspective order and control are the preferred state of affairs and conflict and power struggles are seen as disruptive and threatening. Therefore conflict must be dealt with as quickly and effectively as possible.

In the time of Jesus there was a distinct separation between the power of the state which was in Roman hands at the time and the power of wisdom and holiness which were closely associated with the temple (cf. Sir 50:1-24). "Scribes who went by the religious traditions of the people were the representatives of Jewish wisdom" (Theissen 1999:101). This historical situation contributed to the way in which the formation and institutionalization of the earliest Jesus movements took place.

In antiquity wisdom and philosophy were mostly associated with the upper classes, because the lower classes had to work for a living and did not have the opportunity to study the traditions, take part in public life and contemplate higher and spiritual values (cf. Sir 38:24-26). Jesus was not of the upper classes and when he taught in the synagogue in Nazareth, the people were offended and he was driven out. He was, after all, probably a carpenter who worked with his hands (see Mark 6:2-3). "The wisdom of Jesus finds a new audience, which like the teacher of this wisdom is really excluded from it by traditional criteria . . . Here it is emphasized that Jesus thus belongs in a general tendency to combine scribal activity and earning one's living and to do away with the elitist limitation of true wisdom to the upper class . . ." (Theissen 1999:102-3). Jesus associated not only with the working people from the lower classes, but also with the traditionally marginalized people such as women (cf. Luke 10:38-42; 15:8-10). His wisdom was not only shared with those who were traditionally excluded, but was directed against those who traditionally had the monopoly on wisdom: the scribes and the interpreters of the law (cf. Luke 11:46, 52; Mark 12:38-40). When wisdom became accessible to the lower classes the form of wisdom changed. Lower-class wisdom with its stories and images from the peasants' world and ideas, transformed the face of traditional wisdom. "The powerful and the rich strive to surround their power and their possessions with the aura of holiness and legitimacy. The wise men and the priests control this aura and it often seduces them into increasing their political power and economic possession. But their real power is the power of definition" (Theissen 1999:107–8).

It has been argued that the development from Jesus as charismatic sage to his post-Easter followers as "itinerant charismatics" on Galilean soil to a more institutionalized setting in Galilean households (as reflected in the Q tradition) coalesces with the "criticism of power with selective adaptation to the power structures of the world" (Theissen 1999:98). John Kloppenborg (2000:195), referring to the work of Ronald Piper (1989, 1995b), describes this phenomenon of "selective adaptation to power structures" as follows:

> Piper adopted my suggestion that the social location reflected in Q's aphoristic sayings was the lower scribal sector of towns and villages—precisely those persons who daily wrote loan, rental, marriage and divorce agreements and who daily came into contact with both poverty and the exploitation of judicial procedures. Piper writes:
>
>> Indeed this sector stands at the interface between local, village social concerns about indebtedness and the administrative structures for dealing judicially with such business and social relations, which inevitably would refer back to the cities. The evidence for lack of confidence in the judicial system, specific fears about "authorities" and a concern to suffer loss rather than seek redress would suggest a clear suspicion about the benefits to be won under higher administrative procedures. This concern may not have been *directly* aimed at Rome, particularly in Galilee, but neither were the structures governing life in Galilee viewed as objects of trust . . . The suspicion about the institutions of power seems to have been sufficiently strong to make voluntary surrender the preferred option (Piper 1995:63; emphasis original).
>
> Piper thus follows a consistent thread of suspicion directed at the official mechanisms of control, and discerns a contrasting strain of hope in God's renewal of society, a renewal in which the poor would acquire honor and dignity (Q 6:20b–21).

Easter Faith as Legitimation of Authority

"God's renewal of society" was brought about by the "resurrection faith" of Jesus followers (also in Q where the resurrection of Jesus was not a central confession and the pivotal point of teaching—see Kloppenborg 2000:359–63). For the Q people Jesus was still the "itinerant sage" among his followers after his death. The kerygmatic tradition of the synoptic gospels produced a different view of Jesus. When considering the influence of Easter on the development of Jesus traditions, critical exegetes began using two terms, namely "historical Jesus" referring to the authentic Jesus and "kerygmatic Christ" referring to *Gemeindebildung* which was the phase after Easter. The concepts "historic" (*proclaimer*) and "kerygmatic" (*proclaimed*) were first used by Martin Kähler (1896). The terms distinguish between the *pre-Easter* and the *post-Easter* Jesus. On account of this distinction researchers realized that the evangelists interpreted Jesus from a post-Easter perspective. In writing from a post-Easter perspective, the evangelists transformed the traditions about Jesus into a narrative. In order to bring the story of Jesus to the point of the Easter event, a story-line (plot) giving reasons why Jesus was killed, was necessary. The theological focus on the cross and resurrection is technically called "kerygma." Mark seems to have been the first author to have developed such a "kerygmatic narrative." Matthew and Luke (as well as John) also adopted this structure. This kerygma can be traced back to before Mark. It originated in the earliest Jesus faction in Jerusalem. Paul also took over this notion from the Jerusalem group. It should, therefore, be taken into account that gospel writers amended the material available to them to be in accord with their intentions and narrative structures.

The saying about the "church" which is built on "Peter" (Matt 16:20) can be used as an example to distinguish between the stadia of the historical Jesus, the post-Easter oral period and the post-Easter written record in Matthew. Historical-critically seen, the saying as a whole cannot be regarded as words of the historical Jesus (cf. Funk and Hoover 1993:207). Since multiple independent documents attest to Peter's primacy among the core group of Jesus followers, it can be regarded as historical. However, on account of the criterion of coherence the primacy of Peter cannot be traced back to the message of Jesus. In Jesus' message of an alternate kingdom of God there is no emphasis on people in primary roles. The fact that

Institutionalization of Authority and the Naming of Jesus

multiple documents attest to Peter's primacy means that it must go back to a very early oral period.

Historical critical research also indicates that the reference to an *assembled faith community* as "church" (ἐκκλησία) does not come from the life situation of the historical Jesus, the pre-Easter disciples or the post-Easter oral period between 30–50 CE. The term ἐκκλησία does not appear in Mark, which was written around 70 CE. Matthew and Luke use the term ἐκκλησία when referring to the Jesus group in contradistinction with the synagogue. The opposition of the synagogue (an exclusive community) forced the community of Jesus followers to clearly define its own identity as a universal (inclusive) believing community. The term ἐκκλησία which had a universal connotation, was used in contradistinction with the term συναγωγή with its connotation of exclusivity (see Schrage 1963:178–202; 1964:798–800).

What becomes clear is that *ekklēsia*, which presupposes and institutionalized structure, is a later development (see Trilling 1978:57–72). The attribution of a primary role to Peter goes back to a very early period of institutionalization. In this early period claims that the resurrected Jesus had appeared to certain people led to the attribution of primary positions to these people in the believing community. Bultmann (1931:260) understood the resurrection of Jesus in the context of what he called the Christ-*Kultlegende*. He argued that the earliest Jesus faction broke away from the Jerusalem temple and began organizing themselves as a separate cultic community. This new cultic community needed officials to facilitate the ceremonies and rituals such as baptism (see Bultmann 1931:261–81) and the eucharist (see Bultmann 1931:282–308). Officials fulfill primary roles in cultic communities. People who could claim that they had received a commission from the *resurrected Jesus* himself became "apostles" (delegates acting on behalf of Jesus; see Luke 6:13; Mark 3:14) and as such fulfilled these primary roles (cf. Schmithals 1986:737–38; Roloff 1965:57–60). This process of becoming a cultic community is part of the process of "christianizing" (*Christianisierung*). Mainville (in Verheyden 1999:976) argues that in "Acts 2, 22–36 Peter places the decisive moment of Jesus' investiture as the Messiah at the resurrection and of this the disciples bear witness (2, 32–33). Corroboration of this view is found in the speech of Paul at Antioch [13:33, 36–37] who follows the same pattern of argumentation . . ." Some of the texts that attest to the attribution of

From Names to Political Titles: Jesus the son of Man as Test Case

primary roles to people who had seen Jesus, also attest to the attribution of honorary titles (*Würdeprädikationen*) to Jesus by these "apostels." Bultmann (1931:310–11), for instance, refers to the *Himmelfahrtslegende* as reported in the Epistula Apostolorum (c. 150 CE; see Hills 1989), where the *apostles* hear angels honouring Jesus by giving him a title after which Jesus commissions them to a missionary task: "Und als er dies sprach, geschah Donner und Blitz und Erdbeben, und es rissen sich die Himmel auf, und es erschien eine lichte Wolke, die ihn emportrug. Und (es ertönten) die Stimmen vieler Engel, indem sie jubelten und lobpriesen und sagten: "Sammle uns, *o Priester*, zum Lichte der Herrlichkeit." Und als sie dem Firmament sich genähert, vernahmen wir seine Stimme. "Gehet hin in Frieden" (my italics).

Bultmann (1931:313) therefore links the legitimation of the commission to missionary work with the stories of the resurrection appearances: "Denn diese Geschichte setzen die universalistische Mission voraus, die durch einen Befehl des Auferstandenen legitimiert wird." These experiences of the Resurrected One go hand in hand with the exaltation of Jesus: "There is a consensus that the first Christians said far more about Jesus than Jesus ever said about himself. Moreover there is also a consensus that the impulse towards this transcending of all the sayings of the historical Jesus came from the Easter appearances" (Theissen 1999:41). However, Theissen states that the experiences of resurrection appearances alone cannot sufficiently explain the exaltation of Jesus. "We have no historical analogies for someone becoming "Messiah" or "Son of Man" or "Son of God" through appearances. Rather, the appearances must have been experienced in the light of particular convictions for them to be able to create the certainty that Jesus has divine status and forms the centre of the religious sign world ... [T]he reconstruction of the sign system came about through *individual* conflicts in the lives of individuals and had consequences for the *social* life of primitive Christian groups" (Theissen 1999:41–42, 45).

Bultmann (1967:46) is well-known for his opinion that, after his death Jesus arose in the kerygma, which means that Jesus lived in the retelling of his story (cf. Marxsen 1976:45–62; Pelser 1997:455–75). This retelling of the Jesus story led to the development of different factions (see Schille 1994:100–112). Some of these factions centred around people who claimed that they had seen the resurrected Jesus (Lüdemann [1994]

1994:68, 100, 170, 176–77). At least two such factions existed at a very early stage: the Peter/James group (in Jerusalem) and the Paul group (in Damascus/Antioch) (see Baur [1853] 1878:44–65). According to Luke, Peter could confirm that the *Kyrios* had *also* appeared to him: λέγοντας ὅτι ὄντως ἠγέρθη ὁ κύριος καὶ ὤφθη Σίμωνι (Luke 24:34). It seems that Paul received this tradition (which probably originated in the Jerusalem faction) that Peter was *the first* to have seen the resurrected Χριστός (1 Cor 15:3). It can be seen in the words εἶτα (then), ἔπειτα (afterwards): ". . . and that [the Lord] appeared to Cephas, *then* (εἶτα) to the twelve [apostles], and *after that* (ἔπειτα) to five hundred brothers simultaneously . . ." (my translation of 1 Cor 15:5–6). Paul does not refer to Mary Magdalene, probably on account of the fact that she was not mentioned in the tradition of the Jerusalem faction. Elisabeth Schüssler Fiorenza (1994:122) calls 1 Corinthians 15:3–8 a "list intended to legitimate male authority."

There is evidence that people who saw the resurrected Jesus described the experience by using honorary titles, such as *Son of Man* (see inter alia Matt 24:30; 27:52–53; 28:16–20). This title denotes a triumphant apocalyptic figure who is expected to inaugurate the alternate kingdom of God which would then replace the emperor's kingdom. Paul (cf. 1 Cor 15:6) received the tradition that James, the brother of Jesus, also claimed to have seen Jesus after his crucifixion. This tradition appears only in Paul and in the dependent text of the Gospel of the Hebrews, fragment 7, preserved by Jerome, *De Viris Illustribus* 2 (see Bultmann 1931:315). The author of the Gospel of Hebrews reported that the resurrected Jesus appeared to James *before* his appearance to "the Twelve" as a group. "The authority of James' upcoming leadership of the Jesus movement in Jerusalem probably depended on his being a primary witness (see 1 Cor 15:6)" (Van Aarde [2001]:366–67). According to the historian, Josephus (Ant 20.197–203), James became an important figure among the officials in Jerusalem.

Apart from these *individual* conflicts, the lack of harmony also had consequences for the "*social* life of primitive Christian groups" (see Theissen 1999:45):

> That is also true of the *social* dimension of Easter faith. The exaltation of the crucified Jesus to divine status had an effect on claims to authority in the primitive Christian community and its influence on the world around. The formula tradition of appearances

already mentions two group appearances alongside individual experiences: one to the Twelve, with whom a claim to leadership of the restored twelve tribes is associated. Probably Peter gathered the Twelve, convinced that they (without Judas) would now be appointed to their promised leadership role. Alongside this, an enigmatic appearance to 5 000 brothers is related [1 Cor 15:6; cf. Acts 2:2-4]—here an egalitarian element in primitive Christianity is addressed with the term "brothers" (the sisters probably included).

The influence of Easter on the development of the Jesus tradition had certain consequences:

- The authentic words and deeds of Jesus can be distinguished from *Gemeindebildung*.
- In earliest Christianity stages of development can be distinguished.
- The oral period between 30 and 50 CE can be distinguished from the written records that originated after 70 CE.
- Certain sources behind the written records (such as the Q tradition) go back to the 50's CE.

The development of the tradition shows that the resurrection appearances, the primary roles given to people in the community of Jesus followers, and the attribution of honorary titles to Jesus are related matters. Theissen (1999:335 n. 8) puts it as follows: "Easter experiences certainly also formed the basis of authority. The battle over authority was a chronic problem of early primitive Christianity. If the Easter appearances had been produced by this social need for recognition, authority and legitimacy, such appearances would have had to have been far more frequent and to have gone on for longer: the presumed sociological factors continued, but they did not produce any more appearances of Christ."

The claim of having seen the resurrected Jesus gave people the right to important positions in the earliest cultic community of Jesus followers. This included the positions of officials, analogous to the official positions found in the Israelite religion and in the Roman Hellenistic religions. In describing their experiences of the resurrected Jesus they made use of honorary titles. These titles are similar to those used for savior figures in the context of Israelite and Roman Hellenistic cultic communities. The attribution of titles to Jesus was often not in accordance with what was implied by the sayings and deeds of Jesus. This can be described as "false attribution," an example of which is how Jesus was portrayed as a messianic figure. During Jesus' lifetime and also in the period of the Jesus movements after his death, the peasantry (also in Herodian Palestine) had a negative experience of kings and kingdoms. There are various reasons for this negative perception. One such contributing factor was that the succession of kings or kingdoms mostly led to the changing of boundaries which, in turn, was often followed by the dispossession of land (Fiensy 1991:21–73).

> The peasants of post-exilic Palestine lived their lives as peasants everywhere, as an endless cycle of planting and harvesting. Always for them there was God, the family, and the land. They earned their subsistence by the sweat of their brow with the help of their children, and in special needs with the help of their extended family members. Most were about equal in wealth and satisfied with what they had. But then the Hellenists came . . . That exploitative efficiency [in which the Hellenists, beginning with the Ptolemies and later the Seleucids, exploited their subject territories—Fiensy] was a challenge of Jewish peasant values—and probably of the values of some in the upper classes as well—of the land (Fiensy 1991:21)

Land tenure had social implications. High taxation led to the loss of land when taxes could not be paid. The loss of land was mostly accompanied by two other social phenomena, the breaking up of families and the enslavement of some members of the family (especially women and children, who would be sold in order that taxes could be paid; see Osiek 2000). The monarchical families were on the top rung of the hierarchical ladder, whereas the peasants were on the lowest rung, on the edge of subsistence. This was also the case in the time when Herod the Great attained political power. "Herod the Great regarded the land as his. He possessed large tracts of land by the time of his death and is known to have confiscated land at will. His economic 'reign of terror' with high taxes and direct expropriation of land 'horrified' his chroniclers [see Strabo 16.2.46—cf. Baron 1952:263; Hengel 1961:329]" (Fiensy 1991:22). Monarchical families did not only come from the Gentile world outside of Palestine. The exploitation and manipulation from above to those below was a common occurrence not restricted to the first century. In the Hebrew Scriptures prophets protested against exploitation by kings in Judea and Israel. Their criticism is related to the expectation of the peasantry that a "popular" king would come from their own ranks (not from the top) who would act as an agent of God (anointed by God). The righteousness of God (δικαιοσύνη/צדק) means that the anointed would protect and take care of the marginalized (cf. Beaton 1999:11–14). David Fiensy (1991:2; 1999:8 n. 16) refers to the work of Redfield (1956:68–84), *Peasant Society and Culture*, which describes "peasant culture" as consisting of "half-culture" and "half-society" (cf. Foster 1967:2–24). These distinctions are related to what is called "great tradition" and "little tradition." When Jesus and the peasantry speak of God, it forms part of the "little tradition." Fiensy (1991:2) describes it as follows:

> The other half of culture in an agrarian society is high culture or learned culture, which Redfield termed the "Great Tradition." The Great Tradition is the tradition of the reflective few, cultivated in schools and temples, the tradition of the philosopher, theologian, or literary man. This tradition is consciously cultivated and handed down. On the other hand the culture of the masses in nondeveloped societies is termed by Redfield the "Little Tradition." The Little Tradition is low culture, folk culture, or popular tradition which is passed on among the unlettered of the village community.

Because Jesus' words and deeds attested to what the peasantry expected of a messianic figure in terms of the "little tradition," the role of messiah was falsely attributed to him. Jesus did not speak about the kingdom of God in terms of monarchical structures, in other words in terms of the "great tradition." The term "the anointed one" ("messiah") is a symbol taken from the "great tradition." In retrospect it seems an anomaly that the peasantry would have attributed titles taken from the "great tradition (*Messiah and Prophet*) to Jesus." The early ("little") Jesus tradition later developed into a "great tradition"—"a selective adaptation to the power structures of the world" (Theissen 1999:98). The question is how this transition affected the meaning of the these titles attributed to Jesus.

The use of Christological honorary titles (*Würdeprädikationen*) for Jesus is an indication of how he was perceived by his followers. There are two facets to this perception. Jesus was perceived in a particular way because of what he said and did. On the other hand, certain things he said and did were highlighted because they were in accordance with the value systems of the people. The exegete can discover more of the nature of value systems by investigating this correlation. This book does not attempt to provide a description of Jesus' views as such, but rather focuses on the investigation of such a correlation. This investigation indicates that Jesus did not use honorary titles in the articulation of his views on, for example, God; the kingdom of God; what discipleship entails; the meaning of his sayings and deeds; his relationship with God and his status and identity in society.

When considering the influence of Easter on the ideological point of view of the early Jesus followers, the following aspects seem relevant:

- the biographical nature of the gospel genre and the narrative structures of the gospels;
- the cultic environment of scribes;
- the process of "christianizing" the Jesus tradition (*Christianisierung*).

A narrative structure was needed in order to convey the *reasons* why Jesus was killed. Whenever the question *why* is asked, a plot becomes necessary. Cultic interests transformed the relevance of the death of Jesus by making use of sacrifice terminology. The interpretation of the death of Jesus from a cultic perspective, necessitated the members of the cult seeing his death as beneficial to them. The process of christianizing is substantiated by attributing the title *Messiah* (*Christ*) to Jesus. A messianic role is, however, at odds with the theme: a sacrifice for the benefit of others. A messiah was expected to bring victory and dominance, not to experience defeat and death.

The cultic environment of the Graeco-Roman world provides the possibility to see "dying" as dialectically connected with its opposite "rising" (see Schweizer [1967] 1970:173-90). Participation in the dying and rising of the cultic hero or god results in participation in the victory of the hero or god. From this perspective the combination of sacrificial terminology and Graeco-Roman imagery is viable. This combination is expressed by attributing additional honorary titles to Jesus in the process of christianizing the Jesus tradition. It is the reason why the titles *Son of God* and *Kyrios* were especially functional in this process.

When using titles such as *Kyrios* and *Son of God* (derived from the emperor cult), the early cultic community of Jesus followers clearly separated themselves from the ideology of the emperor cult. Jesus' vision of an *alternate* kingdom (as expressed in aphoristic symbols and healing activities) provided the setting for understanding God's reign and sovereignty. In this cult the values of inclusiveness and egalitarianism make it possible for the destitute and slaves to participate in the dying and rising of the cultic hero on an equal level with those of noble birth. This resulted in conflict with the customs of the emperor cult and a tense relationship with the temple and synagogue authorities.

All cults, including the "Christian cult," need officials to preside in their cultic activities. Cultic officials in the ἐκκλησία facilitated the people's participation in cultic activities. Similarly, scribes were needed in the "Christian" cult as in other cults. Their task was to interpret the holy writings and to codify the cultic activity. The cultic hero was given the position of ultimate "law-giver" and "priest" and the position of the officials was that of representatives of the cultic hero, law-givers and priests. Names were given both to the cultic hero and to the representatives in order to express these functions. Positions, names and functions were based on the sayings and deeds of the "founder" of the cult. In historical Jesus research this has been called "false attribution."

In my discussion on false attribution the following elements were identified:

- The process of false attribution occurred against the background of the dispossession of land and the disruption of families.
- The sayings and deeds of Jesus as the "founder" of the "Christian cult" were originally transmitted in a peasant culture that conceptualized the world in terms of the "little tradition" (using concepts from agrarian society and not concepts of the ruling classes).
- The "little tradition" was domesticated by scribes who conceptualized their world in terms of the "great tradition" (using terminology of schools, temples and empires).
- This "domestication" of the Jesus tradition relates to the crossing of the boundaries between in-group and out-group (horizontal boundaries) and those between higher status positions and lower ones (vertical boundaries).
- *Würdeprädikationen* used for Jesus, are terms that originated in the "great tradition" and were used to express the "little tradition."

The potential conflict inherent in early Christian scribal activity can be illustrated by means of a study of the Christological honorary titles (*Würdeprädikation*). The use of titles for Jesus ("great tradition") is grounded in the words and deeds of Jesus that were originally spoken, performed and transmitted in terms of the peasant culture ("little tradition"). The difference between the interests of the "great tradition" and "little tradition" can also become clear when the titles of Jesus are studied. Focusing on the title *Son of Man* as case study, the following becomes clear:

- seen from a diachronic perspective, the use of the title *Son of Man* indicates an ideological conflict between the "great tradition" and the "little tradition";
- seen from a synchronic perspective, the interrelatedness between the title *Son of Man* and other names that were used for Jesus indicate a conflict between Jesus' understanding (point of view) of God and that of the followers of Jesus;
- both the conflict between the "great tradition" and the "little tradition" and that between Jesus and the Jesus followers can be explained sociologically by interpreting this *conflict* in terms of conflict theory and the social theory of the institutionalization of charismatic authority.

Jesus the Son of Man

Rudolf Bultmann's (1931:117, 129, 163) rather challenging point of view on the use of the title *Son of Man* is that Jesus used the title to refer prophetically to someone who was still to come and not to himself. The followers of Jesus, however, identified this *Son of Man* figure with Jesus. Norman Perrin (1965-1966:105-55; 1966:17-28), Philip Vielhauer (1975:124-47) en J Dominic Crossan (1991:238-55) argue that Jesus never used "son of man" as a *title*. However, according to Crossan Jesus did refer to the figure "son of man" mentioned in Daniel 7:11-14, but not as a self-reference. In this passage the expression is not used as a title. Later Jesus' followers also made use Daniel 7:11-14, but understood "son of man" as a title and identified Jesus with this figure. According to Crossan, the use of the title *Kyrios* as a reference to a coming "apocalyptic judge" (see Cullmann 1958:153; Duling and Perrin 1994:223) by Hellenistic-Judean followers of Jesus facilitated the identification of Jesus *Messiah* with Jesus, *Son of Man*. It is Vielhauer's (1975:124-47) opinion that the earliest Jesus faction in Jerusalem used the title *Son of Man* to describe Jesus on account of their experience of Easter. Perrin's point of view is similar to that of Vielhauer. He also sees the use of the title *Son of Man* as an attempt by Jesus' followers to make sense of the death of Jesus. By identifying Jesus with the *Son of Man* the Jesus followers expressed their faith that Jesus was vindicated by his victory over death. Hans Conzelmann's (1969:135-36) evaluation of the evidence shows a somewhat different nuance. He is of the opinion that Jesus did not refer to the figure "son of man" at all. According to Conzelmann, scholars who state that he did (e.g., Sanders 1985, 1993; Boring 1982; Higgins 1980), incorrectly identify Jesus' sayings of the *Kingdom of God* with sayings on the *Son of Man* in the gospel tradition. The concept "Kingdom of God" and the title *Son of Man* refer to two entirely different matters.

Bultmann' perspective on Jesus as apocalyptic prophet forms the background of his opinion that Jesus did refer to a "son of man" figure. Crossan (1983), in his work on the parables, and Leif Vaage (1994), in his work on the Q tradition, both concluded, however, that Jesus was not an apocalyptic figure. The Jesus Seminar (see Miller 2000:1-18; Schmidt 2000:19-38), building on this work, confirmed their results and demonstrated that Jesus' perspective on the Kingdom of God was that of a present reality and not as a future entity. They illustrated the socio-cultural and socio-political consequences of Jesus' view on the Kingdom of God as a present reality over against a type of kingdom that is represented and embodied by an emperor.

My investigation follows the work of Adela Collins (1996:139-58) in her contention that Jesus used the expression "son of man" not in a titular way but generically, meaning "humankind." Collins clearly indicates how the this use of "son of man" developed into a titular usage in which Jesus is identified with the Son of Man. Collins has not, however, conceded that Jesus conceptualized from an apocalyptic perspective. I will show that Jesus' use of the expression "son of man" should be understood in the context of the "little tradition" which was reinterpreted in terms of the "great tradition" in a titular way. I argue that this transition from "little tradition" to "great tradition" can be seen as *false attribution*, which can be understood against the background of the *dispossession of land* and the *breaking up of the extended family*. The disruption of land and family meant that the lives of peasants were severely affected. The sayings and deeds of Jesus as the "founder" of the "Christian cult" should be understood in the context of peasant culture. Jesus sayings and deeds have their oral history within the "little tradition." After Jesus' death when his followers reorganized themselves into a cultic community, they gave Jesus the position of "founder of the cult." This they did by making use of honorary titles. At this stage the "little tradition" was reconceptualized in terms of the "great tradition."

The Greek idiom used for "son of man" in the gospel tradition is ὁ υἱὸς τοῦ ἀνθρώπου. In terms of first century Greek, it could be literally translated as "the son of *the* man," meaning nothing more than "*the* man's son." Although it later became an idiom on account of its usage as a title, the expression would not normally be used in Greek. On account of the fact that the phrase is found in Daniel 7:11–14, it has been thought that the Greek phrase might be an incorrect translation of the Hebrew *ben ha-'adam* or the Aramaic *bar 'nosha/bar nosha*. Because this expression is rarely found in the definite form in Hebrew or Aramaic, the indefinite forms *ben 'adam* and *bar nosh* were also investigated. Vermes (1967:310; 1973:160–91) found that the use of the expression in the literature of normative Judaism (Talmud Yerushalmi, targumim, and midrashim) can shed light on the meaning of the expression in formative Judaism and in the New Testament. Researchers such as Veilhauer (1965:57–58), Perrin (1965:150–55) and Tödt ([1959] 1965) agree with Vermes and this is also the chosen approach for this investigation (Fitzmyer [1968:426–27] however disagrees.)

Vielhauer and Tödt found seventy-four Son of Man sayings in the New Testament and one that is relevant in the Gospel of Thomas (cf. Schwartz 1986:11–12). Some of the sayings represent a (post-Easter) reflection *by Jesus* on his coming, passion, death and resurrection (cf. Bultmann 1931:161–79). Other *Son of Man* sayings are categorized by Bultmann as "legendary sayings."[1] Collins (1996:145) is of the opinion that these sayings could contain early traditions, but she finds categories

---

1. According to Bultmann (1931:163): "in denen die Person Jesu eine wesentliche Rolle spielt, und die ich *a parte potiori* Ich-Worte nenne."

(see Bultmann 1931:73) such as "legal sayings and church rules," "wisdom sayings" and "prohetic and apocalyptic sayings" more helpful (Collins 1996:146-48, 148-51, 151-52). The following discussion of examples from these categories will demonstrate the *institutionalization of charismatic authority*.

According to Bultmann (1931:138-61) two of the 74 *Son of Man* sayings can, in their present form, be categorized as "legal sayings" (*Gesetzesworte*) or "church rules" (*Gemeinderegeln*) (cf. Collins 1996:146). One of these *logia* can be found in the story of the healing of the paralytic in Mark 2:1-12 and another in Q 12:10. In Mark this story also takes the form of a *controversy dialogue*. In the narrative structure of Mark the controversy began when Jesus taught (*edidasken*) in the synagogue in Capernaum (Mark 1:22). It was a controversy between Jesus and the scribes (*hoi grammateis*) (Mark 1:22) and was caused by Jesus' teaching (*hē didachē*). From a social-scientific perspective the controversy can be seen as a challenge-riposte about honor. The dispute is about the nature of Jesus' *authority* (Mark 1:27): "What is this? A new teaching—and with what authority!" The story of Jesus healing the paralytic (Mark 2:1-12) is, in a way, an extension of this controversy in Capernaum in the narrative structure of Mark (cf. Mark 2:1 where it is expressly stated that the healing of the man with the evil spirit also took place in Capernaum). In the second story (Mark 2:1-12) Jesus' honor is expressed with a *title* just as it was in the first story (Mark 1:21-28). In the first story the title is *the Holy One of God* (Mark 1:24) and in the second it is *the Son of Man* (Mark 2:10).

Earlier I compared the *Wurdeprädikation* "the Holy One of God" with the title "Son of the Mighty One" in the story of the healing of the Gerasene demoniac (Mark 5:1-20). The expression "Holy One" was understood as an acknowledgement that Jesus was a *sage* with divine authority. Such an explanation is congruent with a controversy dialogue. The *Sitz im Leben* of the story of the healing of the Gerasene Demonic (Mark 5:1-20) is not the *conflict* between Jesus' teaching and the teachings of other scribes, but rather the *conflict* between Jesus as *Son of the Mighty One* and the Roman *legion* as the representatives of their gods. The *Sitz im Leben* in which the title *Son of Man* functions in Mark 2:1-12 is also one of conflict. This *logion* is found in Mark 2:10: "But that you may know that *the Son of Man* has *authority* [*exousia*] on earth to forgive sins . . . He [Jesus] said . . ."

Geza Vermes (1973:163–68) is of the opinion that here "son of man" is an expression of a self-awareness of authority. Jeremias (1967:165 n. 9), Fitzmyer (1968:426–27), Borsch (1967:23 n. 4), Colpe (1972:403–4), and Casey (1976:147–54) do not agree, but rather see this as a titular use of Son of Man. To me this is an example of the *institutionalization of charismatic authority*. A development of the tradition can be clearly seen. Firstly, Jesus used the expression "son of man" in a generic way (indefinite form) (cf. Vermes1967:311–19). It referred to Jesus as a *wisdom teacher* with *charismatic authority*. Traces of this early tradition can be seen in the story of the healing of the man with the evil spirit (Mark 1:21–28). The wisdom teaching of Jesus as charismatic figure subverted the conventional wisdom/order according to which only *priests* had the authority to facilitate reconciliation for people's sins in order to receive forgiveness (see Num 15:25). John the Baptist also circumvented the structures of the temple when he encouraged people to let themselves be baptized in order for their sins to be forgiven (Mark 1:4). By using the generic forms *ben 'dam* or *bar nosh* Jesus taught that any person could forgive the sins of another. "In no case is the speaker set off from other human beings as distinctive in any way. If Mark 2:10, therefore, represents an older Semitic saying, it would have meant 'human beings have authority on earth to forgive sins'" (Collins 1996:147). According to Casey (1976:46) the "son of man" in this verse only refers to *healers*. If this were the case, however, John the Baptist who was not a healer, would be excluded from baptizing and forgiving sins. Jesus obviously went along with what John the Baptist did, since he himself came to be baptized (for the authenticity of this story see Funk 1999:11). Colpe (1972:430–31) is of the opinion that the *authority* (*exousia*) to forgive sins could only belong to *Jesus*. Such authority would no longer be *auctoritas*, but, on account of its exclusivity, would have become *potestas*. "Power" in this sense of the word indicates *inequality*, in which case *conflict* can be expected (see my earlier discussion). This can be seen in the narrative structure of the Gospel of Mark where the healing of the paralytic is transformed into a controversy dialogue between *scribes*. This *Sitz im Leben* is no longer similar to that of the historical Jesus. In the aftermath of the destruction of the temple in 70 CE, "Christian scribes" find themselves in controversy with "Judean scribes" in Galilee.

In the context of such scribal activity it can be expected that there would be dispute as to the interpretation of Numbers 15:25: "the priest shall make atonement for all the congregation of the people of Israel, and they shall be forgiven" (RSV). In a post-Easter "Christian" cultic setting it can be expected that Jesus would be presented as the "ultimate priest." Examples from Qumran (11QMelchizedek) indicate that a *royal figure* who is simultaneously represented as the *priest* of "God Most High" was known in the context of first-century scribal activity (see Kobelski 1981). This theme can also be found in Psalm 110:4b: "You are a priest forever, in the order of Melchizedek." In Mark 12:35-38 Jesus is identified with this royal priestly figure and his *teaching* (*hē didachē*) (Mark 12:35) is contrasted with that of the *scribes* (*hoi grammateis*) who wear "royal" robes (στολαί) (Mark 12:38) and go around the (Greco-Roman) *agoras* in order that they could be greeted and receive honor: "Watch out for the teachers of the law. They like to walk around in flowing robes and be greeted in the market-places, and have the most important seats in the synagogues and the places of honor at banquets. They devour widows' houses and for a show make lengthy prayers. Such men will be punished most severely" (Mark 12:38-40).

This pronouncement of judgment is probably a post-Easter projection back to Jesus of the *conflict* that was experienced in post-Easter times, and was directed at the opponents in their post-Easter situation. Jesus, honored with the title *Son of Man*, functions as a *judge*. This *power* (*potestas*) of Jesus is already reflected in the story of the healing of the paralytic in Mark 2:1-12 when Jesus is given the *authority* to forgive sins. We can conclude, therefore, that the use of the title *Son of Man* in Mark 2:10 is an illustration of the *institutionalization of charismatic authority*: Jesus as wisdom teacher subverted conventional wisdom by taking the *power* to forgive sins from the priests and giving this authority to any person (ὁ υἱὸς τοῦ ἀνθρώπου in an indefinite generic form). In a post-Easter "Christian" cultic setting Jesus was honored with the title Son of Man and the *power* that he took from the priests was given to him as the "ultimate" king-priest!

A similar development can be seen in Q 12:10 (another example of a "legal saying" or "church rule"—cf. also Käsemann 1954-55:248-60). The development here is also from the *Sitz im Leben Jesu* to a *Sitz im Leben ecclesiae*. It is generally accepted that Luke was more conservative than Matthew in the use of the source material of the second recension of Q (Q³) (see Kloppenborg 2000:88). *Synagogical controversy* (see Luke 12:11)

129

Institutionalization of Authority and the Naming of Jesus

will then more likely be the setting in which the Sayings Gospel Q interpreted the Son of Man logion than Matthew's (apocalyptic) Beelzebub discourse (see Matt 12:22–37). Q 12:10 reads as follows: "And everyone who speaks a word against the Son of Man will be forgiven, but anyone who blasphemes against the Holy Spirit will not be forgiven" (NIV). The similar logion in Mark (see Mark 3:28–29) does not contain the title Son of Man. It is possible that the Markan logion could have been taken from Q^2 (see my earlier discussion), while Luke and Matthew made use of Q^3. Mark 3:28–29 reads: "All sins and blasphemies will be forgiven *the sons of men* (τοῖς υἱοῖς τῶν ἀνθρώπων), as many as they commit; but whoever blasphemes against the Holy Spirit will not have forgiveness forever" (RSV). According to Collins (1996:148) the similar variant in *Didache* 11:7b is an indication "that the Markan form is not idiosyncratic." This earlier tradition behind Mark (and *Didache*) also places the following on the lips of Jesus: "if *a human* sins against *another human*, forgiveness is available . . ." (Collins 1996:148, my italics). If this *logion* can traced back to the formative stratum of the Q tradition, it represents a similar kind of subversive wisdom as discussed earlier: the act of forgiveness is a general human matter and not limited to priests. In the context of Q^2, and even more so in Q^3 it can be expected that this type of teaching would be subjected to the interpretation of the Scriptures since Q^2 and Q^3 (and Mark and Matthew) probably originated in the context of scribal activity and the controversy between "Christian" scribes and Pharisaic scribes. Collins (1996:148) is of the opinion that 1 Samuel 2:25 could have played a role in this regard: "If a man [*ben 'adam*] sins against another man [*ben 'adam*], God may mediate for him; but if a man sins against the Lord, who will intercede for him?" (RSV). If Mark 3:28–29 reflects an earlier (Q) tradition, the expression "sons of men" was used in the indefinite generic form and not as a titular reference to Jesus. Q^3 (= Luke 12:10) which has a synagogical controversy as *Sitz im Leben*, draws the *logion* into a context of whether or not Jesus' teaching could be acknowledged. In this context Jesus is honoured with the title Son of Man. Casey (1976:147–54; cf. 1979:229; Bauckham [1985] 1995:245–55) concludes that the "original" form of the logion in Aramaic had "two levels of meaning" (see Collins 1996:148 n. 35). According to him the saying refers to sins against people in general in the first place, and in the second place to sins against Jesus as the Son of Man. Casey supposes that the Greek translators were unaware of this ambivalence in the Aramaic and interpreted it solely as a reference to Jesus as the Son of Man. Collins (1996:148) asks why such a "shift" from the generic use of the expression "son of man" to Jesus as the Son of Man would have taken place:

> It is possible that Jesus spoke such a saying, using the generic or indefinite Semitic idiom, and that it gave rise to the variants. But this reconstruction leaves unanswered the question why someone who handed on the saying made a shift from speaking about humans or men in general to speaking of Jesus as *the* human or the Son of Man. Was the shift due to a mistake in translation? Did some oral performer or scribe simply not know Hebrew or Aramaic very well? Such an explanation is conceivable, but resorting to it seems desperate, tendentious, or both.

It is possible that a *scribe* could have made an error in the process of translation or perhaps did not know Hebrew or Aramaic very well. Another possible explanation of the use of the title *Son of Man* in Q³ could be the previously mentioned probability that a subversive wisdom saying of Jesus developed into the *titular false attribution* of honoring (ὁμολογέω) or renouncing (ἀπαρνέομαι) Jesus as Son of Man (Luke 12:8). Jesus' generic use of sins against people in general that can be forgiven by God (according to 1 Sam 2:25) is, in the context of scribal activity, applied in such a way that Son of Man (as God's "mediator") could forgive sins committed against him (Jesus as the Son of Man), but not sins against God (substituted by τὸ ἅγιον πνεῦμα).

Two of the seventy-four Son of Man sayings belong to the category "proverbs" (see Collins 1996:148–51). Bultmann (1931:73) discusses these sayings under the heading *Logien* (*Jesu als Weisheitslehrer*). One of them can be found in the Markan (and parallels) controversy dialogue about Sabbath observance (Mark 2:23–28) and the other is a Q aphorism (Luke 9:58//Matt 8:20). In the controversy dialogue the challenge-riposte between Jesus and the Pharisees is decided with a Son of Man logion which is a reference to Scriptures: "The sabbath came into being for the sake of τὸν ἄνθρωπον [*the* man] and not ὁ ἄνθρωπος [*the* man] for the sake of the sabbath; so ὁ υἱὸς τοῦ ἀνθρώπου [the Son of Man] is *lord* [κύριός] even of the sabbath" (Mark 2:27–28); translation by Collins 1996:149; my additions).

Collins (1996:149) describes the *Sitz im Leben* of this saying in the context of the Gospel of Mark as follows: "The controversy dialogue itself probably was composed in a post-Easter situation in which followers of Jesus claimed *his authority* in order to settle disputes over sabbath observance. The *Son of Man* saying, although attached to the narrative at a relatively late date, *could itself be early, even a saying of Jesus*" (my italics). I choose for the argument that the "indefinite generic form" of the expression "son of man" can be traced back to Jesus, but that the titular use of *Son of Man* in connection with Jesus was false attribution on account of post-Easter scribal activity. This process can be understood in the light of the influence of Easter on the Jesus tradition and also in the light of the process of *institutionalization of charismatic authority* seen against the background of *conflict*.

Collins (1996:149) probably has a point when she says: "If Jesus said something like Mark 2:27-28, using an Aramaic phrase like בר נש [*bar nosh*], he probably used it in the generic sense. We thus arrive at a point similar to the conclusion of the discussion of the saying about the word spoken against the Son of Man. There is a gap between Jesus' generic use of an Aramaic term and the Gospels' quasi-titular use of a corresponding Greek term."

One of the authentic elements in the life of the historical Jesus was his repudiation of regulations regarding the observance of the sabbath (see Bultmann [1960] 1965b:11). It is possible that Jesus based his point of view on the observance of the sabbath on the Genesis motif (Gen 2:2-3). Another possibility is that the scriptural reference to Genesis first appeared when Jesus' teachings were contextualized by scribes in a post-Easter setting with a controversy dialogue as *Sitz im Leben*. Be that as it may, the notion that the sabbath originated at a certain stage of human history, is an allusion to Gen 2:2-3.

When the story of creation (as told in Genesis 2) is remembered, the Greek word for the "first human being" (ὁ ἄνθρωπος) is, at the same time, a generic indication for humanity in general (בר אדם). To be κύριος of the sabbath is a reference to God's command in Genesis 1:28 to rule over creation (see Collins 1996:149). Bultmann (1931:112) points out that a similar saying was known to normative Judaism, namely that the sabbath was given for people and not people for the sabbath. It can be deduced, therefore, that the expression that Jesus as Son of Man (ὁ υἱὸς τοῦ ἀνθρώπου) is ruler over the sabbath (Mark 2:27-28) reflects a similar context of scribal activity. In my opinion this is another instance of the *institutionalization of charismatic authority*. Jesus, the sage, subverted the conventional order regarding the regulations for observing the sabbath. When his followers at a much later stage find themselves in a dispute concerning the Scriptural grounding of Jesus' wisdom, they change Jesus' reference to the "son of man" in the indefinite generic form to a *logion* in which Jesus is honoured with the title *Son of Man*. This titular use of the expression in a conflict situation gives Jesus the *potestas* to be κύριος over the sabbath and to change the regulations according to his wisdom.

Another example of a wisdom saying that underwent a similar process, is Q 9:58: "Foxes have holes and birds of the air have nests, but ὁ υἱὸς τοῦ ἀνθρώπου has nowhere to lay his head" (translation by Collins 1996:150). An aphorism with similar content can also be found in the Gospel of Thomas (logion 86) where it is introduced with the formula: "Jesus said." In Q[3] (also used by Luke *and* Matthew), this logion concludes a short narrative (confirmed by the similarity between Matthew and Luke). Previously I argued that the *biographical* framework that can be found in Q should be seen as a post-Easter addition to the Q tradition. Here, too, there is evidence of an earlier Jesus tradition, also indicated by the parallel in the Gospel of Thomas. Multiple independent witnesses confirm the authenticity of the Jesus *logion* (see Funk 1999:23) which was later placed in a biographical framework. The uncomplicated introduction to the *logion* in Thomas 86 indicates an earlier aphoristic form.

Bultmann (for the Greek, see Bultmann 1931:102 note 2) points out a parallel saying in Plutarch's Life of Tiberius. It is a speech about land reform which argues that soldiers of the emperor had the right to receive land that was taken from others. Tiberius was the emperor when the teachings of the historical Jesus were heard. Previously I indicated the relevance of the issue of the dispossession of land for the understanding of the conflict between the peasants and the élite. Tiberius declared: "The wild beasts inhabiting Italy have holes, their places of rest and refuge, but those who fight and die for Italy have no share in it except air and light and are forced to wander unsettled with their wives and children" (see Collins 1996:150). This saying of Tiberius was probably well-known among the peasants during the time of Jesus. Antagonism towards Roman and Herodian authorities on account of the dispossession of land and the resulting disintegration of families, was to be expected (see Fiensy 1991:21). One cannot know whether Jesus had the saying of Tiberius in mind, however. It is possible that a similar wisdom saying of Jesus could have been taken over in the Q tradition and only later, when placed in a biographical context, made to resonated with the saying of Tiberius. Bultmann (1931:102) is of the opinion that the Jesus saying reflected a type of folk-pessimism, such as for example Job 3:25–26 and Ecclesiastes 3:19. The latter reads as follows: "For the fate of the *sons of men* and the fate of beasts is the same; as one dies, so dies the other. They all have the same breath, and man has no advantage over the beasts; for all is vanity" (RSV, my italics).

This wisdom saying subverts the conventional wisdom that human beings were given a higher position in the hierarchy than animals in the order of creation. Another reason for this higher position, according to conventional wisdom, is that human beings find meaningful existence in dyadic relationships with other relatives in a household. "Subversive wisdom" could be expected from the historical Jesus who was a wandering sage without family ties. According to Collins (1996:150) the following wisdom saying from Job 3:25–26 can be seen as a reflection of the kind of wisdom that can be expected from Jesus: "For the thing that I fear comes upon me, and what I dread befalls me. I am not at ease, nor am I quiet; *I have no rest*; but trouble comes" (RSV, my italics). The version of *Thomas* 86 of this Jesus saying is: "But the Son of Man has nowhere to lay his head *and rest*." The version in Q 9:58 ("Foxes have holes and birds of the air have nests, but the *Son of Man* [ὁ υἱὸς τοῦ ἀνθρώπου] has nowhere to lay his head") suggests a differentiation between human beings and animals.

A development can clearly be traced from a wisdom saying in which Jesus as *charismatic figure* refers to *humanity* in general, to Q^3 which identifies the Son of Man with Jesus. Possibly Q^2 already contained this transition, but if so, the tradition was either unknown to Mark or he chose not to take it over. It is possible that such a tradition could have been transmitted and interpreted in various ways during the process of the development of the tradition. Collins (1996:150) formulates it as follows: "Such folk pessimism could easily be adapted to a philosophically dualistic, apocalyptic or gnostic perspective, in which humanity has no home or rest in this world, but does find such in the heavenly world." It is also possible that this tradition could have been taken over in circumstances where poverty was the result of, among other things, the dispossession of land and where the disintegration of families could have been a dire problem. A comparison could be drawn between the saying of Jesus (the "little tradition" of the peasant culture) and the saying of Tiberius. In the formative stratum of the Q tradition themes such as poverty, discipleship and Jesus' vision of an alternate kingdom were integrated (see Jacobson 1992:50). As Jesus sayings became further removed from the "little tradition" and were increasingly domesticated into the "great tradition" of school, temple and scribal activity, the attribution of *titles* to Jesus is to be expected. This is probably what happened with the saying in Q 9:58.

In the previous discussion of the history of the Q traditions, it became clear that Q^2 originated in a context of *conflict* with the Second Temple ideology and Q^3 in the Galilean/Syrian region in a more Hellenistic context after the destruction of Jerusalem in 70 CE. At this stage of the tradition history the Q community defines its own identity and orientation as "wandering itinerants" (cf. Crossan 1997:21-53). At this time opposing Judean oriented scribes in places such as Capernaum, Bethsaida and Chorazin were also judged by means of apocalyptic woes (see Luke 10:13-15). It is therefore understandable that Jesus sayings about, for example, *discipleship*, were associated with *homeless itinerancy*. By drawing Jesus into their context they gave their own ideology greater authority. By reinterpreting the *logia* of Jesus as though the Son of Man said them, they anticipated their own vindication. After all, it would be the victorious Son of Man figure who would eventually triumph over suffering and judge the "enemies."

Luke took over this Q^3 tradition and gave it a functional position at the beginning of his travel narrative (Luke 9:51—19:44). *Imitatio Jesu* is the theme with which Luke calls upon the followers of Jesus to travel with him to Jerusalem. The disciples are asked to count the cost of their discipleship (see Luke 9:57-62; 14:25-35). It could be that his fate would become their fate: "As they were walking along the road, a man said to him, 'I will follow you wherever you go.' Jesus replied: 'Foxes have holes and birds of the air have nests, but *the Son of Man* has no place to lay his head'" (NIV, my italics).

> In any case, if the saying goes back to Jesus, it most likely referred to human beings in general, or to Jesus' experience as typical of

humanity. At some point, the reference to the generic human being was transformed into a reference to Jesus as a particular individual who is without an abode for a specific reason: his sense of vocation, a lifestyle which was a prophetic symbolic action, or the result of hostility to his person or work. At the latest, this transformation occurred when the saying was placed in a pronouncement story concerning discipleship, such as the one preserved in Q. In this context, the life of the disciple is to be homeless in imitation of Jesus' life. (Collins 1996:150–51)

Sixteen of the seventy-four Son of Man sayings in the gospel tradition belong to the group of "prophetic and apocalyptic sayings" (Collins 1996:151). "Four of these could well have been formulated by the author of the Gospel in which they appear; three by Matthew (16:28; 24:30a; 25:31) and one by Luke (17:22). Another four are older than the Gospels in which they appear, but are probably post-Easter formulations (Matt 10:23; Mark 14:21 par.; Luke 6:22; 21:36). The origin of the remaining eight is ambiguous" (Collins 1996:151). According to Bultmann (1931:117, 129, 163) some of the "prophetic and apocalyptic" *Son of Man* sayings could have originated with Jesus, for instance Luke 12:8–9; Mark 8:38 par.; Matthew 24:27 par. Bultmann (1931:163) is uncertain whether Matthew 24:37–39 par. and 24:43–44 par. should be included. It has been posited earlier that Bultmann (1956:90–110) saw these logia of Jesus as a "prophet" referring to someone else as the *apocalyptic Son of Man*, while Jesus' followers identified him with the Son of Man figure. This can especially be seen in Mark 8:38 par. and Luke 12:8–9.

The discussion of Luke 12:10 as a Q tradition argued that Jesus probably did not have the title Son of Man in mind for himself, but that the later Q tradition attributed "titular authority" to Jesus. When Luke took over Q 12:10 and added vv. 8–9 as introduction, he took it for granted that Jesus was the Son of Man. The titular references to the *Son of Man* in Luke 12:8–9 need not be traced back to Jesus. They could simply be the addition of the evangelist. A similar case can be argued for Mark 8:38. Vielhauer (1975:124–47) sees no convincing argument either for or against any of the titular references to the Son of Man originating with Jesus. Such an argument does not take the indefinite generic form of some "son of man" references as possibly authentic Jesus sayings, into account.

I agree that there is no strong argument for Jesus using the title Son of Man in his "little tradition." On the other hand, seeing the "prophetic and apocalyptic" sayings as articulation of the "great tradition" and as examples of the *institutionalization of Jesus' charismatic authority*, provides a sociological explanation for the *conflict* situation of the post-Easter followers of Jesus. This is the case especially when the use of "Christological titles" for Jesus is *demystified* from a postmodern perspective. The title of Ragnar Leivestad's (1968) article, "Der apokalyptische Menschensohn: Ein theologisches Phantom" is rather telling; but to see no "grounds" in the Jesus tradition why the post-Easter followers of Jesus institutionalized his *charismatic authority*, is taking the argument too far. It is possible to argue that 'n similar process could have taken place in the Judean-Hellenistic context where the expression *Son of Man* could have been used as a title (cf. Casey's 1976 discussion of the use of "Son of Man" in the Similitudes of Enoch). It would, however, lie beyond the scope of this book. "It is well known that the community at Qumran and at least some early followers of Jesus believed that the scriptures were written for *their* benefit and prophesied events which *they* were experiencing and other events *they* expected to occur in the near future" (Collins 1996:154, my italics).

The early followers of Jesus believed that his authority which they acknowledged, came from God. The Son of Man title is expression of the belief that he would appear on the clouds along with holy angels: "he comes in his Father's glory with the holy angels" (Mark 8:38b). The process of the *institutionalization of charismatic authority* was not limited to Jesus, however. It also happened with other figures, such as Moses. An author of tragedies called Ezekiel (c. 200 BCE) (see Snell 1971:1:292) writing about the Exodus, described a dream of Moses. He saw a "man" sitting on a throne on Mount Sinai. This man beckoned to Moses and gave him a crown and a scepter after which he disappeared from the scene. Moses' authority was institutionalized by God and the place of God as acting subject was taken by the "institute." This is similar to what happened when Jesus became Son of Man on account of God's intervention when Jesus triumphed over death by means of the resurrection.

Bibliography

Abel, E. L. 1974. The Genealogies of Jesus ὁ Χριστός. *NTS* 20:203–10.
Adam, A. K. M. 1995. *What Is Postmodern Biblical Criticism?* GBS. Minneapolis: Fortress.
Alexander, Loveday. 1986. "Luke's Preface in the Context of Greek Writing." *NovT* 28:48–74.
Allegro, J. M. 1956. *The Dead Sea Scrolls.* Harmondsworth, UK: Penguin.
Allison, D. C. 1984. "Elijah Must Come First." *JBL* 103:256–58.
———. 1993. *The New Moses: A Matthean typology.* Minneapolis: Fortress.
———. 1997. *The Jesus Tradition in Q.* Harrisburg, PA: Trinity.
———. 1998. *Jesus of Nazareth: Millenarian Prophet.* Minneapolis: Fortress.
Alvis, J. 1995. *Divine Purpose and Heroic Response in Homer and Virgil: The Political Plan of Zeus.* Lanham, MD: Rowman & Littlefield.
Appelbaum, S. 1976. "The Social and Economic Status of the Jews in the Diaspora." In *The Jewish People in the First Century: Historical Geography, Political History, Social, Cultural and Religious Life and Institutions,* edited by S. Safrai and M. Stern, 2:701–27. Compendia Rerum Iudaicarum ad Novum Testamentum, Section One. Philadelphia: Fortress.
Appiah, K. A. 1991. "Is the 'Post' in 'Postmodernism' the 'Post' in 'Postcolonial'?" *Critical Inquiry* 17:360–67.
Assmann, J. 1992. *Das kulturelle Gedächtnis: Schrift, Erinnerung und politische Identität in frühen Hochkulturen.* Munich: Beck.
Aune, D. E. 1981. "The Problem of the Genre of the Gospels: A Critique of C. H. Talbert's *What is a gospel?*" In *Gospel Perspectives, II: Studies of History and Tradition in the Four Gospels,* edited by R. T. France and D. Wenham, 9–60. Sheffield, UK: JSOT Press.
Austin, J. L. 1962. *How to Do Things with Words.* Oxford: Clarendon.
Arnal, W. E. 2001. *Jesus and the Village Scribes: Galilean Conflicts and the Setting of Q.* Minneapolis: Fortress.
Bauckham, R. A. [1985] 1995. "The Son of Man: 'A Man in My Position' or 'Someone'?" In *The Historical Jesus,* edited by Craig A. Evans and Stanley E. Porter, 23–33. A Sheffield Reader. Sheffield, UK: Sheffield Academic.
Bauer, D. R, 1988. *The Structure of Matthew's Gospel: A Study in Literary Design.* Decatur, GA: Almond.
Baur, F. C. [1853] 1878. *The Church History of the First Three Centuries.* Vol. 1. Translated by A. Menzies. Edinburgh: Williams & Norgate.
Baron, S. W. 1952. *The Social and Religious History of the Jews.* Vol. 1. New York: Columbia University Press.

Bibliography

Barton, Stephen C. 1997. "Social-scientific criticism." In *Handbook to Exegesis of the New Testament*, edited by Stanley E. Porter, 277–89. NTTS 25. Leiden: Brill.

Beaton, R. 1999. "Messiah and justice: A key to Matthew's use of Isaiah 42:1–4?" *JSNT* 75:5–23.

Berger, K. 1984. "Hellenistische Gattungen im Neuen Testament." In *ANRW* II.25.2:1031–432.

Berger, P. 1967. *The Sacred Canopy: Elements of a Social Theory of Religion*. Garden City, NY: Doubleday.

Berger, P., and T. Luckmann. 1975. *The Social Construction of Reality: A Treatise in the Sociology of Knowledge*. Harmondsworth, UK: Penguin.

Bergman, J. 1968. *Ich bin Isis: Studien zum memphitischen Hintergrund der griechischen Isisaretalogien*. Acta Universitatis Upsaliensis. Historia Religionum 3. Uppsala/Lund: Berlingsha Boktrycheriet.

Best, E. 1983. *Mark: The Gospel as Story*. Studies of the New Testament and Its World. Edinburgh: T. & T. Clark.

Betz, H. D. 1968. "Jesus as Divine Man." In *Jesus and the Historian: Written in Honor of Ernest Cadman Colwell*, edited by F. Thomas Trotter, 114–33. Philadelphia: Westminster.

Betz, O. 1972. "The Concept of the So-called 'Divine Man' in Mark's Christology." In *Studies in New Testament and Early Christian Literature: Essays in Honour of Allen P. Wikgren*, edited by David E. Aune, 229–51. NovTSup 33. Leiden: Brill.

Bickerman, E. J. 1988. *The Jews in the Greek Age*. Cambridge: Harvard University Press.

Bilezikian, G. G, 1977. *The Liberated Gospel: A Comparison of the Gospel of Mark and Greek Tragedy*. Grand Rapids: Baker.

Black, Matthew. 1966. *The Dead Sea Scrolls and Christian Doctrine*. Ethel M. Wood Lecture Delivered before the University of London on 8 February 1966. London: Athlone.

———. 1984. "'Not peace but a sword': Matt 10:34ff; Luke 12:51ff." In *Jesus and the Politics of His Day*, edited by E. Bammel and C. F. D. Moule, 287–94. Cambridge: Cambridge University Press.

Blau, P. M. 1963. "Critical Remarks on Weber's Theory of Authority." *American Political Science Review* 57:305–16.

Blau, P. M., and J. W. Moore. 1970. "Sociology." In *A Reader's Guide to the Social Sciences*, edited by B. F. Hoselitz, 1–40. New York: Free Press.

Bock, Darrell L. 1987. *Proclamation from Prophecy and Pattern: Lucan Old Testament Christology*. JSNTSup 12. Sheffield: JSOT Press.

Bolkestein, H. [1939] 1967. *Wohltätigkeit und Armpflege im vorchristlichen Altertum: Eine Beitrag zum Problem "Moral und Gesellschaft."* Groningen: Bouma.

Bonz, Marianne Palmer. 2000. *The Past as Legacy: Luke-Acts and Ancient Epic*. Minneapolis: Fortress.

Borg, M. J. 1984. *Conflict, Holiness and Politics in the Teachings of Jesus*. Studies in the Bible and Early Christianity 5. New York: Mellen.

———. [1987] 1991. *Jesus: A New Vision—Spirit, Culture, and the Life of Discipleship*. San Francisco: Harper.

———. 1994. *Meeting Jesus Again for the First Time*. San Francisco: Harper.

———. 1999a. "Seeing Jesus: Sources, Lenses, and Method." In *The Meaning of Jesus: Two Visions*, by Marcus J. Borg and N. T. Wright, 3–14. San Francisco: HarperSanFrancisco.

———. 1999b. "Jesus Before and After Easter: Jewish Mystic and Christian Messiah." In *The Meaning of Jesus: Two Visions*, Marcus J. Borg and N. T. Wright, 53–76. San Francisco: HarperSanFrancisco.
Boring, M. Eugene. 1982. *Sayings of the Risen Jesus: Christian Prophecy in the Synoptic Tradition*. SNTSMS 46. Cambridge: Cambridge University Press.
———. 1984. *Truly Human/Truly Divine: Christological Language and the Gospel Form*. St. Louis: CBP.
Bornkamm, Günther. [1960] 1963. "End-expectation and Church in Matthew." In *Tradition and Interpretation in Matthew*, by Gunther Bornkamm, Gerhard Barth, and Heinz Joachim Held. Translated by P. Scott, 15–51. NTL. London: SCM.
Borsch, Frederick H. 1967. *The Son of Man in Myth and History*. NTL. Philadelphia: Westminster.
Bossman, David. 1979. "Ezra's Marriage Reform: Israel Redefined." *BTB* 9:32–38.
Bousset, William. [1913] 1926. *Kyrios Christos: Geschichte des Christusglaubens von den Anfängen des Christentums bis Irenaeus*. FRLANT 4. Göttingen: Vandenhoeck & Ruprecht.
Bovon, Francois. 1983. *Luke the Theologian: Thirty-three Years of Research (1950–1983)*. PTMS 12. Allison Park, PA: Pickwick Publications.
Brandon, S. G. F. 1967. *Jesus and the Zealots: A Study of the Political Factor in Primitive Christianity*. Manchester: Manchester University Press.
Braun, H. 1957. "Der Sinn der neutestamentlichen Christologie." *ZTK* 54:341–77.
Brettler, Marc Zvi. 1995. *The Creation of History in Ancient Israel*. London: Routledge.
Breytenbach, A. P. B. 1997a. "Die herfsfees en die koningsrite by Bet-El as interteks van Amos 7:10–8:14 en Hosea 9:1–9." *HvTSt* 53:513–28.
———. 1997b. "Meesternarratiewe, kontranarratiewe en kanonisering: 'n Perspektief op sommige profetiese geskrifte." *HvTSt* 53:1157–86.
Brink, A. P. 1987. *Vertelkunde: 'n Inleiding tot die lees van verhalende tekste*. Pretoria: Academica.
Brooks, C., and Robert Penn Warren. 1970. *Modern Rhetoric*. New York: Harcourt.
Brown, Raymond E. 1957. "The Messianism of Qumran." *CBQ* 19:53–82.
———. [1977] 1978. *The Birth of the Messiah: A Commentary on the Infancy Narratives in Matthew and Luke*. Garden City, NY: Doubleday.
Brownlee, William H. 1956–57. "Messianic Motifs of Qumran and the New Testament." *NTS* 3:12–30, 195–210.
Bultmann, Rudolf. [1921] 1931. *Die Geschichte der synoptischen Tradition*. 2nd ed. FRLANT 12. Göttingen: Vandenhoeck & Ruprecht.
———. [1923] 1967. "Die religionsgeschichtliche Hintergrund des Prologs zum Johannesevangelium." In *Exegetica: Aufsätze zum Neuen Testaments*, 10–35. Tübingen: Mohr/Siebeck.
———. [1926] 1988. *Jesus*. Neuausgabe. Tübingen: Mohr/Siebeck.
———. [1949] 1956. *Primitive Christianity in Its Contemporary Setting*. Translated by R. H. Fuller. London: Thames & Hudson.
———. [1951] 1974. *Theology of the New Testament*, Vol. 1. Translated by Kendrick Grobel. London: SCM.
———. [1958] 1968. *Theologie des Neuen Testaments*. 6th ed. Tübingen: Mohr/Siebeck.
———. 1965a. "Antwort an Ernst Käsemann." In *Glauben und Verstehen* 4:190–98. Tübingen: Mohr/Siebeck.

Bibliography

———. [1960] 1965b. *Das Verhältnis der urchristlichen Christusbotschaft zum historischen Jesus.* 4th ed. Heidelberg: Carl Winter Universitätsverlag.

———. 1967. "Neues Testament und Mythologie: Das Problem der Entmythologisierung der neustamentlichen Verkündigung." In *Kerygma und Mythos, I: Ein theologisches Gespräch,* edited by H.-W. Bartsch, 15-48. Hamburg-Bergstedt: Reich.

———. [1976] 1985. *The Second Letter to the Corinthians.* Translated by Roy A. Harrisville. Minneapolis: Augsburg.

Burridge, Richard A. [1992] 1999. *What Are the Gospels? A Comparison with Graeco-Roman Biography.* SNTSMS 70. Cambridge: Cambridge University Press.

Cain, M. 1999. *Jesus the Man: An Introduction for People at Home in the Modern World.* Sonoma, CA: Polebridge.

Carney, T. F. 1975. *The Shape of the Past: Models and Antiquity.* Lawrence, KS: Coronado.

Casey, Maurice. 1976. "The Son of Man Problem." *ZNW* 67:147-54.

———. 1979. *Son of Man: The Interpretation and Influence of Daniel 7.* London: SPCK.

Charlesworth, James H. 1996. *Jesus' Jewishness: Exploring the place of Jesus in Early Judaism.* New York: Crossroad.

Christ, F. 1970. *Jesus Sophia: Die Sophia Christologie bei den Synoptikern.* ATANT 57. Zurich: TVZ.

Cimok, F. [1993] 1998. *Pergamum.* Istanbul: A. Turizm Yayinlari.

Cohen, J. D. 1992. "The Place of the Rabbi in Jewish Society of the Second Century." In *The Galilee in Late Antiquity,* edited by Lee I. Levine, 157-73. New York: Jewish Theological Seminary.

Cohn-Sherbock, Dan. 1997. *The Jewish Messiah.* Edinburgh: T. & T. Clark.

Collins, A. Y. 1996. "The Origin of the Designation of Jesus as 'Son of Man.'" In *Cosmology and Eschatology in Jewish and Christian Apocalypticism,* 139-58. JSJSup 50. Leiden: Brill.

Collins, J. J. 1984. *The Apocalyptic Imagination: An Introduction to the Jewish Matrix of Christianity.* New York: Crossroad.

———. 1995. *The Scepter and the Star: The Messiahs of the Dead Sea Scrolls and Other Ancient Literature.* New York: Doubleday.

Colpe, Carsten. 1972. "huios tou anthropou[set macron over 1st o]." In *TDNT* 8:403-4.

Combrink, H. J. B. 1983. "The Structure of the Gospel of Matthew as Narrative." *TynBul* 34:61-90.

Conzelmann, Hans. 1954. *Die Mitte der Zeit: Studien zur Theologie des Lukas.* BHT 17. Tübingen: Mohr/Siebeck.

———. [1959] 1973. *Jesus.* Translated by I. McLuskey and F. McLuskey with J. M. Robinson. San Francisco: Harper & Row.

———. [1967] 1969. *An Outline of the Theology of the New Testament.* Translated by John Bowden. London: SCM.

———. 1969. *Geschichte des Urchristentums.* GNT 5. Göttingen: Vandenhoeck & Ruprecht.

Coote, R. B., and M. P. Coote. 1990. *Power, Politics, and the Making of the Bible: An Introduction.* Minneapolis: Fortress.

Coser, L. A. 1964. *The Functions of Social Conflict.* International Library of Sociology and Social Reconstructions. New York: Free Press.

———. 1968. "Conflict: Social Aspects." In *International Encyclopedia of the Social Sciences,* edited by D. L. Sills, 3:232-36. New York: Macmillan.

Cox, P. 1983. *Biography in Late Antiquity: A Quest for the Holy Man*. Transformation of the Classical Heritage 5. Berkeley: University of California Press.

Cromhout, M. 2007. *Jesus and Identity: Reconstructing Judean Ethnicity in Q*. Matrix. Eugene, OR: Cascade Books.

Crossan, J. D. 1983. *In Fragments: The Aphorisms of Jesus*. Reprint, Eugene, OR: Wipf & Stock, 2008.

———. 1991. *The Historical Jesus: The Life of a Mediterranean Jewish Peasant*. San Francisco: HarperSanFranciso.

———. 1994a. *Jesus: A Revolutionary Biography*. San Francisco: HarperSanFrancisco.

———. 1994b. "The Historical Jesus in Earliest Christianity." In *Jesus and Faith: A Conversation on the Work of John Dominic Crossan*, edited by J. Carlson and R. A. Ludwig, 1–21. Maryknoll, NY: Orbis.

———. 1994c. "The Infancy and Youth of the Messiah." In *The Search for Jesus: Modern Scholarship Looks at the Gospels*, edited by Hershel Shanks, 59–81. Washington DC: Biblical Archaeology Society.

———. 1994d. *The Essential Jesus: Original Sayings and Earliest Images*. San Francisco: HarperSanFrancisco.

———. 1997. "Jesus and the Kingdom: Itinerants and Householders in Earliest Christianity." In *Jesus at 2000*, edited by Marcus J. Borg, 21–53. Boulder, CO: Westview.

———. 1998. *The Birth of Christianity: Discovering What Happened in the Years Immediately after the Execution of Jesus*. San Francisco: HarperSanFrancisco.

Cullmann, O. 1948. *Die Tauflehre des Neuen Testaments*. AThANT 12. Zurich: TVZ.

———. [1955] 1958. *Die Christologie des Neuen Testaments*. Tübingen: Mohr/Siebeck.

Dahl, Nils Alstrup. [1958] 1983. "The Purpose of Mark's Gospel." In *The Messianic Secret*, edited by Christopher Tuckett, 29–34. IRT 1. Philadelphia: Fortress.

Dahrendorf, R. 1958. "Towards a Theory of Social Conflict." *Journal of Conflict Resolution* 2:170–83.

———. 1959. *Class and Class Conflict in Industrial Society*. Stanford: Stanford University Press.

———. 1965. *Gesellschaft und Freiheit*. Sammlung Piper. Munich: Piper.

———. 1968a. "Out of Utopia." In *Essays in the Theory of Society*, 107–28. London: Routledge & Kegan Paul.

———. 1968b. "On the Origins of Inequality among Men." In *Essays in the Theory of Society*, 151–78. London: Routledge & Kegan Paul.

Dalman, G. [1889] 1902. *The Words of Jesus: Considered in the Light of Post-biblical Jewish Writings and the Aramaic Language*. Translated by D. M. Kay. Edinburgh: T. & T. Clark.

Daube, D. 1973. *The New Testament and Rabbinic Judaism*. New York: Arno.

Davies, P. R. 1987. *Behind the Essenes: History and Ideology in the Dead Sea Scrolls*. BJS 94. Atlanta: Scholars.

———. 1997. "Whose History? Whose Israel? Whose Bible? Biblical Histories, Ancient and Modern." In *Can a "History of Israel" Be Written?*, edited by Lester L. Grabbe, 104–22. JSOTSup 245. Sheffield, UK: Sheffield Academic.

Davies, S. L. 1994. *New Testament Fundamentals*. Rev. ed. Sonoma, CA: Polebridge.

Davies, W. D. 1991. *The Territorial Dimension of Judaism: With a Symposium and Further Reflections*. Minneapolis: Fortress.

Bibliography

Davies, W. D., and D. C. Allison. [1988] 1997. *A Critical and Exegetical Commentary on the Gospel according to Saint Matthew*. Vol. 1, *Introduction and Commentary on Matthew I–VII*. ICC. Edinburgh: T. & T. Clark.

———. [1991] 1998. *A Critical and Exegetical Commentary on the Gospel according to Saint Matthew*. Vol. 2, *Introduction and Commentary on Matthew VIII–XVIII*. ICC. Edinburgh: T. & T. Clark.

Deissmann, Adolf. [1927] 1965. *Light from the Ancient East*. Reprinted, Grand Rapids: Baker.

Derrett, J. D. M. 1997. "The Prayer in Gethsemane (Mk 13:35–36)." *Journal of Higher Criticism* 4.1:78–88.

Dewey, Joanna. [1973] 1995. "The Literary Structure of the Controversy Stories in Mark 2:1–3:6." In *The Interpretation of Mark*, edited by W. R. Telford, 141–52. 2nd ed. Studies in New Testament Interpretation. Edinburgh: T. & T. Clark.

Dibelius, Martin. [1919] 1934. *From Tradition to Gospel*. Translated by B. L. Woolf. London: Nicholson & Watson.

———. 1932. *Jungfrauensohn und Krippenkind: Untersuchungen zur Geburtsgeschichte Jesu im Lukas-Evangelium*. Heidelberg: Winters.

Dittenberger, W. 1960. *Sylloge Inscriptionum Graecarum*, Volume 2. 4th ed. Hildesheim: Olms.

Dodd, C. H. [1935] 1936a. *The Parables of the Kingdom*. Reprinted (revised). London: Nisbet.

———. 1936b. *The Apostolic Preaching and Its Developments*. London: Hodder & Stoughton.

———. [1936] 1956. *The Apostolic Preaching and Its Developments*. New York: Harper.

Dormeyer, D. 1989. *Evangelium als literarische und theologische Gattung*. EdF 263. Darmstadt: Wissenschaftliche Buchgesellschaft.

Douglas, M. 1973. *Implicit Meanings: Essays on Anthropology*. London: Routledge & Kegan Paul.

Downing, F. G. 1988. *Christ and the Cynics: Jesus and Other Radical Preachers in First-Century Tradition*. JSOT Manuals 4. Sheffield, UK: Sheffield Academic.

Duling, D. C. 1991. "Matthew's Son of David in Social Science Perspective: Kinship, Kingship, and Magic. Unpublished paper presented at the First International Conference on the New Testament and Social Sciences at Medina del Campo, Spain.

———. 1999. "The Jesus Movement and Social Network Analysis (Part I: The Spatial Network)." *BTB* 29:156–75.

Duling, D. C., and N. Perrin. [1974] 1994. *The New Testament: Proclamation and Parenesis, Myth and History*. 3rd ed. Fort Worth: Harcourt Brace.

Dunn, J. D. G. 1975. *Jesus and the Spirit*. London: SCM.

———. 1980. *Christology in the Making: An Inquiry into the Origins of the Doctrine of the Incarnation*. London: SCM.

———. 1991. *The Parting of the Ways: Between Christianity and Judaism and Their Significance for the Character of Christianity*. London: SCM.

———. 1994. "The Making of Christology—Evolution or Unfolding?" In *Jesus of Nazareth: Lord and Christ; Essays on the Historical Jesus and New Testament Christology*, edited by J. B. Green and M. Turner, 437–52. Grand Rapids: Eerdmans.

———. 1999. *The Theology of the Apostle Paul*. Edinburgh: T. & T. Clark.

Du Toit, A. B. 1999. "What Has Tarsus to Do with Jerusalem?" Unpublished paper, SNTS Annual Meeting, University of Pretoria, August 1999.

Eagleton, T. 1976. *Criticism and Ideology: A Study in Marxist Literary Theory.* London: Verso.
———. 1983. *Literary Theory: An Introduction.* Minneapolis: University of Minnesota Press.
Eden, P. T., editor. 1984. *"Apocolocyntosis," by Seneca.* Cambridge Greek and Latin Classics. Cambridge: Cambridge University Press.
Eilberg-Schwartz, H. 1990. *The Savage in Judaism: An Anthropology of Israelite Religion and Ancient Judaism.* Bloomington: Indiana University Press.
Eisenstadt, S. N. 1968. "Weber and Modern Sociology." In Max Weber, *On Charisma and Institution Building: Selected Papers,* edited by S. N. Eisenstadt. Chicago: University of Chicago Press.
Ellingworth, P. 1994. "Christology: Synchronic or Diachronic?" In *Jesus of Nazareth: Lord and Christ; Essays on the Historical Jesus and New Testament Christology,* edited by Joel B. Green and M. Turner, 489–500. Grand Rapids: Eerdmans.
Elliott, J. H. 1985. Review of *The First Urban Christians* by Wayne A. Meeks. *Religious Studies Review* 11:329–35.
———. 1993. *What Is Social-scientific Criticism?* GBS. Minneapolis: Fortress.
Elsas, C. 1993. "Herrscherkult." In *HRWG* 3:115–22.
Ernst, J. 1989. *Johannes der Täufer: Interpretation—Geschichte—Wirkungsgeschichte.* BZNW 53. Berlin: de Gruyter.
Eschenburg, T. 1976. *Über Autorität.* Frankfurt: Suhrkamp.
Esler, P. F. [1987] 1996. *Community and Gospel in Luke-Acts: The Social and Political Motivations of Lucan Theology.* SNTSMS 57. Reprinted. Cambridge: Cambridge University Press.
Etzioni, A. 1961. *A Comparative Analysis of Complex Organizations: On Power, Involvement, and Their Correlates.* New York: Free Press.
———. 1968. *The Active Society: A Theory of Societal and Political Processes.* London: Macmillan.
Feine, P. 1934. *Theologie des Neuen Testaments.* 6th ed. Leipzig: Hinrichs.
Fiensy, D. A. 1991. *The Social History of Palestine in the Herodian Period: The Land Is Mine.* Studies in the Bible and Early Christianity 20. Lewiston, NY: Mellen.
———. 1999. "Leaders of Mass Movements and the Leader of the Jesus Movement." *JSNT* 74:3–27.
Fink, C. F. 1968. "Some Conceptual Difficulties in the Theory of Social Conflict." *Journal of Conflict Resolution* 12:412–60.
Fitzmyer, J. A. 1968. Review of Matthew Black, *An Aramaic Approach to the Gospels and Acts.* 3rd ed. *CBQ* 30:426–27.
———. 1989. *Luke the Theologian: Aspects of His Teaching.* London: Chapman.
Foster, G. M. 1967. "What Is a Peasant?" In *Peasant Society: A Reader,* edited by J. M. Potter et al., 2–14. Boston: Little, Brown.
Foucault, M. 1972. *The Archaeology of Knowledge.* Translated by A. M. Sheridan Smith. New York: Harper & Row.
———. 1980. "Power Strategies." In *Power/Knowledge: Selected Interviews and Other Writings 1972–1977,* edited by Colin Gordon. Translated by Colin Gordon et al. New York: Pantheon.
Freyne, S. 1980. *Galilee from Alexander the Great to Hadrian, 323 BCE to 135 CE: A Study of Second Temple Judaism.* Wilmington, DE: Glazier.

Bibliography

———. 1988. *Galilee, Jesus, and the Gospels: Literary Approaches and Historical Investigations*. Philadelphia: Fortress.
Friedrich, C. J. 1958. "Authority, Reason and Discretion." In *Authority*, edited by C. J. Friedrich, 27–48. Nomos 1. Cambridge: Harvard University Press.
Friedrich, Gerhard. 1956. "Beobachtungen zur messianischen Hohepriestererwartung in den Synoptikern." *ZTK* 53:265–311.
Funk, R. W. 1996. *Honest to Jesus: Jesus for a New Millennium*. San Francisco: HarperCollins.
Funk, R. W., R. W. Hoover, and The Jesus Seminar. [1993] 1997. *The Five Gospels: The Search for the Authentic Words of Jesus*. New York: Macmillan.
Funk, R. W., and The Jesus Seminar. 1998. *The Acts of Jesus: What Did Jesus Really Do?* San Francisco: HarperSanFrancisco.
———. 1999. *The Gospel of Jesus according to the Jesus Seminar*. Sonoma, CA: Polebridge.
Galtung, J. 1990. "International Development in Human Perspective." In *Conflict: Human Needs Theory*, edited by John Burton, 301–35. Conflict Series 2. Basingstoke, UK: Macmillan.
Gärtner, B. 1965. *The Temple and the Community in Qumran and the New Testament: A Comparative Study in the Temple Symbolism of the Qumran Texts and the New Testament*. SNTSMS 1. Cambridge: Cambridge University Press.
Gennep, A. van. 1961. "On the Rites of Passage." In *Theories of Society: Foundations of Modern Sociological Theory* 1:950. New York: Free Press of Glencoe.
Gennep, F. O. van. 1989. *De terugkeer van de verloren vader: Een theologisch essay over vaderschap en macht in cultuur en christendom*. Baarn: Ten Have.
Gerhardsson, Birger. 1986. *The Gospel Tradition*. Coniectanea biblica: New Testament Series 15. Lund: Gleerup.
Geyser, A. S. 1945. "Die vroegste heidenberig oor Christus en die Christene." *HvTSt* 2.1:5–16.
———. 1956. "The Youth of John the Baptist: A Deduction from the Break in the Parallel Account of the Lucan Infancy Story." *NovT* 1:70–75.
———. 1986. "Israel in the Fourth Gospel." *Neotestamentica* 2:13–20.
Geyser, P. A. 1999a. "Die hermeneutiese uitgangspunte in die 'nuwe historiese' benadering tot Jesus-studies." DD diss., University of Pretoria.
———. 1999b. "Bronne vir Jesus-studies." *HvTSt* 55.1:3–21.
———. 2000. "Waarom Jesus-studies?" *HvTSt* 56.1:63–83.
Goodenough, E. R. 1962. *An Introduction to Philo Judaeus*. Oxford: Blackwell.
Gottwald, N. K. 1979. *The Tribes of Yahweh: A Sociology of the Religion of Liberated Israel, 1250–1050 BC*. London: SCM.
Gottwald, N. K., editor. 1983. *The Bible and Liberation: Political and Social Hermeneutics*. Maryknoll, NY: Orbis.
Goulder, Michael D. 1983. "From Ministry to Passion in John and Luke." *NTS* 29:561–68.
———. 1989a. *Luke: A New Paradigm*. Vol. 1, Part 1, *The Argument*. Part 2, *Commentary: Luke 1.1—9.50*. JSNTSup 20. Sheffield, UK: Sheffield Academic.
———. 1989b. *Luke: A New Paradigm*. Vol. 2, Part 2 (cont.). *Commentary: Luke 9.51—24.53*. JSNTSup 20. Sheffield, UK: Sheffield Academic.
Gowan, D. E. 1986. *Eschatology in the Old Testament*. Philadelphia: Fortress.
Gräbe, I. 1986. "Narratologiese ondersoek en eksegese van die boodskap van die evangelies." *HvTSt* 42:151–68.
Green, J. B. 1997. *The Gospel of Luke*. NICNT. Grand Rapids: Eerdmans.

Bibliography

Grenfell, B. P. et al., editors. 1898–1927. *The Oxyrhynchus Papyri*. 17 vols. London: Egypt Exploration.

Grillmeier, A. 1965. *Christ in Christian Tradition: From the Apostolic Age to Chalcedon (451)*. Translated by J. S. Bowden. London: Mowbray.

Grundmann, Walter. 1956. "Sohn Gottes: Ein Diskussionsbeitrag." *ZNW* 47:113–33.

———. 1959. "Fragen der Komposition des lukanischen Reiseberichts." *ZNW* 50:252–70.

Gunneweg, H. J., and Walter Schmithals. [1980] 1982. *Authority*. Translated by John E. Steely. Biblical Encounter Series. Nashville: Abingdon.

Hadas, M., and M. Smith. 1965. *Heroes and Gods: Spiritual Biographies in Antiquity*. Religious Perspectives 13. London: Routledge & Kegan Paul.

Hahn, F. [1963] 1974a. *Christologische Hoheitstitel: Ihre Geschichte im frühen Christentum*. 4th ed. FRLANT 83. Göttingen: Vandenhoeck & Ruprecht.

———. 1974b. "Methodologische Überlegungen zur Ruckfrage nach Jesus." In *Rückfrage nach Jesus: Zur Methodik und Bedeutung der Frage nach dem historischen Jesus*, edited by K. Kertelge, 11–77. 2nd ed. QD 63. Freiburg: Herder.

Hanson, K. C., and Oakman, D. E. 1998. *Palestine in the Time of Jesus: Social Structures and Social Conflicts*. Minneapolis: Fortress.

Hare, D. R. A. 1967. *The Theme of Jewish Persecution of Christians in the Gospel according to St. Matthew*. SNTSMS 6. Cambridge: Cambridge University Press.

———. 1990. *The Son of Man Tradition*. Minneapolis: Fortress.

Harper, G. McL. Jr. 1928. *Village Administration in the Roman Province of Syria*. Princeton: Princeton University Press.

Harris, M. J. 1992. *Jesus as God: The New Testament Use of "Theos" in Reference to Jesus*. Grand Rapids: Baker.

Hartmann, H. 1964. *Funktionale Autorität: Systematische Abhandlung zu einem soziologischen Begriff*. Soziologische Gegenwartsfragen 22. Stuttgart: Kohlhammer.

Heitmuller, W. 1912. "Zum Problem Paulus und Jesus." *ZNW* 13:320–37.

Hekman, Susan J. 1983. *Weber, the Ideal Type, and Contemporary Social Theory*. Notre Dame: University of Notre Dame Press.

Hengel, M. 1961. *Die Zeloten*. AGSU 1. Leiden: Brill.

———. [1968] 1981. *The Charismatic Leader and His Followers*. Translated by J. C. Greig. Edinburgh: T. & T. Clark.

———. 1973. *Judentum und Hellenismus: Studien zu ihrer Begegnung unter besonderer Berücksichtigung Palästinas bis zur Mitte des 2.Jh.s v. Chr.* WUNT 10. Tübingen: Mohr/Siebeck.

———. [1973] 1974a. *Judaism and Hellenism*. Translated by John Bowden. Philadelphia: Fortress.

———. 1974b. *Property and Riches in the Early Church*. Translated by John Bowden. London: SCM.

———. 1976. *Juden, Griechen und Barbaren: Aspekte der Hellenisierung des Judentums in vorchristlicher Zeit*. SBS 76. Stuttgart: KBW.

Herder, J. G. [1780–81] 1879. "Das Studium der Theologie betreffend." In *Herders Sämmtliche Werke*. Vol. 10. Edited by B. Suphan. Berlin: Weidmann.

Herion, G. A. 1986. "The Impact of Modern and Social Science Assumptions on the Reconstruction of Israelite History." *JSOT* 34:3–33.

Higgins, A. J. B. 1980. *The Son of Man in the Teaching of Jesus*. SNTSMS 39. Cambridge: Cambridge University Press.

Bibliography

Hills, Julian. 1989. *Tradition and Composition in the Epistula Apostolorum.* Philadelphia: Fortress.
Hoffmann, Paul. [1992] 1994. "The Redaction of Q and the Son of Man: A Preliminary Sketch." In *The Gospel behind the Gospels: Current Studies on Q*, edited by Ronald A. Piper, 159–98. NovTSup 75. Leiden: Brill.
Holmberg, Bengt. 1978. *Paul and Power: The Structure of Authority in the Primitive Church as Reflected in the Pauline Epistles.* Coniectanea Biblica: New Testament Series 11. Lund: Gleerup.
———. 1990. *Sociology and the New Testament: An Appraisal.* Minneapolis: Fortress.
Holtzmann, Heinrich Julius. 1863. *Die synoptische Evangelien: Ihr Ursprung und geschichtlicher Charakter.* Leipzig: Engelmann.
Horbury, William. 1998. *Jewish Messianism and the Cult of Christ.* London: SCM.
Horrell, David G. [1997] 1999a. "Introduction—Social scientific Interpretation of the New Testament: Retrospect and Prospect." In *Social-scientific Approaches to New Testament Interpretation*, edited by David G. Horrell, 3–27. Edinburgh: T. & T. Clark.
———. [1997] 1999b. "Leadership Patterns and the Development of Ideology in Early Christianity." In *Social-scientific Approaches to New Testament Interpretation*, edited by David G. Horrell, 309–38. Edinburgh: T. & T. Clark.
Horsley, Richard A. 1979. "Josephus and the Bandits." *Journal of Jewish Studies* 10:37–63.
———. 1991. "The Q People: Renovation, not Radicalism." *Continuum* 1:49–63.
———. 1994. "The Death of Jesus." In *Studying the Historical Jesus*, edited by Bruce Chilton and Craig A. Evans, 395–422. NTTS 19. Leiden: Brill.
———. 1995. "Social Conflict in the Synoptic Sayings Source Q." In *Conflict and Invention: Literary, Rhetorical and Social Studies on the Sayings Gospel Q*, edited by John S. Kloppenborg, 37–52. Valley Forge, PA: Trinity.
———. 1996. *Archaeology, History, and Society in Galilee: The Social Context of Jesus and the Rabbis.* Valley Forge, PA: Trinity.
———. 2007. *Scribes, Visionaries and the Politics of Second Temple Judea.* Louisville: Westminster John Knox.
Horsley, Richard A., and John S. Hanson. 1985. *Bandits, Prophets, and Messiahs: Popular Movements in the Time of Jesus.* Minneapolis: Fortress.
Howell, David B. 1990. *Matthew's Inclusive Story: A Study in the Narrative Rhetoric of the First Gospel.* JSNTSup 42. Sheffield: JSOT Press.
Huntress, E. 1935. "'Son of God' in Jewish Writings prior to the Christian Era." *JBL* 54:117–23.
Hurtado, Larry. 1979. "New Testament Christology: A Critique of Bousset's Influence." *TS* 40:306–17.
Jacobson, Arland D. 1978. "Wisdom Christology in Q." PhD dissertation, Claremont.
———. 1982. "The Literary Unity of Q." *JBL* 101:365–89.
———. 1992. *The First Gospel: An Introduction to Q.* Foundations and Facets Series. Reprinted, Eugene, OR: Wipf & Stock, 2005.
Jamieson-Drake, D. W. 1991. *Scribes and Schools in Monarchic Judah: A Socio-archeological Approach.* JSOTSup 109. Sheffield: Almond.
Jeremias, Joachim. [1936] 1966. Die Salbungsgeschichte Mk. 14, 3–9." In *und Zeitgeschichte*, 107–15. Göttingen: Vandenhoeck & Ruprecht.
———. 1952. "*pais Theou.*" In *Theologisches Wörterbuch zum Neuen Testament*, Vol. 5. Edited by Gerhard Friedrich, 698–713. Stuttgart: Kohlhammer.

———. 1953. "Kennzeichen der *ipsissima vox* Jesu." In *Synoptische Studien*, edited by Alfred Winkenhauser, 86-93. Munich: Zink.

———. 1958. *Heiligengräber in Jesu Umwelt (Mt. 23,29; Lk. 11,47): Eine Untersuchung zur Volksreligion der Zeit Jesu*. Göttingen: Vandenhoeck & Ruprecht.

———. 1960. "Der gegenwärtige Stand der Debatte um das Problem des historischen Jesus." In *Der historische Jesus und der kerygmatische Christus*, edited by H. Ristow and K. Matthiae, 12-25. Berlin: Evangelische Verlagsanstalt.

———. [1962] 1969. *Jerusalem zur Zeit Jesu: Eine kulturgeschichtliche Untersuchung zur Neutestamentlichen Zeitgeschichte*. 3rd ed. Göttingen: Vandenhoeck & Ruprecht.

———. [1962] [1967] 1969. *Jerusalem in the Time of Jesus: An Investigation into Economic and Social Conditions during the New Testament Period*. London: SCM.

———. 1967. Älteste Schicht der Menschensohn-Logien. *ZNW* 58:159-72.

———. 1969. *Jerusalem in the Time of Jesus: An Investigation into Economic and Social Conditions during the New Testament Period*. Philadelphia: Fortress.

Jeppesen, K. 1994. "Then Began Men to Call upon the Name of Yahweh: An Idea." In *In the Last Days: On Jewish and Christian Apocalyptic and Its Period*, edited by K. Jeppesen et al., 158-63. Aarhus: Aarhus University Press.

Jervell, Jacob. 1962. *Luke and the People of God: A New Look at Luke-Acts*. Minneapolis: Augsburg.

Kähler, Martin. [1896] 1969. *Der sogenannte historische Jesus und der geschichtliche, biblische Christus*. Neu herausgegeben von E. Wolf. 4th ed. Munich: Kaiser.

Käsemann, Ernst. [1954] 1960a. "Das Problem des historischen Jesus," in *Exegetische Versuche und Besinnungen*, Erster Band, 187-214. Göttingen: Vandenhoeck. [Originally published in *ZTK* 51:125-53.]

———. 1960b. Die Anfänge christlicher Theologie. *ZTK* 57: 162-85.

———. 1954-55. "Sätze heiligen Rechtes im Neuen Testament." *NTS* 1:248-60.

Kee, Howard Clark. 1973. "Aretology and Gospel." *JBL* 92:402-22.

———. 1989. *Knowing the Truth: A Sociological Approach to New Testament Interpretation*. Minneapolis: Fortress.

Kenney, W. 1966. *How to Analyze Fiction*. New York: Monarch.

Kippenberg, Hans G. 1978. *Religion und Klassenbildung im antiken Judäa: Eine religionssoziologische Studie zum Verhältnis von Tradition und Gesellschaftlicher Entwicklung*. SUNT 14. Göttingen: Vandenhoeck & Ruprecht.

Kirk, Alan. 2005. "The Memory of Violence and the Death of Jesus in Q." In *Memory, Tradition, and Text: Users of the Past in Early Christianity*, edited by Alan Kirk and Tom Thatcher, 191-206. SemeiaSt 52. Atlanta: Society of Biblical Literture.

Kingsbury, Jack Dean. 1975. *Matthew: Structure, Christology, Kingdom*. London: SPCK.

———. 1977. *Matthew: A Commentary for Preachers and Others*. London: SPCK.

———. 1981. *Jesus Christ in Matthew, Mark, and Luke*. Proclamation Commentaries. Philadelphia: Fortress.

———. 1986. *Matthew as Story*. Philadelphia: Fortress.

Kloppenborg, John S. 1987. *The Formation of Q: Trajectories in Ancient Wisdom Collections*. Studies in Antiquity and Christianity. Philadelphia: Fortress.

———. 1988. *Q Parallels: Synopsis, Critical Notes & Concordance*. Sonoma, CA: Polebridge.

———. 1991. "Literary Convention, Self-evidence and the Social History of the Q People." *Semeia* 55:77-102.

———. 1993. "The Sayings Gospel Q: Recent Opinion on the People behind the Document. *Currents in Research: Biblical Studies* 1:9-34.

Bibliography

———. 1999. "Patronage Avoidance in James." *HvTSt* 55:755–94.
———. 2000. *Excavating Q: The History and Setting of the Sayings Gospel*. Minneapolis: Fortress.
Kobelski, Paul J. 1981. *Melchizedek and Melchiresa*. CBQMS 10. Washington, DC: Catholic Biblical Association.
Koester, Helmut. 1971a. "One Jesus and Four Primitive Gospels." In *Trajectories through Early Christianity*, James M. Robinson and Helmut Koester, 158–204. Philadelphia: Fortress.
———. 1971b. "Jesus as the Divine Man (Aretologies)." In *Trajectories through Early Christianity*, James M. Robinson and Helmut Koester, 187–193. Philadelphia: Fortress.
———. 1990. *Ancient Christian Gospels: Their history and Development*. Philadelphia: Trinity.
———. 1992. "Jesus the Victim." *JBL* 111:3–15.
———. 1994. "The Historical Jesus and the Historical Situation of the Quest: An Epilogue." In *Studying the Historical Jesus*, edited by Bruce Chilton and Craig A. Evans, 535–46. NTTS 19. Leiden: Brill.
Köhler, K. 1901. "Abba, Father, Title of Spiritual Leader and Saint." *Jewish Quarterly Review* 13:567–80.
Kriesberg, Louis. 1973. *The Sociology of Social Conflicts*. Englewood Cliffs, NJ: Prentice-Hall.
Kruger, P. 2000. "Sosiologiese en antropologiese insigte en die studie van die Hebreeuse Bybel: 'n Bestekopname." *HvTSt* 56.1:137–73.
Kuhn, H.-W. 1971. *Ältere Sammlungen im Markusevangelium*. SUNT 8. Göttingen: Vandenhoeck & Ruprecht.
Kuhn, K.G. 1954–55. "Die beiden Messias Aarons und Israels." *NTS* 1:168–79.
Kümmel Werner Georg. 1934. "Jesus und der jüdische Traditionsgedanke." *ZNW* 33:105–30.
———. 1950. "Das Gleichnis von den bösen Weingärtnern (Mark 12,1–9)." In *Aux sources de la tradition chrétienne: Mélanges Offerts à M. Goguel*, 120–31. Neuchâtel.
Kundera, Milan. [1967] 1992. *The Joke*. Translated by A. Asher. London: Faber & Faber.
Leivestad, R. 1968. "Der apokalyptische Menschensohn: Ein theologisches Phantom." *Annual of the Swedish Theological Institute (in Jerusalem)* 6:49–105.
Lemche, Niels Peter. 1996. *Die Vorgeschichte Israels: Von den Anfängen bis zum Ausgang des 13. Jahrhunderts v. Chr.* Biblische Enzyklopädie 1. Stuttgart: Kohlhammer.
Lemmen, M. M. W. 1990. *Max Weber's Sociology of Religion: Its Method and Content in the Light of the Concept of Rationality*. Hilversum: Gooi & Sticht.
Lenski, Gerhard E. 1966. *Power and Privilege: A Theory of Social Stratification*. New York: McGraw-Hill.
———. 1985. "A Theory of Inequality." In *Three Sociological Traditions: Selected Readings*, edited by R. Collins, 89–116. New York: Oxford University Press.
Lenski Gerhard et al. [1970] 1995. *Human Societies: An Introduction to Macrosociology*. 7th ed. New York: McGraw-Hill.
Levine, Lee I. 1992. "The Sages and the Synagogue in Late Antiquity." In *The Galilee in Late Antiquity*, edited by Lee I. Levine 201–22. New York: Jewish Theological Seminary.
Loffreda, Stanislao. [1993] 1997. *Recovering Capharnaum*. 2nd ed. Studium Biblicum Franciscanum Guides 1. Reprinted. Jerusalem: Franciscan.

Lohmeyer, Ernst. 1922. "Die Verklärung Jesu nach dem Markus-Evangelium." *ZNW* 21:185-215.

———. 1936. *Galiläa und Jerusalem*. FRLANT 34. Göttingen: Vandenhoeck & Ruprecht.

———. [1951] 1953. *Das Evangelium des Markus*. 12th ed. KEK 1/2. Göttingen: Vandenhoeck & Ruprecht.

Lohr, C. H. 1961. "Oral Techniques in the Gospel of Matthew." *CBQ* 23:403-35.

Lüdemann, Gerd. [1994] 1994. *The Resurrection of Jesus: History, Experience, Theology*. Translated by John Bowden. Minneapolis: Fortress.

Luhmann, N. 1970. "System der Gesellschaft." In *Zur Theorie der Institution*, edited by H. Schelsky, 27-41. Interdisziplinäre Studien 1. Düsseldorf: Bertelsmann.

Lührmann, Dieter. 1969. *Die Redaktion der Logienquelle*. WMANT 33. Neukirchen-Vluyn: Neukirchener.

Luz, Ulrich. [1965] 1983. "The Secrecy Motif and the Marcan Christology." In *The Messianic Secret*, edited by Christopher Tuckett, 75-96. IRT 1. Philadelphia: Fortress.

Lyotard, Jean-Francois. 1984. *The Postmodern Condition: A Report on Knowledge*. Translated by Geoff Bennington and Brian Massumi. Theory and History of Literature 10. Minneapolis: University of Minnesota Press.

———. 1993. *The Postmodern Explained: Correspondence, 1982-1985*. Translated and edited by Julian Pefanis and Morgan Thomas. Minneapolis: University of Minnesota Press.

Mack, Burton L. 1988. *A Myth of Innocence: Mark and Christian Origins*. Philadelphia: Fortress.

———. 1993. *The Lost Gospel Q: The Book of Christian Origins*. San Francisco: HarperSanFrancisco.

Malbon, Elizabeth Struthers. [1982] 1995. "Galilee and Jerusalem: History and literature in Marcan Interpretation." In *The Interpretation of Mark*, edited by W. R. Telford, 253-68. 2nd ed. Studies in New Testament Interpretation. Edinburgh: T. & T. Clark.

Malina, Bruce J. 1988. "A Conflict Approach to Mark 7." *Foundations & Facets Forum* 4/3:3-30.

———. [1981] 1993. *The New Testament World: Insights from Cultural Anthropology*. 2nd ed. Louisville: Westminster John Knox.

———. 1993b. *Windows on the World of Jesus: Time Travel to Ancient Judea*. Louisville: Westminster John Knox.

———. 1996. *The Social World of Jesus and the Gospels*. London: Routledge.

Malina, Bruce J., and Jerome H. Neyrey. 1988. *Calling Jesus Names: The Social Value of Labels in Matthew*. Sonoma, CA: Polebridge.

Malina, Bruce J., and Richard L. Rohrbaugh. 1992. *Social Science Commentary on the Synoptic Gospels*. Minneapolis: Fortress.

Mandelbaum, Maurice. 1977. *The Anatomy of Historical Knowledge*. Baltimore: John Hopkins University Press.

Manson, T. W. [1937] 1949. *The Sayings of Jesus: As Recorded in the Gospels according to St Matthew and St Luke Arranged with Introduction and Commentary*. First published as Part II of *The Mission and Message of Jesus*. London: SCM.

Marshall, I. Howard. 1967. "The Development of Christology in the Early Church." *Tyndale Bulletin* 18:77-93.

———. [1970] 1992. *Luke: Historian and Theologian*. Reprinted. Guernsey, UK: Paternoster.

Bibliography

———. [1976] 1977. *The Origins of New Testament Christology*. Second printing. Leicester, UK: InterVarsity.

———. [1976] 1990. *The Origins of New Testament Christology*. Updated ed. Issues in Contemporary Interpretation. Leicester, UK: InterVarsity.

Marxsen, Willi. 1976. "Jesus—Bringer oder Inhalt des Evangeliums?" In *Die Sache Jesu geht weiter*, 45–62. Gütersloher Taschenbücher 12. Gütersloh: Gütersloher.

Matera, Frank J. [1988] 1995. "The Prologue as the Interpretative Key to Mark's Gospel." In *The Interpretation of Mark*, edited by W. R. Telford, 289–306. 2nd ed. Studies in New Testament Interpretation. Edinburgh: T. & T. Clark.

McKay, H. 1998. "Ancient Synagogues: The Continuing Dialectic between Two Major Views." *Currents in Research: Biblical Studies* 6:103–42.

McKerrow, R. 1999. "Contemporary Rhetorical Theory: A Reader." In *Critical Rhetoric: Theory and Practice*, edited by J. L. Lucaites et al., 441–63. New York: Guilford.

McVann, Mark. 1991. "Baptism, Miracles, and Boundary Jumping in Mark." *BTB* 21:151–57.

Mercer, Samuel A. B. 1942. *Horus, Royal God of Egypt*. Grafton, MA: Society of Oriental Research.

Mettinger, T. N. D. 1971. *Solomonic State Officials: A Study of the Civil Government Officials of the Israelite Monarchy*. Coniectanea Biblica: Old Testament Series 5. Lund: Gleerup.

Miller, Robert J. 2000. "The Case for the Non-apocalyptic Jesus. Unpublished paper presented at the Westar Institute's Jesus Seminar, 1–5 March 2000, Santa Rosa, California.

Mödritzer, Helmut. 1994. *Stigma und Charisma im Neuen Testament und seiner Umwelt: Zur Soziologie des Urchristentums*. NTOA 28. Göttingen: Vandenhoeck & Ruprecht.

Montgomery, J. A. [1907] 1968. *The Samaritans: The Earliest Jewish Sect. Their History, Theology and Literature*, with an introduction by A. S. Halkin. New York: Ktav.

Moore, George Foot. [1927] 1962. *Judaism in the First Centuries of the Christian Era: The Age of the Tannaim*, vol. 1. Cambridge: Harvard University Press.

Moore, Stephen D. 1989. *Literary Criticism and the Gospels: The Theoretical Challenge*. New Haven: Yale University Press.

Mowinckel, Sigmund. [1951] 1956. *He That Cometh*. Translated by G. W. Anderson. Nashville: Abingdon.

Muhly, J. D. [1973] 1976. *Copper and Tin: The Distribution of Metal Resources and the Nature of the Metals Trade in the Bronze Age*. New Haven: Yale University Press.

Murphy-O'Connor, Jerome. [1980] 1998. *The Holy Land: An Oxford Archaeological Guide from earliest times to 1700*. 4th ed. Oxford Archaeological Guides. Oxford: Oxford University Press.

Myers, Ched. [1988] 1992. *Binding the Strong Man: A Political Reading of Mark's Story of Jesus*. Maryknoll, NY: Orbis.

Mylonas, G. E. 1961. *Eleusis and the Eleusinian Mysteries*. Princeton: Princeton University Press.

Nader, Laura, and Harry F. Todd Jr., editors. 1978. *The Disputing Process: Law in Ten Societies*. New York: Columbia University Press.

Neusner, Jacob. 1982. *Formative Judaism: Religious, Historical, and Literary Studies*. BJS 37. Chico, CA: Scholars.

———. [1984] 1988. *Judaism in the Beginning of Christianity*. Second printing. Philadelphia: Fortress.

———. 1991. *An Introduction to Judaism: A Textbook and Reader.* Louisville: Westminster John Knox.

Newman, B. M. [1971] 1993. *A Concise Greek-English Dictionary of the New Testament* Stuttgart: Deutsche Bibelgesellschaft.

Neyrey, Jerome H. 1991. "The Symbolic Universe of Luke-Acts: 'They turn the world upside down.'" In *The Social World of Luke-Acts: Models for Interpretation*, edited by Jerome H. Neyrey, 271–304. Peabody, MA: Hendrickson.

———. 1998. "Questions, *Chreiai*, and Challenges to Honor: The Interface of Rhetoric and Culture in Mark's Gospel." *CBQ* 60:657–81.

———. 2004. *Render to God: New Testament Understandings of the Divine.* Minneapolis: Fortress.

Oakman, Douglas E. 1996. "The Ancient Economy." In *The Social Sciences and New Testament Interpretation*, edited by Richard L. Rohrbaugh, 126–43. Peabody, MA: Hendrickson.

———. 1999. "The Lord's Prayer in Social Perspective." In *Authenticating the Words of Jesus*, edited by Bruce Chilton and Craig A. Evans, 137–86. NTTS 28.1. Leiden: Brill.

Oldfather, C. H. 1935. *Diodorus of Sicily*, with an English translation. LCL. Cambridge: Harvard University Press.

Ord, David R., and Robert B. Coote. 1994. *Is the Bible True? Understanding the Bible Today.* Maryknoll, NY: Orbis.

Orton, David E. 1989. *The Understanding Scribe: Matthew and the Apocalyptic Ideal.* JSNTSup 25. Sheffield, UK: Sheffield Academic.

Osborne, Grant R. 1994. "Structure and Christology in Mark 1:21–45." In *Jesus of Nazareth: Lord and Christ; Essays on the Historical Jesus in New Testament Christology*, edited by Joel B. Green and Max Turner, 147–63. Grand Rapid: Eerdmans.

Osiek, Carolyn. 1993. "The Women at the Tomb: What Are They Doing There?" *Ex Auditu* 9:97–107.

———. 2000. "From Women and Slaves to Women Slaves: The Neglected Minority." Unpublished paper discussed at the March 2000 Meeting of the Context Group, Portland, Oregon.

Overholt, Thomas W. 1996. *Cultural Anthropology and the Old Testament.* GBS. Minneapolis: Fortress.

Overman, J. Andrew. 1990. *Matthew's Gospel and Formative Judaism: The Social World of the Matthean Community.* Minneapolis: Fortress.

Parsons, Talcott.1937. *The Structure of Social Action.* New York: McGraw-Hill.

———. 1977. *The Evolution of Societies*, edited and with an introduction by J. Toby. Prentice-Hall Foundation of Modern Sociology Series. Englewood Cliffs, NJ: Prentice-Hall.

Patterson, Stephen J. 1993. *The Gospel of Thomas and Jesus.* Foundations & Facets Reference Series. Sonoma, CA: Polebridge.

———. 1998. *The God of Jesus: The Historical Jesus and the Search for Meaning.* Harrisburg, PA: Trinity.

Perdue, Leo G. 2008. "Sages, Scribes, and Seers in Israel and the Ancient Near East: An Introduction." In *Scribes, Sages, and Seers: The Sage in the Eastern Mediterranean World*, edited by Leo G. Perdue, 1–34. FRLANT 219. Göttingen: Vandenhoeck & Ruprecht.

Perrin, Norman. 1965–66. "Mark XIV.62: The End Product of a Christian Pesher Tradition." *NTS* 12:150–55.

———. 1966. "The Son of Man in Ancient Judaism and Primitive Christianity: A Suggestion." *BR* 11:27–28.
———. 1969. *What Is Redaction Criticism?* GBS. Philadelphia: Fortress.
Petersen, Norman R. 1978a. "'Point of View' in Mark's Narrative." *Semeia* 12:97–121.
———. 1978b. *Literary Criticism for New Testament Critics*. GBS. Philadelphia: Fortress.
———. 1985. *Rediscovering Paul: Philemon and the Sociology of Paul's Narrative World*. Reprinted, Eugene, OR: Wipf & Stock, 2008.
Piper, Ronald A. 1989. *Wisdom in the Q-tradition: The Aphoristic Teaching of Jesus*. SNTSMS 61. Cambridge: Cambridge University Press.
———. 1995a. The Language of Violence and the Aphoristic Sayings in Q: A Study of Q 6:27–36." In *Conflict and invention: Literary, Rhetorical and Social Studies on the Sayings Gospel Q*, edited by John S. Kloppenborg, 53–72. Valley Forge, PA: Trinity.
———, editor. 1995b. *The Gospel behind the Gospels: Current Studies on Q*. NovTSup 75. Leiden: Brill.
Polag, Athanasius. 1982. *Fragmenta Q*. Neukirchen-Vluyn: Neukirchener.
Preuss, H. D. 1978. *Eschatologie im Altem Testament*. Wege der Forschung. Darmstadt: Wissenschaftliche Buchgesellschaft.
Rawlinson, A. E. J. 1926. *The New Testament Doctrine of Christ*. London: Longmans Green.
Recaniti, Francois. 1987. *Meaning and Force: The Pragmatics of Performative Utterances*. Cambridge Studies in Philosophy. Cambridge: Cambridge University Press.
Redfield, Robert. 1956. *Peasant Society and Culture*. Chicago: University of Chicago Press.
Redman, Charles L. 1978. *The Rise of Civilization: From Early Farmers to Urban Society in the Ancient Near East*. San Francisco: Freeman.
Reed, Jonathan L. 1994. "Places in Early Christianity: Galilee, Archaeology, Urbanization, and Q." PhD diss., Claremont Graduate School.
Reicke, Bo. 1959. "Instruction and Discussion in the Travel Narrative." *Studia Evangelica* 1:206–16.
Reitzenstein, Richard. 1910. *Die hellenistischen Mysterienreligionen: Ihre Grundgedanken und Wirkungen*. Berlin: Teubner.
Robbins, Vernon K. 1975. "The We-Passages in Acts and Ancient Sea Voyages." *BR* 20:5–18.
———. 1978. "By Land and Sea: The We-Passages and Ancient Sea Voyages." In *Perspectives on Luke-Acts*, edited by Charles H. Talbert, 215–42. Danville, VA: Association of Baptist Professors of Religion.
———. 1984. *Jesus the Teacher: A Socio-Rhetorical Interpretation of Mark*. Philadelphia: Fortress.
Robinson, J. A. T. 1957–1958. "Elijah, John and Jesus: An Essay in Detection." *NTS* 4:263–81.
Robinson, James M. 1970. "On the *Gattung* of Mark (and John)." In *Jesus and Man's Hope*, edited by Donald G. Miller and Dikran Y. Hadidian, 1:99–129. Pittsburgh: Pittsburgh Theological Seminary.
———. 1971a. "The Johannine Trajectory." In *Trajectories through Early Christianity*, James M. Robinson and Helmut Koester, 232–68. Reprinted, Eugene, OR: Wipf & Stock, 2006.
———. 1971b. "LOGOI SOPHON: On the Gattung of Q." In *Trajectories through Early Christianity*, by James M. Robinson and Helmut Koester, 71–113. Reprinted, Eugene, OR: Wipf & Stock, 2006.

Rogerson John W. 1989. "Anthropology and the Old Testament." In *The World of Ancient Israel: Sociological Anthropological and Political Perspectives*, edited by R. E. Clements, 17–31. Cambridge: Cambridge University Press.

Rohrbaugh, Richard L. 1984. "Methodological Considerations in the Debate over the Social Class Status of Early Christians." *JAAR* 52:519–46.

———. 1987. "'Social Location of Thought' as a Heuristic Construct in New Testament Study." *JSNT* 30:103–19.

Roloff, Jürgen. 1965. *Apostolat—Verkündigung—Kirche*. Gütersloh: Mohn.

———. 1999. "The Question of Criteria in Jesus Research: From Dissimilarity to Plausibility." *Review of Theological Literature* 1.1:54–58.

Rostovtzeff, M. 1922. *A Large Estate in Egypt in the Third Century B.C.: A Study in Economic History*. University of Wisconsin Studies in the Social Sciences and History 6. Madison: University of Wisconsin Press.

Runciman, W. G. 1968. "Class, Status and Power." In *Social Stratification*, edited by J. A. Jackson, 25–61. Sociological Studies 1. London: Cambridge University Press.

Runia, K. 1988. "God and Man in Philo of Alexandria." *JTS* 39:48–75.

Runia, David T. 1993. *Philo in Early Christian Literature: A Survey*. CRINT Section 3: Jewish Traditions in Early Christian Literature 3. Assen: Van Gorcum.

Saldarini, Anthony J. [1988] 2001. *Pharisees, Scribes, and Sadducees in Palestinian Society: A Sociological Approach*. Reprinted with a foreword by James VanderKam. Biblical Resource Series. Grand Rapids: Eerdmans.

Sand, Alexander. 1974. *Das Gesetz und die Propheten: Untersuchungen zur Theologie des Evangeliums nach Matthäus*. Biblische Untersuchungen 11. Regensburg: Pustet.

Sanders, E. P. 1985. *Jesus and Judaism*. Philadelphia: Fortress.

———. 1993. *The Historical Figure of Jesus*. New York: Penguin.

Sanders, E. P., and M. Davies. [1989] 1996. *Studying the Synoptic Gospels*. 5th impression. London: SCM.

Schaberg, Jane. 1985. "Daniel 7, 12 and the New Testament Passion-Resurrection Predictions." *NTS* 31:208–22.

Schams, Christine. 1998. *Jewish Scribes in the Second-Temple Period*. JSOTSup 291. Sheffield, UK: Sheffield Academic.

Scheffler, Eben. 1993. *Suffering in Luke's Gospel*. ATANT 81. Zurich: TVZ.

Schelsky, Helmut. 1965a. "Ist die Dauerreflexion institutionalisierbar? Zum Thema einer modernen Religionssoziologie." In *Auf dem Suche nach Wirklichkeit: Gesammelte Aufsätze*, 250–75. Düsseldorf: Bertelsmann.

———. 1965b. "Über die Stabilität von Institutionen, besonders Verfassungen: Kulturanthropologische Gedanken zu einem rechtssoziologischen Thema. in *Auf der Suche nach Wirklichkeit: Gesammelte Aufsätze*, 33–55. Düsseldorf: Bertelsmann.

———. 1970. "Zur soziologischen Theorie der Institution." In *Zur Theorie der Institution*, edited by Helmut Schelsky, 9–26. Düsseldorf: Bertelsmann.

Schenk, Wolfgang. 1981. *Synopse zur Redenquelle der Evangelien*. Düsseldorf: Patmos.

Schille, Gottfried. 1994. "Die Jesusbewegung und die Entstehung der Kirche." *Theologische Literatur Zeitung* 119:100–12.

Schmidt, D. D. 1990. *The Gospel of Mark*. Scholars Bible. Sonoma, CA: Polebridge.

———. 2000. "Finding a Non-apocalyptic Jesus." Unpublished paper presented at the Westar Institute's Jesus Seminar, 1–5 March 2000, Santa Rosa, California.

Schmidt, K. L. 1919. *Der Rahmen der Geschichte Jesu: Literarkritische Untersuchungen zur ältesten Jesusüberlieferung*. Berlin: Trowitzsch.

Bibliography

Schmithals, Walther. 1972a. *Jesus Christus in der Verkündigung der Kirche: Aktuelle Beiträge zum notwendige Streit um Jesus*. Neukirchen-Vluyn: Neukirchener.

———. 1972b. Der Markusschluß: Die Verklärungsgeschichte und die Aussendung der Zwölf." *ZTK* 69:379–411.

———. 1986. *Das Evangelium nach Markus: Kapitel 9, 2–16, 20*. 2nd ed. ÖTK 2/2.. Gütersloh: Gütersloher.

———. 1987. "Der Konflikt zwischen Kirche und Synagoge in Neutestamentlicher Zeit." In *Altes Testament und christliche Verkündigung: Festschrift für Antonius H. J. Gunneweg zum 65. Geburtstag*, edited by M. Oeming and A. Graupner, 366–86. Stuttgart: Kohlhammer.

———. 1994. *Theologiegeschichte des Urchristentums: Eine problemgeschichtliche Darstellung*. Stuttgart: Kohlhammer.

Schneider, G. 1977. "Zur Bedeutung von *kathexēs* im lukanischen Doppelwerk." *ZNW* 68:128–31.

Schönberger, O. 1990. *Apocolocyntosis Divi Claudii, Lucius Annaeus Seneca: Einführung, Text und Kommentar*. Würzburg: Königshausen & Neumann.

Schrage, W. 1963. "'Ekklesia' und 'Synagoge': Zum Ursprung des urchristlichen Kirchenbegriffs." *ZTK* 60:178–202.

———. 1964. "*sunagōgē* et al." In *Theologisches Wörterbuch zum Neuen Testament*, vol. 7. Edited by Gerhard Friedrich. Stuttgart: Kohlhammer.

Schulz, S. 1971. *Q—Die Spruchquelle der Evangelisten*. Zurich: TVZ.

Schürer, E. [1884–1924] 1979. *The History of the Jewish People in the Age of Jesus Christ (175 B.C.—A.D. 135)*, Vol 2. A new English version revised and edited by Geza Vermes et al. Edinburgh: T. & T. Clark.

Schürmann, H. 1975. "Beobachtungen zum Menschensohn-Titel in der Redequelle." In *Jesus und der Menschensohn: für Anton Vögtle*, edited by Rudolf Pesch et al., 124–47. Freiburg: Herder.

Schüssler Fiorenza, Elisabeth. 1985. "De-centering Biblical Interpretation." *JBL* 107:1–17.

———. 1994. *Jesus: Miriam's Child, Sophia's Prophet; Critical Issues in Feminist Christology*. New York: Continuum.

———. 1999. *Rhetoric and Ethic: The Politics of Biblical Studies*. Minneapolis: Fortress.

Schwartz, G. 1986. *Jesus "der Menschensohn": Aramaistische Untersuchungen zu den synoptischen Menschensohnworten Jesu*. BWANT 6. Stuttgart: Kohlhammer.

Schweizer, Eduard. 1957. "Der Glaube an Jesus den 'Herrn' in seiner Entwicklung von den ersten Nachfolgern bis zur hellenistischen Gemeinde." *EvT* 17:7–21.

———. [1967] 1970. "Dying and Rising with Christ." In *New Testament Issues*, edited by Richard Batey, 173–90. London: SCM.

Scobie, C. H. H. 1973. "The Origins and Development of Samaritan Christianity." *NTS* 19:390–414.

Scott, B. B. [1989] 1990. *Hear Then the Parable: A Commentary on the Parables of Jesus*. Minneapolis: Fortress.

Scott, J. C. 1977. "Protest and Profanations: Agrarian Revolt and the Little Tradition." *Theory and Society* 4:1–38, 211–246.

———. 1998. *Seeing Like a State: How Certain Schemes to Improve the Human Condition Have Failed*. Yale Agrarian Studies. Yale ISPS Series. New Haven: Yale University Press.

Searle, J. R. 1969. *Speech Acts: An Essay in the Philosophy of Language*. Cambridge: Cambridge University Press.

———. 1979. "The Logical Status of Fictional Discourse." In *Expression and Meaning: Studies in the Theory of Speech Acts*, 58–75. Cambridge: Cambridge University Press.
Sellin, G. 1978. "Komposition, Quellen und Funktion des lukanischen Reiseberichts (Lk. IX.51—XIX.28)." *NovT* 20:100–135.
Sheres, Ita, and Anne Kohn Blau. 1995. *The Truth about the Virgin: Sex and Ritual in the Dead Sea Scrolls*. New York: Continuum.
Shils, E. 1965. "Charisma, Order and Status." *American Sociological Review* 30:199–213.
Sim, D. C. 1996. *Apocalyptic Eschatology in the Gospel of Matthew*. SNTSMS 88. Cambridge: Cambridge University Press.
———. 1998. "Are the Least Included in the Kingdom of Heaven? The Meaning of Matthew 5:19." *HTS* 54:573–87.
———. 2000. "The Sword Motif in Matthew 10:34." *HTS* 56:84–104.
Smith, Morton. 1959. "What Is Implied by the Variety of Messianic Figures?" *JBL* 78:66–72.
———. 1971. "Prolegomena to a Discussion of Aretalogies, Divine Man, the Gospels and Jesus." *JBL* 90:174–99.
Snell, Bruno, editor. 1971. *Tragicorum Graecorum Fragmenta*. Göttingen: Vandenhoeck & Ruprecht.
Standartinger, Angela. 1995. *Das Frauenbild im Judentum der hellenistischen Zeit: Ein Beitrag anhand von "Joseph & Aseneth"* AGJU 26. Leiden: Brill.
———. 1996. "From Fictional Texts to Socio-historical Context: Some Considerations from a Textcritical Perspective on Joseph and Aseneth." In *SBL 1996 Seminar Papers*, 303–18. Atlanta: Scholars.
Stauffer, E. [1941] 1948. *Die Theologie des Neuen Testaments*. 4. vols. Gütersloh: Mohn.
Stegemann, E. W., and W. Stegemann. 1995. *Urchristliche Sozialgeschichte: Die Anfänge im Judentum und die Christusgemeinden in der mediterranen Welt*. Stuttgart: Kohlhammer.
Stenger, Werner. 1988. *"Gebt dem Kaiser, was des Kaisers ist . . . !": Eine socialgeschichtliche Untersuchung zur Besteuerung Palästinas in neutestamentilicher Zeit*. Athenäums Monografien: Theologie 68. Frankfurt: Athenaum.
Stern, M. 1976. "Aspects of Jewish Society: The Priesthood and Other Classes." In *The Jewish People in the First Century: Historical Geography, Political History, Social, Cultural and Religious Life and Institutions*, edited by S. Safrai et al., 2:561–630. CRINT Section 1. Amsterdam: Van Gorcum.
Sternberg, M. 1985. *The Poetics of Biblical Narrative: Ideological Literature and the Drama of Reading*. Indiana Literary Biblical Series. Bloomington: Indiana University Press.
Sternberger, D. 1968. "Legitimacy." In *International Encyclopedia of the Social Sciences* 9: 244–48. New York: Macmillan
Strack, H. L., and P. Billerbeck. 1922–1928. *Kommentar zum Neuen Testament aus Talmud und Midrasch*. 4 vols. Tübingen: Mohr.
———. 1956. *Kommentar zum Neuen Testament aus Talmud und Midrasch*. Vol. 5. Rabbinischer Index, edited by Joachim Jeremias. Tübingen: Mohr/Siebeck.
———. 1961. *Kommentar zum Neuen Testament aus Talmud und Midrasch*. Vol. 6, *Verzeichnis der Schriftgelehrten, Geographisches Register*, edited by Joachim Jeremias. Tübingen: Mohr/Siebeck.
Strecker, G. [1964] 1983. "The Theory of the Messianic Secret in Mark's Gospel." In *The Messianic Secret*, edited by Christopher Tuckett, 49–64. IRT 1. Philadelphia: Fortress.
Talbert, C. H. 1978. *What Is a Gospel? The Genre of the Canonical Gospels*. London: SPCK.

Bibliography

Talmon, S. 1978. "The 'Comparative Method' in Biblical Interpretation: Principles and Problems." In *1977 Congress Volume: Göttingen*, 320–56. Leiden: Brill.
Tannehill, Robert C. [1977] 1995. "The Disciples in Mark: The Function of a Narrative Role." In *The Interpretation of Mark*, edited by W. R. Telford, 169–96. 2nd ed. Studies in New Testament Interpretation Edinburgh: T. & T. Clark.
———. 1985. "Israel in Luke-Acts: A Tragic Story." *JBL* 104:69–85.
———. 1986. "Rejection by Jews and Turning to Gentiles: The Pattern of Paul's Mission in Acts." In *Society of Biblical Literature Seminar Papers Series 25*, edited by Kent H. Richards, 130–41. Atlanta: Scholars.
Tarn, W. W. 1952. *Hellenistic Civilization*. London: Methuen.
Tatum, W. Barnes. 1994. *John the Baptist and Jesus: A Report of the Jesus Seminar*. Sonoma, CA: Polebridge.
———. 1999. *In Quest of Jesus*. Rev. ed. Nashville: Abingdon.
Taylor, L. R. [1931] 1981. *The Divinity of the Roman Emperor*. Garland Library of Latin Poetry. Philological Monographs 1. Reprinted, Chico, CA: Scholars.
Tcherikover, V. A., and A. Fuks, editors. 1957. *Corpus Papyrorum Judaicarum*, Vol 1(6). Cambridge: Harvard University Press.
Theissen, G. [1975] 1979. "Die soziologische Auswertung religiöser Überlieferungen: Ihre methodologischen Probleme am Beispiel des Urchristentums." In *Studien zur Soziologie des Urchristentums*, 35–54. WUNT 19. Tübingen: Mohr/Siebeck.
———. [1979] 1983. *Studien zur Soziologie des Urchristentums*. Tübingen: Mohr/Siebeck.
———. 1989. *Lokalkolorit und Zeitgeschichte in den Evangelien: Ein Beitrag zur Geschichte der synoptischen Tradition*. NTOA 8. Göttingen: Vandenhoeck & Ruprecht, 1989
———. [1989] 1992. *The Gospels in Context: Social and Political History in the Synoptic Tradition*. Edinburgh: T. & T. Clark.
———. 1995a. "'Geben ist seliger als nehmen' (Apg 20, 35): Zur Demokratisierung antiker Wohltätermentalität im Urchristentum." In *Kirche, Recht und Wissenschaft, F.S. Albert Stein*, edited by A. Boluminski, 195–215. Neuwied: Luchterhand.
———. 1995b. "Urchristlicher Liebeskommunismus: Zum 'Sitz im Leben' des Topos in Apg 2, 44 und 4, 32." *Texts and Contexts: Biblical Texts in Their Textual and Situational Contexts*, edited by T. Fornberg and D. Hellholm, 689–711. Oslo: Scandinavian University Press.
———. [1999]. "Die politische Dimension der Verkündigung Jesu." Paper presented at the Internationales Symposium, Jesus in neuen Kontexten: Sozialwissenschaftlichen Perspektiven der Jesusforschung, Evangelische Akademie Tutzing, 25–27 June 1999.
———. 1999. *A Theory of Primitive Christian Religion*. Translated by John Bowden. London: SCM.
Theissen, Gerd, and Dagmar Winter. 1997. *Die Kriterienfrage in der Jesusforschung: Von Differenzkriterium zum Plausibalitätskriterium*. NTOA 34. Göttingen: Vandenhoeck & Ruprecht.
Thiselton, Anthony C. 1992. *New Horizons in Hermeneutics: The Theory and Practice of Transforming Biblical Reading*. London: HarperCollins.
———. 1994. "Christology in Luke, Speech-Act Theory, and the Problem of Dualism in Christology, after Kant." In *Jesus of Nazareth: Lord and Christ; Essays on the Historical Jesus and New Testament Christology*, edited by J. B. Green and M. Turner, 453–72. Grand Rapids: Eerdmans.
Thompson, Thomas L. 1999. *The Bible in History: How Writers Create a Past*. London: Cape.

Bibliography

Toby, Jackson. 1977. "Parsons' Theory of Societal Evolution." In *The Evolution of Societies*, by T. Parsons, edited and with an introduction by J. Toby, 1–23. Prentice-Hall Foundations of Modern Sociology Series. Englewood Cliffs, NJ: Prentice-Hall.

Tödt, H. E. 1959. *Der Menschensohn in der synoptischen Überlieferung*. Göttersloh: Mohn.

Tolbert, M. A. 1989. *Sowing the Gospel: Mark's World in Literary-Historical Perspective*. Minneapolis: Fortress.

Trilling, W. 1978. "Implizite Ekklesiologie: Ein Vorschlag zum Thema 'Jesus und die Kirche.'" In *Die Botschaft Jesu: Exegetische Orientierung*, 57–72. Freiburg: Herder.

Tuckett, C. M. 1996. *Q and the History of Early Christianity: Studies on Q*. Peabody, MA: Hendrickson.

Turner, J. H. 1978. *The Structure of Sociological Theory*. Revised edition. Dorsey Series in Sociology. Homewood, IL: Dorsey.

Uro, R. 1987. *Sheep among the Wolves: A Study of the Mission Instructions of Q*. AASF. Humanarum Litterarum 47. Helsinki: Suomalainen Tiedeakatemia.

Uspenski, B. A. 1973. *A Poetics of Composition: The Structure of the Artistic Text and Typology of a Compositional Form*. Translated by V. Zavarin and S. Wittig. Berkeley: University of California Press.

Vaage, L. E. 1991. "The Son of Man Sayings in Q: Stratigraphical Location and Significance." *Semeia* 55:103–29.

———. 1994. *Galilean Upstarts: Jesus' first followers according to Q*. Valley Forge, PA: Trinity.

Van Aarde, A. G. 1982. "The Portrait of the Disciples and the Structure of Matthew 13:53—17:27. *Neot* 16:21–34.

———. 1994. *God-With-Us: The Dominant Perspective in Matthew's Story, and Other Essays*. HvTStSup 5. Pretoria: Periodical Section of the Nederduitsch Hervormde Kerk van Afrika.

———. 1998. "Matthew 27:45–53 and the Turning of the Tide in Israel's History." *BTB* 28: 16–26.

———. 2001. *Fatherless in Galilee: Jesus as Child of God*. Harrisburg, PA: Trinity.

———. 2005. "Resolving Communication Disturbances in Luke 12:35–48 through Narratology." In *One Text, a Thousand Methods: Studies in Memory of Sjef van Tilborg*, 161–78, edited by U. Berges and P. Chatelion Counet, 177–95. Biblical Interpretation Series 71. Boston: Brill.

Van Eck, E. 1995. *Galilee and Jerusalem in Mark's Story of Jesus: A Narratological and Social Scientific Reading*. HvTStSup 7. Pretoria: University of Pretoria.

Van Huyssteen, J. W. V. 1988. "Paradigms and Progress: Inference to the Best Explanation." in *Paradigms and Progress in Theology*, edited by J. Mouton et al., 81–90. HSRC Studies in Research Methodology 5. Pretoria: Human Sciences Research Council.

Van Zyl, S., and A. G. Van Aarde. 1997. "Die Lukaanse Jesusbeeld: In dialoog met Wilhelm Bousset se "Kyrios Christos". *HvTSt* 53: 185–208.

Verheyden, J. 1999. "The Unity of Luke-Acts." *IITS* 55.964–79.

Vermes, G. 1967. "The Use of *bar nosh/bar nasha* in Jewish Aramaic, in *An Aramaic Approach to the Gospels and Acts*, by M. Black, appendix C. 3rd ed. Oxford: Clarendon.

———. 1973. *Jesus the Jew: A Historian's Reading of the Gospels*. London: Collins.

———. 1993. *The Religion of Jesus the Jew*. Minneapolis: Fortress.

Via, D. O. 1975. *Kerygma and Comedy in the New Testament: A Structuralist Approach to Hermeneutic*. Philadelphia: Fortress.

Bibliography

Vielhauer, P. 1975. "Beobachtungen zum Menschensohn-Titel in der Rede(n)quelle." In *Jesus und der Menschensohn: Festschrift für A. Vögtle*, edited by R. Pesch and, R. Schnackenburg, 124–47. Freiburg: Herder.

Vivas, E. 1968. "Literary Classes: Some Problems." *Genre* 1: 97–105.

Vledder, E-J 1997. *Conflict in the Miracle Stories: A Socio-exegetical Study of Matthew 8 and 9*. JSNTSup 152. Sheffield: Sheffield Academic.

Von Wahlde, U. C. 1981–82. "The Johannine 'Jews': A Critical Survey. *NTS* 28:33–60.

Vorster, W. S. 1980. "Mark: Collector, Redactor, Author, Narrator?" *Journal for Theology of Southern Africa* 31:46–61.

———. 1981. "The Function of the Use of the OT in Mark." *Neot.* 14:62–72.

———. 1982. "De taal van het Nieuwe Testament." In *Inleiding tot de studie van het Nieuwe Testament*, edited by A. F. J. Klein, 32–42. Kampen: Kok.

———. 1986a. "Die Brief aan Rheginos: Oor geloof en rede en die opstanding." *HvTSt* 42:211–28.

———. 1986b. The New Testament and narratology. *Journal of Literary Studies /Tydskrif vir Literatuurwetenskap* 2:42–62.

———. 1987. "Characterization of Peter in the Gospel of Mark." *Neot.* 21:57–76.

———. [1987] 1995. "Literary reflections on Mark 13:5–37: A Narrated Speech of Jesus." In *The Interpretation of Mark*, edited by W. R. Telford, 269–88. 2nd ed. Studies in New Testament Interpretation. Edinburgh: T. & T. Clark.

Waetjen, H. C. 1999. *Praying the Lord's Prayer: An Ageless Prayer for Today*. Harrisburg: Trinity.

Walsh, J. P. M. 1987. *The Mighty from Their Thrones: Power in the Biblical Tradition*. OBT. Philadelphia: Fortress.

Weber, M. 1962. *Basic Concepts in Sociology*. Translated and introduced by H. P. Secher. London: Owen.

———. [1947] 1968a. *Max Weber on Charisma and Institution Building: Selected Papers Edited and with an Introduction by E. N. Eisenstadt*. Heritage of Sociology. Chicago: University of Chicago Press.

———. 1968b. *Economy and Society: An Outline of Interpretive Sociology*, Vol. 1. Edited by G. Roth and C. Wittich. Berkeley, CA: University of California Press.

Weeden, T. J. 1971. *Mark—Traditions in Conflict*. Philadelphia: Fortress.

Weinfeld, M. 1972. *Deuteronomy and the Deuteronomistic School*. Oxford: Clarendon.

Weisman, Z. 1984. "The Prophetic Pattern of Anointing Kings in Ancient Israel." in *Monarchies and Socio-religious Traditions in the Ancient Near East*, edited by H. I. H. Prince Takahito Mikasa, 21–26. Bulletin of the Middle Eastern Culture Center in Japan 1. Wiesbaden: Harrassowitz.

Weiss, Z. et al. 1996. *Zippori National Park*. The Israel National Parks Authority, Marketing Division, Education & Guidance Department.

West, C. 1985. "The Politics of American Neo-pragmatism." In *Post-analytic Philosophy*. New York: Columbia University Press.

———. 1989. *The American Evasion of Philosophy: A Genealogy of Pragmatism*. The Wisconsin Project on American Writers. Madison: University of Wisconsin Press.

White, L. M. 1986. "Sociological Analysis of Early Christian Groups: A Social Historian's Response. *Sociological Analysis* 47:249–66.

Whitelam, K. W. 1986. "Recreating the History of Israel." *JSOT* 35:45–70.

Williams, R. 1977. *Marxism and Literature*. Marxist Introductions. Oxford: Oxford University Press.

Wilson, R. R. 1984. *Sociological Approaches to the Old Testament*. GBS. Philadelphia: Fortress.
Winch, P. G. 1958. "Authority." In *The Symposia Read at the Joint Session of the Aristotelian Society and the Mind Association*, 225-40. Proceedings of the Aristotelian Society. Supplementary Vol. 1. London: Harrison.
Windisch, H. 1925. "Friedensbringer—Göttessöhne: Eine religions-geschichtliche Interpretation der 7. Seligpreisung." *ZNW* 24:240-60.
Wink, W. 1968. *John the Baptist in the Gospel Tradition*. SNTSMS 7. London: Cambridge University Press.
Wlosok, A., editor. 1978. *Römischer Kaiserkult*. Wege der Forschung 372. Darmstadt: Wissenschaftliche Buchgesellschaft.
Wolterstorff, N. 1980. *Works and Worlds of Art*. Clarendon Library of Logic and Philosophy. Oxford: Clarendon.
Woude, A. S. van der. 1957. *Die messianischen Vorstellungen der Gemeinde von Qumrân*. SSN 3. Leiden: Brill.
Wrede, W. [1901] 1971. *The Messianic Secret*. Translated by J. C. G. Greig. London: Clarke.
———. 1904. "Zur Messiaserkenntnis der Dämonen bei Markus." *ZNW* 5:169-77.
Wright, E. O. 1979. *Class Structure and Income Determination*. Institute for Research on Poverty Monograph Series. New York: Academic Press.
Wright, N. T. 1992. *Who Was Jesus?* London: SPCK.
———. 1996. *Jesus and the Victory of God*. Christian Origins and the Question of God 2. London: SPCK.
———. 1999. "Knowing Jesus: Faith and History." In *The Meaning of Jesus: Two Visions*, by M. J. Borg and N. T. Wright, 15-27. San Francisco: HarperSanFrancisco.
Wrong, D. H. 1979. *Power: Its Forms, Bases, and Uses*. Key Concepts in the Social Sciences. New York: Harper & Row.
Wulfing von Martitz, P. 1969. "Sub verbo *huios, huiothsia*." *Theologisches Wörterbuch zum Neuen Testament*, Vol. 8. Edited by Gerhard Friedrich. Stuttgart: Kohlhammer.
Zahavy, T. 1990. *Studies in Jewish Prayer*. Studies in Judaism Lanhan, MD: University Press of America.
Zeller, D. 1982. "Redaktionsprozesse in wechselnder 'Sitz im Leben' beim Q-Material." In *Logia: Les paroles de Jésu—The Sayings of Jesus*, edited by J. Delobel, 395-409. BETL 59. Leuven: Leuven University Press.
———. 1985. "Entrückung zur Ankunft als Menschensohn (Lk 13,34f.; 11,29f.)." In *À cause de l'Evangile*, 513-30. Lectio Divina 123. Paris: Cerf.
———. 1992. "Eine weisheitliche Grundschrift in der Logienquelle?" In *The Four Gospels, 1992: Festschrift Franz Neirynck*, edited by F. van Segbreck et al., 1:389-401. 3 vols. BETL 100. Leuven: Leuven University Press.
Ziegler, K., editor. 1969. "Marcus Coriolanus." In *Plutarchi vitae paralelae* 1.2:183-226. 4th ed. Teubner Leipzig: Teubner.
Zimmermann, H. [1967] 1974. *Neutestamentliche Methodenlehre: Darstellung der historisch-kritischen Methode*. 4th ed. Stuttgart: Katolisches Bibelwerk.

www.ingramcontent.com/pod-product-compliance
Lightning Source LLC
Chambersburg PA
CBHW050817160426
43192CB00010B/1794